Mary Rose

MARY ROSE

The Evolution of Love and Medicine
in Victorian New Orleans

Carol Bloom Paine

Granddaughter of Mary Rose

Rev. date: 10/09/2013

To order additional copies of this book, contact:
Xlibris LLC
1-888-795-4274
www.Xlibris.com
Orders@Xlibris.com
140349

Contents

PROLOGUE

In 1980 my father decided to sell the Victorian mansion in which he had grown up and raised his family. It was purchased by his father in 1906 to please his new bride, Mary Rose, according to her, because it had palm trees in front of it. It is a beautiful home that stands out among many beautiful homes on Saint Charles Avenue.

Going through seventy years of family heirlooms was a monumental job. Among the things I scavenged from the findings was a scrapbook made by my grandfather that held newspaper clippings dating from the 1880's until his death. There were also letters and telegrams and programs glued inside. It even had two pages of four leaf clovers that he had picked in England while on his honeymoon. Unfortunately, although the newspaper articles included the dates, the names of the papers were omitted and there were over ten newspapers listed in New Orleans at that time. I also found a box filled with the articles that Popsy, Dr. Bloom, had published in numerous medical journals. We had grown up with many of the quaint artifacts of his trade stashed in closets and drawers around the house.

The more I delved into the scrapbook, the more I realized his story had to be shared, not only with family, but with the whole world. I know that my father had donated most of Popsy's medical books to Tulane University where he had obtained his medical degree, but when I went to the Tulane Library to do research about him, I could barely find his name mentioned.

Unfortunately Popsy died before I was born, but Mary Rose (Granny) lived on until 1958. I remember her well, because she lived with us and told us many of the stories I have shared in this book. She also compiled a biography of Popsy to be published in *The National Cylopedia of American Biography*, which filled in some of the early information about his birth, but far from completed the story. As you can tell from the extensive bibliography, I did a lot of research to verify information.

Many of the names are actual people who deserve credit for changing medicine and culture in New Orleans, and others have been completely made up. The list of real people is in Appendix One. Some of the names you will recognize. All of the others are figments of my imagination. In researching this story I have met many wonderful people who have given me insight into the people and places included. My visit to Touro Infirmary archives led me to meet a distant cousin who is the archivist there. Visiting the archives of Longue Vue Gardens, I saw a picture of my great aunt for the first time, and she looks just like my sister, Elizabeth. It has been a challenging, but rewarding adventure, and I only regret that it took me so long to finally sit down and put it to paper.

New Orleans has a language all its own. I have included a glossary of unusual terms that may help you understand some of the expressions. I also have included some of the German, French, and Hebrew words, and translated them to the best of my knowledge. Please be assured that some of this story is pure fiction, in fact, all of the conversations are. I researched for several years to try to put the historical facts into play, but wanted to add the color that makes for an interesting historical novel.

Some of my friends suggested that I really needed to spice it up, but if you would have known my straight-laced grandmother from Boston you would know she would haunt me to this day if I had done such to sully her name. I hope you enjoyed her story.

CHAPTER ONE

The Orphan

Philadelphia had been so cold that winter, and there had been so much sickness. That seemed to make it even colder when people were sick and could not give you hugs or snuggle with you to keep you warm. Diphtheria! What a hideous word that was, and even more hideous disease. It took both of her parents and two of her siblings. They kept talking about how strong she had been through all of the turmoil, but all she wanted to do was cry. And she did cry a lot, but only in private. They were not about to know how lost and alone she felt. She would show them.

And now she was headed to Boston. It was her first time out of Philadelphia. She wondered if she would ever return. She was going to live in a convent, of all things! They had tried placing her with other family members, but she was a bit too strong willed. They all blamed it on her bright red curly hair. They claimed that it was a touch the devil had given her to warn those who met her that they had better beware. But her Daddy saw it differently. At her birth he had exclaimed, "Finally I have my rose. I knew when I married an Irish woman, one day she would give me a redhead. This one will be called Mary Rose." She was his favorite and he spoiled her from the time she was born. That was part of the problem: this five year old needed special handling. Her oldest sister, Elizabeth, had joined the order of the Daughters of Charity two years before, and her convent had an orphanage attached to it. There Mary Rose would learn discipline. Her sister would be nearby to keep a close eye on her, and give her moral support when needed.

Elizabeth held Mary Rose's hand tightly as they climbed the steps of their Pullman car. What a pair they must have been! Elizabeth with her huge cornette headdress and voluminous blue habit, and tiny little Mary Rose with her brilliant red curls spilling from her blue bonnet. This would be quite an adventure. There were so many things to see and smell that Mary Rose had never seen before, but Elizabeth would not allow any dawdling or gawking. She basically had dragged her through the train station. The good sisters had taught her to keep her head down, walk swiftly, and never make eye contact with strangers. Mary Rose had a lot to learn.

Mary Rose had learned so much in her brief five years. Her life used to be so simple, until the day her mom came home complaining of being tired. She never complained. She went directly to bed without preparing supper or even saying the family prayers. She had watched her mom's throat swell up to the point she could not talk or eat or even drink. They all said she probably got the disease from helping the poor children at the church. Not long after that her dad also became sick. It was so sad to see the two of them, ashen, holding hands, lying side by side on their death bed. They all said it was unusual for older people to get the disease. It usually killed children under ten. The doctor could only give them the laudanum to dull the pain, and hope that their bodies were strong enough to fight off the infection.

The funerals followed. Then the extended family descended on them trying to decide who would live with whom, and who was going to take what with them. Her mother would have hated to see the circus that ensued. Elizabeth, who was 18, was already living in the convent in Boston. Edward, 16, would stay in Philadelphia with Uncle James and Aunt Sarah. He was already working in the textile business that his father and uncle had been so successful in running. Clara at 12 was going to stay with Uncle John and Aunt Mary. Veronica, 8, was going to live in New York City with Uncle Patrick and Aunt Jillian.

And then there was Mary Rose, the baby. At five, she was a very curious child and wanted to know and see everything. At first, she stayed with Edward at Uncle James' house, but Aunt Sarah was too high strung for her constant questions and mischief making. Next came Uncle David and Aunt Corrine. That lasted about two weeks, before Aunt Corrine had to be put on medication for her nerves.

And now Mary Rose was on her way to Saint Mary's Home in Boston. Her sister, Elizabeth, was assigned to the orphanage and arrangements had been made that Elizabeth would be the supervising sister in Mary Rose's dormitory. That meant she would sleep in an adjoining room which would have eleven other little girls. Possibly this would ease the adjustment from being the spoiled favorite to being an orphan. The family did not know what else to do with her.

As they boarded the train, the conductor showed them to their private quarters. The dear sisters had insisted on Elizabeth accepting that luxury.

They had wanted Sister Francis to accompany her. It was most unusual for a sister to travel alone, but Elizabeth had insisted on going to Philadelphia for the funeral, and knew that she might be away from the convent for several months, because she would need to take care of all the family arrangements. She was the oldest and felt responsible for her younger siblings. There were so many decisions to make. It would be good to get back to the convent where she would only take orders, and not have to make any decisions.

Their "private quarters" was a tiny cubicle about five feet long and four feet wide. It was currently made up for day travel with a comfortable chaise, but would convert to two bunks for the night. A sliding door opened into the room which could be secured. A large window allowed you to watch the scenery pass, and curtains draped it, so they could have some semblance of privacy. A wood stove at the end of the car heated it. There were two tiny washrooms, one at either end of the car. Gas lights illuminated the corridor. It was the ultimate of luxurious travel. Elizabeth had packed enough food for them for their journey so they would rarely have to leave their cubicle until they reached Boston. The train did include a dining car, but the sisters were not allowed to eat in public. In fact, it was breaking the rules for Elizabeth to eat in front of Mary Rose, but that would be a minor infraction. Mary Rose could not be left alone. The whole journey should take about 15 hours. The trip was a little over 300 miles, but there were four or five stops along the way, including a very long one in New York City.

Little did Elizabeth realize how difficult it would be to keep Mary Rose in the tiny cubicle for such a long time. She wanted to meet the other travelers. She wanted to find out where they were from and where they were going. They all seemed so friendly. They gave her the biggest smiles. One nice lady even gave her a peppermint. As soon as the train left the station, Elizabeth opened the curtains so they could see the changing landscape. Mary Rose insisted on making hourly trips to the restroom at the end of the car. Each trip down the car was a new adventure for her.

"Elizabeth, when I grow up I want to travel all over the world and see everything there is to see."

"We will see what God has in store for you, Mary Rose. Perhaps he wants you to be one of his missionaries and travel to darkest Africa to convert the heathens!

"By the way, Mary Rose, once we arrive in Boston, you may no longer call me Elizabeth. I am Sister John. When I joined the Daughters of Charity they proudly gave me Saint John's name. I am not sure which Saint John. There were several of them, but they were all very good men who loved Jesus very much."

"But John is a boy's name and your name has always been Elizabeth."

"As a Daughter of Charity I gave up all worldly things. My old name, Elizabeth, reminds me of those worldly things. Now that my name is Sister John, I can concentrate on loving Jesus as much as the saints do, and focus entirely on helping the poor."

"Elizabeth, er . . . , Sister John, do you think one day you will be a saint?"

"I sure hope so, Mary Rose, and I hope you will be one too."

"Do you think Momma and Daddy are in heaven with Jesus?"

"Oh, Mary Rose, I think they are in heaven with Jesus, watching down on us making our way to Boston. But you never can be too sure, so let us say a prayer for them right now, and whenever that thought crosses your mind, say another prayer for them."

At that time the porter came in to adjust the cabin for sleeping. He pulled down the top bunk and set out the fresh linens. This was one of the features the new trains took great pride in offering.

Mary Rose and Elizabeth prepared for bed, said their prayers and turned in for the evening as the motion of the train lulled them quickly to sleep. Mary Rose dreamed of all the places she would go, including heaven.

The habit commonly worn by the Daughters of Charity

CHAPTER TWO

Entering Medical School

"Pa, that Maurice fellow sure has been hanging around here a lot. I think he has sweet eyes for Hannah," said Jeff sheepishly.

"Oh, dat vould be a match made in heaven," said Isaac, grinning broadly. "You know he came over from der old country just like I did. In just ten years he has vorked hard to become a very successful business man in der cotton trade. It is high time ve married her off! She turns eighteen dis year. I tink your stepmother is already planning the vedding. Now ve need to find a nice Jewish girl for you."

"Maurice is indeed a shrewd businessman, and he has always been very pleasant. But, Pa, I am glad you brought that up. On my own, I have applied and have been accepted to the medical school at the University of Louisiana. I have followed your advice and worked hard for you as a merchant, but my heart is not in it. Your business is doing wonderfully, and Louis does not need me around to help. Young Arthur seems to really love working in the business, too. Now that I have reached twenty-one, I want to follow my heart. I have saved up enough money to pay for my tuition and upkeep for my four years of training. I hope you will give me your blessing," said Jeff.

"And just vaste all that you learned in Vicksburg? I sent you dere to make you one of the best merchants in the South. You vere to be my pride and joy. Vhen you vere born, I named you after our brave president, knowing that you vere bound for greatness. How can you disappoint your poor father so? I vas afraid something vas wrong. Vhile you ver in Vicksburg, I received letters from Mr. Sartorius saying that you ver spending all of your free time at the City Hospital. He indicated that you had very little interest in the cotton trade, but ver totally absorbed by the practice of medicine. I thought you vould outgrow your crazy fantasies about being a doctor. I have seen that collection of books you have on medicine. It is a vonder you even have to go to medical school. I tink you probably already learned all there is to know. Go and be der doctor you have always dreamed of being. Dere is no point in fighting it any longer."

"Thank you, Pa! I will make you proud of me," said Jeff as he hugged his father.

"Harrumph! But tell me exactly what it will entail. Vill you remain in New Orleans?"

"Yes, Pa, all of the studies are done at the school which is at the Charity Hospital, where I will have to live. The first two years will be mostly class work, and lab work. Luckily the supply of cadavers at Charity is endless. In other medical schools, the students have to rob graves to get their specimens to study, but at Charity there are many indigents and transients who have no one to claim their bodies, and we are allowed to study them. After the first two years, we go into the hospital and begin our internship. It will take four years to complete the program and become a doctor.

"There are so many good things going on at the medical schools. Since the carpetbaggers left and Governor Nicholls took office, conditions have really changed around the hospital. It used to be a 'hell hole,' but he has cleaned it up and made sure it is supplied with the food and material needed for good patient care. This is the time to be there and help it grow. Requirements at the school have also become much stricter. They are talking about establishing a bona fide ambulance service that would transport patients to the hospital. Dr. Miles, the house surgeon, is really pushing the board of directors to implement it. He is going to the east coast next year to study the ambulances at the hospitals and see what he thinks will work for us."

"Jeff, vat do you tink it will be like to work with dose 'sisters' with deir big sail hats? Won't dey distract you into tinking you are at der yacht club instead of in a hospital?

"Oh, Pa, the Daughters of Charity I have met have been wonderful. They have devoted their lives to taking care of the poor and downtrodden. After a while, you do not even notice those silly cornettes they wear."

"Jeff, how much time have you been spending around dat hospital?"

"Every chance I get, Pa. They even let me watch surgeries. I saw a man's leg amputated just yesterday. There is so much to learn."

"When does dis school start?"

"I begin in September—next month. It will be long hours and lots of studying, but maybe one day I will even be able to save your life. Who knows? I do plan to squeeze in time to take my boat out on the lake. The dear sisters' habits will remind me to nourish my body also, and nothing nourishes me more than sailing across the Ponchartrain. Only this time I will not be working for you like I have since I returned from Vicksburg."

"You ver vonderful at inspiring the darkies to vork hard as they cut the cypress trees on the north shore. You have demonstrated your leadership ability. Your crews were always the ones dat out produced any other, and seemed to stay healthier. Perhaps you do have a knack for taking care of people. You also developed some ingenious ways of hauling der trees out of der swamps. I even hear dat you have a technique for scaring away der snakes and alligators!"

"Oh, Pa, you know how those darkies make up stories. I read to them about how they should take care of themselves, and a lot of them are heeding my advice. Most of them have never been read to before. They are like children with their eyes wide open, grabbing every word."

"Vell, it seems ve are going to have a doctor in der family. If you are going to be a doctor, you had better be der best you possibly can be. Maybe you can find out how to cure some of der scourges dat are always running rampant in our city," said Pa. "Let us go share der news with der rest of der family."

CHAPTER THREE

Medical School

The fifth of the Charity Hospitals of New Orleans had been built in 1832. The four previous ones had been washed away by floods or hurricanes or burned to the ground. This one was a huge building, three stories tall, with the top two being reserved for patients. The lower floor was for admitting,  doctors' offices, the medical school's classrooms and library. The second floor was strictly for women, who were divided into four wards: one for women of good character, one for women of ill-repute, the third for women with surgical or obstetrical problems, and the last for women of color. The top floor was for the male patients. The Daughters of Charity had been brought in to manage it in 1834. A brochure describing the hospital bragged that it had more wounds, fractures, dislocations, other injuries, and disease requiring surgery than any other hospital in America. Its capacity was over 1000 patients.

Medical school lived up to its promise of hard work. The first two years flew by with intense study and very little free time. Jeff did get to watch surgeries, and was required to follow the doctors as they made their rounds. One of the instructors had graduated just four years earlier. His name was Dr. Rudolph Matas, and his specialty was anatomy. By the time students completed his course, they were familiar with every bone, muscle, nerve, gland and organ in the human body. Dr. Matas was a free thinker who was always trying to find better ways to do surgery. He felt strongly that every doctor needed to understand the human body inside and out, and he made sure the students he taught did.

During his second year of training, Jeff's sister, Hannah, married Maurice Stern. The wedding was the social event of the year. Isaac Bloom tried to show how wealthy he had become. For a wedding gift, he gave them a lovely home, as he said, big enough to raise lots and lots of children.

By his third year of medical school, life changed drastically. To become an intern a student had to pass a stringent examination. Once that was accomplished, the studying was over and the real work began. Interns were on call seven days a week. They were like assistant doctors, and actually treated patients.

It so happens that this was also the year that Paul Tulane bequeathed $1.25 million dollars to establish the Tulane University of Louisiana. The Medical Department of the University of Louisiana, formerly dependent on state aid and tuition dollars, became a part of the private Tulane University.

In 1885 the ambulance service was finally begun, and was manned by the interns. This was a relished duty, to get to drive the fastest horses in the city and rush to the aid of some poor dying person. Only the driver and one intern rode on the ambulance. Real doctors did not come along, so the intern had to study the patient's symptoms and provide them with their first line of medical care. They even called you doctor. As a third year student, Jeff was delighted to accept this assignment, and often used whatever pull he could to make sure he was on the roster. The ambulance itself was a specially designed draft wagon. Just the ride was the thrill of a lifetime. The challenge was to get to the injured party as quickly as possible. Too often, the patient died before they arrived, or felt much better and refused to go with them. In either case, the intern felt like he had failed his assignment.

The four years of medical school flew by, and Jeff was totally surprised at graduation when Governor Samuel Douglas McEnery presented him with the handsome heavy gold Administrator's Medal, bearing the inscription: "Awarded to Jefferson Davis Bloom by the Board of Administrators, in token of highest standing in the outgoing class of students." The reverse side was engraved with: "Charity Hospital, *Palman qui meruit ferat*, New Orleans, Louisiana 1886."

"Jeff, I am so proud of you. Not only did you complete der four years of study, you did so in exemplary style, receiving top honors," said his father as he presented him with a brass handled walking stick engraved with his new name, Dr. Jefferson D. Bloom.

"Thank you, Pa." Jeff was overwhelmed at the pride in his father's eyes, something he had not seen for such a long time. But his father quickly changed the subject.

"Now it is time for you to get serious about finding a nice Jewish girl to marry and settling down and giving me some more grandchildren. Hannah's little Edgar is bright as can be. I really like being a Grandpa. Hannah and Maurice are planning another tour of Europe soon. I hate to see them leave."

"Well, Dad, I do not think I will have time for wives and babies quite yet. Next week I start as assistant house surgeon at Touro Infirmary."

"At least dat is a Jewish hospital, and I have been working on der board of directors dere. You von't have to fool with all dose nuns with der sails on deir heads. Maybe you vill be able to meet der future Mrs. Bloom dere. It is much smaller dan Charity, but I tink you can do a great job dere too. I understand dat Dr. Loeber is a very strong taskmaster. He vill keep you on your toes."

"Perhaps, it will be very different working in a private hospital where the patients can actually pay their way. Charity has so many immigrants and dock workers. They come in with all kinds of unimaginable diseases. Doctors come from all over to study some of our cases. It is most challenging."

"I have been reading in der paper about all dose new diseases. Just do not name any of dem after me! You have been lucky you have not come down vith something no civilized person has ever seen before."

"That is part of the excitement at Charity. You never know what new disease we will find tomorrow. With the medical school on the premises, there is a lot of research into what causes some of those diseases. They are in the process of putting together a laboratory just to try to isolate the causes of different diseases. We have already isolated scurvy and pellagra as diseases resulting from poor nutrition. Those are things you cannot catch. But for others, we are finding specific germs. Some travel in the air, some in water, and some in milk.

"And that is what I think I will miss the most, the stories of the patients and all the places they have been. One of the things I hope to do, when I have time, is to travel the world. My patients have told me about their homelands and the sights they have seen that I cannot wait to see. I may just hop on a steamer like you did and head over to the old country and meet all of our relatives you left behind so many years ago. But that will come later. I still have a lot to learn about being a doctor."

"I left der old country vit my brother because the French army was going to draft us and make us kill Germans. I am a German. How could I kill Germans? Alsace, vhere ve lived, is on der border and keeps changing hands. Right now der French own it, but dat could change. Ve did not leave on a lark to see der world. Ve left to save our own lives. Someday, maybe I vill go back and see all der people ve left behind, but not until Alsace is a part of Germany again."

CHAPTER FOUR

Touro Infirmary

"Dr. Loeber, it is such a pleasure to be here at Touro. My father is delighted that I have been offered the position as your assistant house surgeon. He speaks very highly of you," said Jeff.

"Jeff, I have also heard much about you, and hope you can teach me a few things. I understand that you are not happy with medicine as it is practiced now and would like to change things, or should I say, improve things."

"Yes, Dr. Loeber. There is so much that needs to be updated. One of the things I am very concerned about is spreading disease from one patient to another. While working at Charity I have seen infections kill too many of our surgery patients. I have read a lot about the use of cotton gauze replacing the sea sponges we have been using to absorb fluids during surgery. It certainly makes sense not to take disease from one patient and place it in another. The sea sponges do their job of absorbing fluids, but are almost impossible to clean thoroughly. I know Dr. Lister promoted the use of carbolic acid in everything, but it tends to destroy the sponges. Boiling also destroys them. Whereas cotton gauze could be easily boiled or, since it is so inexpensive, it can simply be disposed of after one use. Using cotton gauze would probably result in much less chance of spreading infections. I would like to implement its use in surgery, and see what kind of effect it has."

"Great idea, Jeff," said Dr. Loeber. "I will look into ordering a supply of it today. But I have another project for you. When Judah Touro bequeathed his fortune to this infirmary in 1852, it was intended to help the poor and destitute of the Jewish population here in New Orleans. We have gotten far away from that. I would like you to devise an outdoor clinic that would be something that indigent people could come to for help when they are sick or injured. For now, this could be set up right outside the back door of the hospital. If necessary, the patient could then be admitted as a charity case. Most of these people, hopefully, will just need minor treatment and then can go home to heal. We will set up operating hours that will not interfere with your regular rounds and surgery."

"Dr. Loeder, what a great idea! So many of the patients I have seen just need to be stitched up, or bandaged. Too often, they do not know where they can go for treatment. When they go untreated for days it only gets worse, and by the time they get to the hospital, it is very serious. I would be delighted to take this assignment," Jeff responded.

"Your father has mentioned to me that he wants you to find the right Jewish lady while you are working here. Would you join us for dinner at my home this Sunday? My wife and I are hosting a little get together for my daughter and several of her friends. Hopefully, one of them will put a twinkle in your eye. My daughter is engaged to be married next month, and her fiancé will be there as well. It is time that we get you fully into the social stream here in New Orleans. You have been buried over at Charity for too long. Perhaps this will be a good introduction," chuckled Dr. Loeber.

"I would be honored to come to dinner Sunday, but, despite my father's desires, I am not sure I am ready to find a wife. Perhaps one of your daughter's friends will change my mind," Jeff smiled.

Life at Touro was much calmer than interning at Charity had been. There were only 120 beds at Touro compared to the 1000 at Charity. The outdoor clinic became widely accepted by the poor Jewish residents. Most of the patients seeking help were there for stab wounds or cuts, a few with gunshot wounds to the extremities, occasionally a patient with more serious injuries or illness arrived. Although the hours for the clinic were widely published, the attendants at the back door knew that if someone came needing immediate attention, they could call Dr. Bloom to see to their care.

In the annual report to the Board of Directors, Dr. Loeber wrote that the mortality rate had dropped, and that a greater number of sick were being treated. He attributed this in part to "the assistance of Dr. Jefferson Bloom, a gentleman in the real sense of the word, and a doctor who loves his profession." He goes on to report that the free clinic for the poor was making the Infirmary much more popular and was giving the interns more material to study. The free clinic was open in the mornings from 10 to 12 on weekdays, and he encouraged the board members to come and observe how much good it was doing.

Jeff earned the respect of Dr. Loeber, who praised him whenever the Board of Directors met. Jeff was always making suggestions about improvements. One of the things Dr. Loeber noticed was his fastidiousness about washing his hands.

"Jeff, what is this with washing your hands? You must do it one hundred times a day. And that stinky brown soap you use! You are going to wear your skin off!" exclaimed Dr. Loeber.

"Dr. Loeber, it only makes sense that if I do not wash my hands I could be spreading infections. So many doctors only wash after surgery. I believe in washing before and after," cited Jeff. "A lot of the books I have read highly recommend using that soap to help kill the germs. It is called Octagon soap. It smells so bad, that even the germs do not like it. I try to wash my hands before and after examining every patient."

Jeff worked long and arduous hours at the Infirmary, but did have time to socialize as well. The debutantes frequently asked him to escort them to their various balls and dances. He purchased a large sailboat that he docked at the yacht club on Lake Ponchartrain. He loved to take long afternoon cruises, and never had difficulty finding friends to join him.

'Touro Infirmary is like milk toast. Nothing exciting ever goes on there. It is the same predictable illnesses day after day. One of our biggest problems is the patients with consumption who are sent from the North to winter here. I do not think their doctors have ever been to New Orleans in January and February for they would know it is not an ideal climate for someone with breathing problems. I am not learning anything, just repeating the same diagnoses over and over. I must get back to Charity—that is where the excitement is,' wrote Jeff angrily in his diary. 'My only accomplishment is housing the outpatient clinic here. I think that is why they hired me. At least it is a start on getting help for some of those who need medical attention, but do not have a family doctor to care for them.'

His two year residency at Touro was ending, and Jeff had applied to serve as an assistant house surgeon to Dr. A. B. Miles at Charity. The house surgeon was the head of the hospital. Dr. Miles was aggressively looking for ways to improve medical practice, and Jeff was eager to be a part of it. The 1890's promised to bring huge changes in treatment procedures. The germ theory was evolving. Louis Pasteur had come up with a cure for rabies. The practice of bleeding patients had finally been eliminated. There was talk of a machine that actually could take a picture of a person's skeleton while he was still in it! Dr. Joseph Lister was always in the headlines with his dramatic reduction in hospital deaths, and his claims that it was all due to cleanliness.

'Wouldn't it be wonderful to be on the cutting edge of surgery?' thought Jeff. He knew that Dr. Matas was constantly trying new techniques in order to have greater success. With the first break in his schedule he went down to the hospital to see if anything had been decided.

* * *

"Dr. Miles, I was hoping I would find you in the hospital this evening." said Jeff. "As you know, I have applied to return to Charity as soon as my residency at Touro is complete. I was wondering if any decision had been made."

"Well, Jeff, I was just preparing a letter requesting that you come by for an interview. However, this could definitely serve as that interview. Tell me, Jeff, why do you want to work with the poor and destitute at Charity rather than the rich and prosperous at Touro?" asked Dr. Miles.

"The good thing about our poor and destitute is that they bring us every possible disease under the sun. It is downright boring working with the rich and prosperous. I feel like I am stagnating at Touro, and cannot wait to get back to being challenged, and Charity always brings its challenges. I read all the journals and try to stay up to date with the newest findings, and I am very excited about testing some of the ideas of the germ theory. So many of our patients die from infections, I am sure there are ways we can eliminate them. How exciting it would be if we could work together to save lives. About fifty percent of our surgery patients die from infections, and from what I already know about you, you feel the same way. You are eager to improve medical practice and are not afraid of making changes to the old procedures."

"Jeff that is just what I wanted to hear. There are so many advances taking place in the medical field and I want Charity to be on the leading edge of change. I need good physicians here who are willing to work hard and take the risks needed to make those changes. Please accept our offer to join the staff at Charity. This time you will be an assistant house surgeon. Now let us talk about what needs to change."

"Thank you, Dr. Miles. You will not regret having faith in me.

"To start with, we have got to prevent the spread of infections. I implemented some techniques at Touro that make a difference. One of the changes is the use of cotton gauze in place of sea sponges to absorb fluids in surgery. The gauze is so inexpensive it can simply be thrown away after each use. I have also found that cleanliness is extremely important in doctors. Dr. Loeder was always teasing me about how much I wash my hands, but I think it makes a difference. As you know there is a whole new germ theory that is widely accepted in Europe. I think we should add some of their strategies to our surgery department.

"Another real concern of mine is the children. They should be housed separately from the adults. I saw young children who had contracted syphilis and gonorrhea just because they were housed near patients who had those dread diseases."

Barely pausing for breath he continued. "We also need to improve the ambulance service. There must be a way that we can get to the patient more quickly. There was a case when I was in med school where the patient was healed and walked away before the ambulance arrived, and there were many cases where the patient died before we arrived. I know you have been investigating the newfangled X-ray machines. What a boon that would be if we could see inside the patient before we start cutting on them!"

"All in good time, Jeff! One of the first things I think we need to work on is setting up an outdoor clinic like you did at Touro. I think that will make medical treatment accessible to many who avoid coming to the hospital itself."

"Absolutely, Dr. Miles, when can I start?"

"Dr. Bloom, as soon as you are released from Touro."

"That will be in two weeks. I can hardly wait."

'Now how am I going to break this news to Pa,' Jeff thought.

* * *

"Pa, I have wonderful news," announced Jeff.

"Aha, you finally met a nice Jewish girl and are ready to get married, eh?" responded Pa.

"No, Pa, I have not been that lucky. There have been lots of nice girls I have met, but Miss Right just has not come along. That will have to come later. But I spoke with Dr. Miles this evening at Charity, and my application for assistant house surgeon has been accepted! That is quite an honor and a privilege to be chosen at my age. Dr. Miles is eager to work with me on implementing many of the changes I have been reading about. I cannot wait to get started."

"Octo libra! And you tought I would be happy to hear dat? You are leaving der prestigious Touro Infirmary to go back to vork vith der hovel at Charity? Are you out of your mind? Has one of dose sailboat wearing nuns cast a spell on you?"

"Pa, you are being ridiculous. The hospital is their life, so they have nothing to distract them from it. They are also good souls who care deeply for their patients. I hope one day you will come and meet some of them. They are really good women."

"Vell, I am not pleased, but you knew I vould not be. You are so different from your brothers and sister. Both Louis and Arthur have done very well in the trade. Hannah has started building her new home on St. Charles Avenue. It will be a mansion three stories tall. You could have made your fortune by now like Maurice has."

"I will have time to make money. There are so many more exciting things to do, like saving lives. Now that my residency is over I will have much more free time to look for the future Mrs. Bloom. I am also looking forward to spending a lot more time on my boat. The girl I marry will have to love the water, too. And she will love to travel. I am eager to go visit the many places that my patients have been telling me about. If you are meeting with a matchmaker for me, please be sure to give him those requirements: beautiful Jewish girl, who knows how to sail and loves to travel."

"And does not mind having a husband who is alvays at der hospital and could be bringing home who knows vhat dread diseases."

"You are so right, Pa. She also has to be intelligent. I want a wife with whom I can carry on a decent conversation."

"A smart wife vill only give you a better argument. You are better off looking for a dumb one who is obedient and villing to serve you."

"Oh no, Pa, I want a partner, someone I can share my life with. Someone who can understand how I feel and help me solve my problems. She should love to read—you know how much I love to read. I will have to think about what other requirements I might have, and get back to you with a list."

CHAPTER FIVE

Charity 1889

"Dr. Bloom, welcome back to Charity," said Sister Agnes. "We are delighted to have you join us again."

"Sister Agnes, it is my pleasure. Where should I begin?"

"Let me take you on the rounds of the facility, and you can see where you are needed the most. I know you are familiar with most of the hospital, but we have made a few changes.

Sister Agnes-Catherine Slavin

"Let us start where I understand you will be in charge of making some changes. This is the area where new patients come into the hospital and are seen by the house surgeon. As you can see, there are patients lined up here with a wide variety of ailments. We have been praying for an outdoor clinic, and we believe you may be the answer to our prayers. I understand you opened one while you were at Touro. We believe it would be better if we could spread the patients out and keep them away from our inmates."

"You flatter me, Sister, although I do not know about divine intervention bringing me here, but I agree completely that the outdoor clinic should be a top priority. The one at Touro enabled us to see many patients with minor problems that would have developed into major problems if not seen by a doctor in the early stages. We also can send the ones who have one of those 'dread' diseases to the pest house.

"What about the pathology lab? I hear you have improved it greatly. I have been reading about the wonderful advances Drs. Koch and Petri have made in isolating germs and trying to find medicines to destroy them. As you know, some people tease me about being a germaphobe. I really feel that we need to control infections as much as possible. Too many of our patients die from them."

"We have acquired two microscopes of varying degrees of quality, and Dr. Lewis has been doing some experimenting there. You will have to check with him on what procedures they are using," said Sister Agnes.

"Another change we made at Touro was using cotton gauze in surgery rather than sea sponges. It is inexpensive and can be disposed of after one use. It seems to have cut down drastically on infections after surgery."

"I think we are going to have to call you Dr. Change. What other breakthroughs have you made in your two years at Touro?" asked the sister.

"Hand washing. Doctors and attendants must wash their hands before and after they touch any patient. We are spreading germs ourselves, and we need to stop. How do I convince all the doctors and caregivers to go along with this? I also want you to order some Octagon soap. It smells awful, but it really kills germs."

"Well, Dr. Bloom that could be a problem. Doctors are not used to taking orders from one another. You had best discuss that with Dr. Miles before you get too far out on a limb and cannot climb back to safety. You need to be able to get along with the other doctors on staff. Our doctors have come a long way from the days of dueling in the courtyards. I certainly do not want to go back to that, but if you start giving them orders, I can see it happening again."

"I have heard about the colorful days here at Charity before the war. Most of the doctors on staff have worked with me in the past. Many were my teachers. I will talk with Dr. Lewis about what strategies we should use.

"The hospital is still divided with the female patients on the second floor and the male patients above on the third floor?"

"Yes, we have made no changes, as far as that goes. We have considered separating patients into wards according to their illnesses, but that has not gotten very far.

"May we go over to the surgical suites? I believe you know Dr. Rudolph Matas from your medical school days. He is making great strides in surgical techniques. You know how ardent a student of the human body he is. He is always trying new ways to treat patients in order to save them."

"One of the reasons I came back to Charity was to be able to work with Dr. Matas. I know what an inspiration he was in medical school. He was not happy with the old methods of letting people heal on their own. He was willing to try new means to help people. I applaud his ability to think clearly and differently and then to try his utmost to save patients and give them a good quality of life."

"I believe he is in surgery right now, but perhaps he is available."

Just as they walked down the hallway to the surgical suite, Dr. Matas came storming out.

"Dios mio! What am I going to do? We just lost another one," exclaimed Dr. Matas.

"Dr. Matas, you must remember Dr. Jeff Bloom from his medical school training. He is rejoining our staff as assistant house surgeon," introduced Sister Agnes.

"Yes, I remember him well. He was one of our most outstanding students. Glad to have you back at Charity, Jeff."

"Dr. Matas, I am sorry to hear you just lost your patient. Can you tell me what happened?" inquired Jeff.

"This was another gunshot wound to the chest and as soon as we open up the chest to repair the damages, the fool stops breathing! I cannot breathe for him, can I?" scoffed Dr. Matas.

"One of the big problems we had to contend with at Touro was opium narcosis, which too often causes the patient to stop breathing. I used the Fell-O'Dwyer apparatus, which is a sort of bellows device, to keep pumping air into and out of the lungs. I wonder if it would also be helpful when you open the chest cavity of a patient?" responded Jeff. "It has worked very successfully on several of my patients. Once the opium wears off, the patient starts breathing on their own. However, you may need to have an attendant pumping at the bellows for quite some time. We need to find an antidote for opium or make paregoric harder to come by. It also would be nice to devise a machine of some sort that would continually pump the lungs with oxygen. If the surgery should not be lengthy, I would think the bellows approach would work."

"Brilliant idea! That is why I so strongly recommended your appointment here. I know that we can work together to come up with new ideas to improve the treatment of our patients. Welcome aboard, Jeff. Please do not hesitate to make suggestions. I am always eager for improvement."

"I am delighted to hear that, because I have so many ideas. However, I know that I will probably have to go slow when presenting them to Dr. Miles. He is progressive in his ideas, but I also know we are on a limited budget. I do not want to flood him with changes all at once. I have made a list of priorities and think I will approach him one at a time with each of them," retorted Jeff.

"That is probably a good idea. He has never been one to hold me back, and I think you will enjoy being here with him in charge."

CHAPTER SIX

Changing Charity

"Dr. Miles, it is so good to be back here at Charity. I am delighted to hear that you have installed a telephone so that emergency patients can call for the ambulance to come get them. That was a huge problem when I was in medical school," said Jeff.

"Oh, that is only one of the changes. We are in an age of change."

"Sister Agnes was telling me about the laboratory to study disease pathogens. I am eager to see what other changes have been made."

"Did Sister Agnes mention the outdoor clinic? That is a top priority. I know you were very successful in getting one started at Touro, and we need to get one here also. Admitting patients with any highly contagious diseases like small pox, yellow fever, or leprosy is a real problem." Dr. Miles shook his head as he went on. "They keep sneaking in on us, and we just have to send them to the pest house as quickly as we can identify their illness. So far we have avoided having any of those illnesses spread widely among our inmates, but, as far as I am concerned, we have been lucky. I am not comfortable relying on luck to ensure our patients' safety. It could totally decimate our population."

"I feel so sorry for those poor people! We had a similar problem at Touro, but the outdoor clinic helped to isolate them quickly before they were admitted to the hospital. Hopefully we can get enough people vaccinated against smallpox that it will not be as much of a problem as it has been in the past. I agree, though, that the pest house is much better prepared to take care of them and to keep their illnesses away from the rest of us.

"I would be honored to set up a clinic here. There is another area in which I need your help. In so many of the articles I have read they insist

30

that hand washing greatly cuts down on the spread of disease. Dr. Loeber teased me constantly because I washed my hands so frequently, before and after seeing each patient. I have found that it reduced the spread of infections substantially. I required it of all my assistants at Touro. I know I cannot require it of all the staff here at Charity, but I was hoping you could help promote that practice."

"Jeff that is just one of the many changes we need to make here. As you requested, we are giving up the sea sponges in lieu of cotton gauze, and hopefully that will make a difference. There are just so many developments in hygiene that could affect our patient care."

"Dr. Miles, I know you also have been talking about starting a nursing school here at Charity. The one we had at Touro was providing the doctors with well-trained assistants. Although the good Sisters are wonderful in their work in the wards, it would be ever so helpful to have trained nurses working in the surgery. Right now, our attendants are learning as they go. I really believe registered nurses could teach us a thing or two as well."

"Actually, Touro can thank us for their nursing school. You may remember we tried to open a nursing school back in 1882. I guess you were in the middle of medical school and may have not been aware of all the outside things that were unfolding. There was a group of women who organized a 'nursing society' which was to be associated with our hospital. It was made very clear that it was no reflection on our dear Daughters of Charity who volunteered their wonderful services. But, during the war, Florence Nightingale stirred up so much excitement about how wonderful it was to be a trained nurse, that nursing schools were cropping up in every hospital. Unfortunately, the dear sisters learned about these plans through an article in one of the newspapers. No one spoke to them directly about it. Then *The Daily Picayune* and *The Weekly* took opposing views. They stirred things up so much, it was quite a row. Dan Holliday, the board vice president, had rounded up enough funds to get the school started, but would only do so with the sisters' approval. The dear sisters refused to approve it saying that they would no longer have control over the teachers or students in this training school, and therefore could not control what went on in the hospital. Sister Agnes said that you just cannot divide the authority and expect proper discipline, and you know what a stickler she is for discipline. As a result, the whole idea was squashed. It ended when the board sued the training school society in civil court. They took their idea and students over to Touro Infirmary, which is why they have a nursing school and we do not."

"Perhaps once everyone has cooled down over this, we can approach this again," said Jeff. "This time we need to make sure the sisters are at the very heart of the decision making process. Sister Agnes and I are on splendid terms. I think she is determined to convert me. Well, I may just have to convert her to some of my ideas too."

"Good luck, Jeff. Might I mention that they also fired the House Surgeon. That is when I was given this position, but the nursing school is one of the changes we are in dire need of here."

'Well,' thought Jeff,' I've never backed off from a challenge.'

CHAPTER SEVEN

Assistant House Surgeon

'October 15, 1890. So many things were happening in medicine it almost boggles the mind,' writes Jeff in his diary. 'Today we got in the newfangled thermometers developed by Sir Thomas Albutt. It is so much better than what we have been using since Dr. Tourere brought his to New Orleans right after the Civil War. The old ones were twelve inches long and took up to 20 minutes to register a patient's body temperature. They were a wonderful tool in helping us track the pace of a fever, but they were very awkward and inefficient. Dr. Albutt's are only six inches long and can record the temperature within five minutes! We are busy training all of the sisters on how to use them so that they can keep accurate readings of our patients' progress. Body temperature seems to be a good indicator of infection.

'Another new piece of equipment is called a stethoscope. We have been using the old heart horns to listen to a patient's breathing and heartbeats, but these new ones connect to both ears and have long rubber tubes that end in a small metal cone. It can easily be placed on various parts of the body to learn about what is going on inside.'

The outdoor clinic had just opened. Two were built, one for women and children and the other for men and boys. They were behind the hospital and each had a set of granite stairs going up into the grand hallway where patients would be evaluated as to how urgent the need for care was. The other job was to make sure that the patient was not suffering from a contagious disease. Those patients were taken by the police to a pest house where they could get treatment. The medical students loved learning their trade on these patients. They were the ones who did the initial evaluations.

One of the most beneficial parts of the free clinics was that many people would come for care. Stab wounds and gunshots were the major problem in the men's clinic. The doctors implored all of the patients to get vaccinated for small pox, but many were frightened of the idea, did not believe it would protect them, and some believed it would hurt them.

Women who were pregnant did not come to the hospital or the free clinic. All maternity care was administered by midwives at home. When a woman had hemorrhaged after giving birth or had other problems she would be brought to the hospital for after care, but deliveries of new babies were not done in the hospital. It was too dangerous to expose a newborn to all the germs in a hospital.

"Jeff, come and see what we have cooked up," shouted Rudolph one morning.

"I feel like you had a part in this coming to be. I have been working with a friend of mine who is very mechanical and we have developed a new breathing machine. It works much like your old bellows except that it is run by a steam engine. It is a little noisy, but it should allow me to open a patient's chest, repair the damage that has been done, close him back up again, and eventually send him on his way. I have a gunshot wound to the chest that I am getting ready to open. Come be my assistant."

"I would love to come observe. What a great idea, Rudy!" commented Jeff. "I love to see your innovations."

"Come on to the surgery. We are getting ready to start."

As they entered the surgery, one med student was in the process of attaching a mask to the head of the patient. Another was standing over the patient compressing the chest in order to try to stop the bleeding.

"You are not going to wash your hands before you start?" asked Jeff.

"There is no time for that. Just put on an apron to try and save your clothes from the mess," responded Rudy. "There will be plenty of time for clean up after we save this fellow's life."

"Tell me, gentlemen, do you know how this fellow ended up with a bullet in his belly?" asked Dr. Matas.

"I understand he was down in Roseville and got into a scuffle with another fellow about who was escorting one of the young 'ladies' down there. Apparently the other fellow won." responded the assistant. "We rushed him here in the ambulance applying constant pressure to the wound. The bleeding has slowed down considerably," responded the student.

"First, we have to keep him breathing. Turn on that confounded noisy machine and let us get a steady flow of air into and out of his lungs. Once that is working, I can open up his chest and see if we can remove the bullet and stitch together whatever it has torn up. This is the cutting edge of medical surgery. The bleeding is not too severe which indicates there may not be much damage inside and perhaps we can save him. Each patient is a new experiment. Chest wounds are usually fatal," added Dr. Matas.

"This is a fascinating piece of equipment, Rudy," commented Jeff. "I imagine it will be a real boon to many types of surgery. I know sometimes the anesthetic used to knock the patient out will overdo itself, and the patient will stop breathing. This machine will not allow that. You have got to have your friend start producing these in quantities for all the hospitals. He could be a very rich man. And you need to write this up for the medical journals. I know there are a lot of doctors that would want to see this."

As the chest was opened, it took only a few minutes to locate the bullet which was lodged between the fourth and fifth rib on the right side. Carefully, Dr. Matas used a forceps to extract the bullet. The damage to the liver was minor. The ribs were not shattered. The pectoral muscle was stitched together and the skin repaired. Formaldehyde was applied to the area to prevent infection, and bandages were applied.

"This young man was very lucky. His opponent must have used a very small caliber gun, such as a derringer, because there was so little damage. If there is no infection problem, he should survive to visit the ladies again, and will probably delight in showing off his scar. Please turn off that contraption, and they can wheel our patient off to the ward to sleep off the ether," instructed Dr. Matas.

"Rudy, that is amazing. I realize this was a minimal gunshot wound, but this is the start of a whole new world in surgery. Things are progressing so rapidly in our world. It is a great time to be in medicine," commented Jeff. "You should come and see what I am doing with broken bones these days. Instead of surgically removing the whole appendage as we have been doing, I take the arm or leg and do my best to get the bones back in place and then wrap it in cloth soaked in plaster of Paris. The cast eventually hardens and the bone will heal itself in just a matter of weeks. It is a relatively simple procedure, but the results are amazing, especially with children. Sometimes it does not heal as well as it should, because we did not get the bone exactly in place, but overall it is much better than losing the arm or leg. I wish we had one of those Roentgen ray machines so that we could actually see what we are doing."

"I know you have been after Dr. Miles for that since you got here. I agree that it would open our eyes to so many things we never knew how to repair. They are very expensive, and I know our budget is limited. Maybe someday . . ."

As Jeff left the surgical wing he ran into his old friend Dr. Michel Boudreaux. "Michel, I have just bought a new boat, and I would love for you to come spend Saturday on the lake with me. Bring along a lady friend and I will arrange a picnic lunch for the four of us. It should be a delightful way to spend the day."

"That sounds wonderful, Jeff. Where do you keep your boat moored?"

"It is out at the Yacht Club, of course. I will be bringing Miss Alice Charbonnet. Have you met her?"

"I do indeed know her. She is a lovely lady. Are you two getting serious?"

"Oh no, Michel, she is a lot of fun to be with and loves to sail. She likes to steer the rudder, but that is as far as it goes. I do not know if I will ever find someone I want to spend the rest of my life with. My father keeps hounding me about finding a wife. Of course, he insists that she must be a good Jewish girl. I cannot tell you how many young ladies have been seated at our dinner table whenever I get a chance to go home for a meal. Pa always seems to have 'der perfect one' there waiting for me. He keeps telling me I am not getting any younger. There is just too little time in the day to even think about marriage and family. I have too much to do at the hospital. That will have to come later."

"Well, I am pretty much in the same boat. All of my spare time is devoted to reading the journals and studying new procedures other doctors are trying. I really do not know anyone I could invite. Perhaps Miss Charbonnet would like to ask a friend? Will you ask her for me?"

"Excellent idea; I will bet there are lots of young ladies who would love to go sailing with the charming Dr. Boudreaux. I will send her a note today, and see if she can suggest a friend."

CHAPTER EIGHT

Lake Pontchartrain

"What a beautiful spring day," commented Miss Alice Charbonnet. "I am so eager to get out in that wonderful yacht of yours, Jeff. Dr. Boudreaux, it is a pleasure to see you again. Beth Doherty was delighted when I invited her to come along. She used to come boating with me and my dad. Daddy always felt I would have more fun if I had a friend along, and Beth loves sailing as much as I do. Her home is just a few blocks away on Coliseum Street."

"Miss Charbonnet, the pleasure is truly mine. Most of my boating has been in a pirogue along Bayou Teche. I have not been sailing very much, but I understand you can teach me how, and now, if Miss Doherty is also an experienced sailor, Jeff will have a trained crew. Perhaps I will just sit back and watch how it is done."

"Small chance of that happening, Michel," responded Jeff. "The girls are indeed experienced at some of the tasks, but I will teach you your duties and I know you are quick witted. There are many jobs that require a bit more dexterity than I would ask of the ladies. You will have to earn your lunch today, but I think you will find it wonderfully relaxing."

"Well, let us get off to the Doherty home. Come on, Big Buck. We have a long way to go today," said Jeff to the horse as he snapped the reins of the carriage. Big Buck took off at a slow trot and the carriage wound its way through the Garden District.

"Miss Charbonnet, tell me a little about your friend, Miss Doherty," quizzed Michel. "What is she like? What does she like to do? What are some of her passions? Does she like to read? Does she enjoy poetry?"

"Well, Dr. Boudreaux, you will just have to ask her those questions yourself. She was born and raised here in New Orleans. In fact, I do not think she has ever left New Orleans. What part of Louisiana are you from? I notice you have a very distinct accent. Can you speak Cajun French?"

"Oui, ma cherie! My grandparents only speak French. They were some of the first to come to Louisiana when they were chased out of Canada. I grew up along the bayous in the southwestern part of the state. I am very fortunate to come to New Orleans to study medicine, but cannot wait to return to my home. We have so few doctors in our rural area; I know I will have a booming practice."

"Well, here we are at the Doherty's. Come and meet Beth's parents. I am sure they will want to size you up and decide if you are worthy of taking their daughter out for a day on the lake," teased Jeff.

"Let me straighten my tie. Miss Charbonnet, do you think I look presentable?"

"You look just wonderful, Dr. Boudreaux. The Doherty's are lovely people. I am sure you will pass inspection," approved Alice.

As the three stood on the porch, the light banter continued. Mr. Doherty opened the door and invited the trio inside.

After introductions were made, Mr. Doherty said "Could I offer you a cup of coffee and a biscuit? You will have a long ride out to the lake, and may need a little extra sustenance. Beth is still getting ready. I have never been able to figure out what it is these women have to do in order to make an appearance. As Alice well knows, Beth loves to go sailing. But Dr. Bloom, tell me about this boat that you are planning to take my daughter out on. Is it seaworthy? You do not have just a little dingy, do you?"

"Mr. Doherty, perhaps you have seen the *Miss Lillian* at the yacht club. She is far from a dingy. I was able to purchase her from a poor bloke who was down on his luck. It almost broke his heart to give her up. He had only had the boat for a year and had resolved all the problems of a new boat. She is a beauty and loves Lake Pontchartrain. If the wind is not blowing, there is a steam engine onboard that will power her home. I prefer to just use the sails, but sometimes nature is not cooperative. Miss Charbonnet can attest, as she has been out with me on several occasions," declared Jeff. "I promise to take the very best care of your daughter. I understand she has been sailing many times before. Are you perhaps a yachtsman as well?"

"In my younger days, I used to sail a lot, but do not have much time for it now."

"Mr. Doherty, Jeff has one of the nicest sailboats at the yacht club. You have nothing to fear about Beth's safety. He is also a master sailor. He learned how from his father who harvested so much of the cypress on the north shore, before and after the war. They had crews traveling across the lake daily. In fact, before Jeff went to medical school, he would supervise the crews. His father frequently comments on what a wonderful job he did, and laments that he gave it all up to go into medicine," added Alice.

"Oh yes, Pa really wanted me to stay in commerce. He even sent me off to Vicksburg to study the cotton market there, but his dreams and mine are very different. Medicine is where I need to be," said Jeff. "Dr. Boudreaux and I have much in common there."

"Oh, here she is now. My dear let me introduce you to our medical staff, Drs. Bloom and Boudreaux. They wish to take you yachting today," quipped Mr. Doherty. "At least if there is an accident of some sort, I know she will get the very best in medical attention."

"How do you do, Dr. Boudreaux? I have had the pleasure of meeting Dr. Bloom on many occasions. Alice has told me about your wonderful boat. Let us waste no time. It is a long ride to the lake and it is such a beautiful day. Do not worry about us, Daddy," said Beth as she quickly pecked her father's cheek and made a dash for the door.

The others followed quickly, hustling into the carriage before Mr. Doherty changed his mind about letting Beth go with them. They waved happily as Big Buck clip clopped down the bricked streets.

"I had my father's cook prepare us a nice picnic lunch, and then I slipped in a couple of bottles of Zinfandel. It should be a perfect day for sailing," added Jeff.

The trip to the lake took well over an hour. The foursome chatted and laughed throughout the journey. As they arrived at the dock, Beth decried, "Oh, Dr. Bloom that is not a boat—that is a ship! How long is it? Could you take it clear to Mexico? Cuba?"

"Well it is thirty feet, but I have never gone beyond the lake yet. I have thought about possibly taking it on an extended voyage, but then I would have to leave the hospital for more than a day or two, and I have difficulty pulling myself away. I am not sure it could survive without me!" teased Jeff.

"Dr. Boudreaux, I hear you grew up in the bayous around Lafayette," remarked Beth.

"First, please call me Michel as my friends do. And no, I do not have webbing between my toes. So many people have heard that about Cajuns! I can maneuver a pirogue with the best of them, but I have never been on a sailboat."

"Are there not a lot of alligators in those waters?" asked Beth.

"Mais oui, they are one of my favorite things to hunt. I grew up catching gators and turtles and frogs. Have you ever had turtle soup? It is a real gourmet delicacy."

"Speaking of food, Michel, help me get the picnic baskets from the carriage. Papa's cook prepared enough for us to spend a week on the boat I believe. I hope all of you brought a hearty appetite."

They boarded *Miss Lillian*, while a groom took the horse and carriage to the nearby stable. Jeff showed Michel the rudiments of raising and lowering the mainstay. They untied from the dock and sailed off. Puffy little clouds filled the sky. The lake waters were relatively calm with the occasional white cap poking its head up. The sails filled quickly and Jeff masterfully steered *Miss Lillian* away from the shoreline towards the north shore. They watched the pelicans perform their precision acrobatics as they dove in a perfect line. A bald eagle soared overhead. A school of mullets seemed to be flying out of the water ahead of their boat.

As they neared the shoreline, Jeff explained, "This has always been one of my favorite spots along the lake front. It has a lovely beach with enough oak trees hung with Spanish moss to provide us with shade should the sun become overbearing. I thought we might dock here for our picnic lunch."

"Exactly where are we?" quizzed Michel.

"Well, this is the village of Mandeville. It was named after Bernard Marigny de Mandeville. He was an enterprising New Orleanian who built a huge sugar plantation near here. As you might guess, he was very French. It is becoming quite a resort town for the people of New Orleans. Just north of here are the famous Abita Springs where throngs of people come for medicinal baths in the mineral springs. The air even smells different here. I have always found it to be a very peaceful place. Just slightly west of here is Madisonville where the huge Jahncke shipyard builds ships for the Navy. There are many rivers and bayous that empty into the lake. I spent many days with crews in those bayous harvesting the cypress trees that are used to build homes in New Orleans. Unfortunately, we would need one of Michel's pirogues to go up those bayous. My boat's draft is a bit too deep."

They found a spot of high land and spread out the blankets and food. The cook had included a variety of cheeses, biscuits with butter and jellies, and fresh tomatoes and cucumbers. The favorite was the strawberries which the cook had gotten from the French Market earlier that morning. After lunch Jeff wandered the area and quickly collected four leaf clovers. He had a knack for finding them, and claimed he could find at least one in every patch of clover. He gave them to Alice and told her to keep them for good luck. They packed up all the picnic materials and boarded the boat for the return trip. They docked just as an afternoon thunderstorm reared its ugly head.

"That is one thing about sailing Lake Pontchartrain. You never know when a storm will brew. You can almost always count on one on a summer afternoon, but I had hoped we would avoid one today," said Jeff. "Let us hope Big Buck does not mind slopping through a few mud puddles."

CHAPTER NINE

Drastic Changes

As the years passed, Jeff became more and more involved with the hospital. He rarely took a day off and Dr. Miles relied on him for many of the duties he had always assumed for himself. He loved doing surgery, mainly because he could see such wonderful results. He became quite good at patching up knife cuts and bullet holes. Many of the patients he treated in the outdoor clinic were the results of hot tempers or too much partying. Charity Hospital saw plenty of both. He also was working wonders with broken bones. Many of the doctors were experimenting with ways to add fluids back into a person once they had suffered dehydration. They were trying a mixture of salt solutions that they thought would supplement the blood supply. The timing of how slowly or quickly to add the fluid seemed to be one of the biggest problems. Although they lost many early patients, without the treatment they would have died much sooner. Success eventually came, and the survival rate grew. They found that using a continuous saline infusion into the patient at a very slow rate during surgery helped the patient recover much faster from the blood loss they would endure. Jeff's patients benefitted from all the new techniques.

They had also been investigating and experimenting with a variety of anesthesias. Ether was a tried and true one, but it had its limitations. A newer technique involved injecting cocaine between the third and fourth vertebrae. This blocked all feeling below the injection site immediately, and gradually extended up to the neck and head. The patient felt no pain at all. They had tested several places for the injections and this seemed to be the very best.

The use of electricity in the operating room was also providing numerous changes. They had learned how to cauterize a blood vessel by applying a mild electrical charge to it. This immediately stopped bleeding. It was quicker and more effective than trying to sew the blood vessels closed.

Dr. Matas was also experimenting with aneurisms. Occasionally, blood vessel walls would weaken and the vessel would balloon out and eventually burst causing internal hemorrhaging. Dr. Matas had developed a technique called obliterative endoaneurismoraphy. He would tie off the balloon, empty it, sew up the vessel, and then remove the sack. Now that he had his breathing machine, he was having great success especially with ones in the chest and stomach areas.

Together the doctors compiled a list of all the implements that would be needed for each of the surgeries they performed, and asked that the nurses have them cleaned and ready for use. The good sisters worked tirelessly in ministering to the patients and helping the doctors in surgery, but their knowledge was very limited. A nursing school would be a huge benefit to the hospital. One day, in 1892, Dr. Miles, Jeff and several other doctors cornered Sister Agnes. They pleaded with her to look into starting a nursing school that she would have complete control over. They desperately needed to have more skilled nurses attending their patients. She agreed, and in 1893 the Charity Hospital Training School for Nurses was opened. The first class had 11 students, four were Sisters of Charity. The nurses had very strict rules. They were up at 5:30, breakfast at 6:30, and report to work at 7. Lights out was at 9. Nurses could receive female visitors in the parlor, no males were allowed. The program lasted 18 months, after which the student would graduate as a registered nurse.

Outbreaks of smallpox had occurred off and on through the years. If a patient was diagnosed with small pox, he was immediately removed from the hospital grounds and sent to what was known as the "pest house." This was a facility provided to take care of patients with very contagious diseases. It was not a nice place to go. The vaccination for smallpox was available to all, and if they could get everyone vaccinated the threat might disappear. The problem was that many were afraid of the vaccination. They were afraid of shots to start with, and many feared that the shot would give them smallpox itself. In order to encourage vaccinations, the doctors of the city went from door to door pleading with the residents and giving vaccinations to everyone who lived in each house. They mapped out the area and each doctor had a certain district they were responsible for covering, in their free time, of course. The result was that most of the incoming small pox patients were from rural areas that had not received the vaccine, but the overall number of patients was reduced from almost 5000 deaths per year before the vaccinations to 160 deaths after. Any patient coming to the outdoor clinic was vaccinated. If you wanted to be treated, you had to be vaccinated.

*   *   *

Bad news intervened on a sunny August morning in 1894. Jeff had been called to Dr. Miles' home in the middle of the night, but it was too late to help him. The death certificate cited the cause of death as typhoid fever and hemorrhaging. As soon as Jeff arrived the hospital was all abuzz. Dr. Miles had passed away during the night, and their leader and friend was no longer with them. The hospital board was scheduled to meet at one that afternoon to determine who would take his place. Dr. Miles had done so much to make Charity Hospital one of the best in the country. Sadness filled the hallways. His shoes would be very difficult to fill.

About four o'clock that afternoon the board of directors called Jeff to their meeting. "Jeff, it has been called to our attention what an outstanding job you have done as assistant house surgeon. We have been discussing who is best suited to replace Dr. Miles, and we know Dr. Miles has been training you to take over his position. We also know that you are a very forward looking physician who is eager to see Charity Hospital maintain its reputation for excellence. In addition, we are aware that you have been trained in commerce, and a significant part of the job of House Surgeon is running an economical business. Funding for the hospital is limited, and the House Surgeon has to make sure that he allocates those funds wisely. Dr. Miles had worked long and hard to bring us up from the depths that once existed here. We will miss him greatly, but we want to continue moving in that direction. After hours of debate we have come to the conclusion that you are the ideal candidate for this position. Are you willing to become our new House Surgeon?" asked Mr. LeBlanc, chairman of the board.

Jeff was dumbfounded. At only 33 years old, such a move was unprecedented. How could he possibly handle all the complexities of the hospital? What about the older doctors who had been on staff for so many more years? How did he handle Sister Agnes and the other sisters who staffed the hospital? They definitely needed special attention. His head was spinning. What an opportunity this would be! And what a huge responsibility!

After taking a seat and composing himself, Jeff responded, "I am so honored by your offer, in fact I am overwhelmed. When called to this meeting, I thought you were looking for input from different doctors as to the direction the hospital should take. In fact, I made some notes on some ideas I have. I never imagined you would be asking me to take Dr. Miles' place. Is this to be a temporary appointment until you find someone more qualified?"

"Absolutely not, this is a permanent position for someone we feel is highly qualified. We want you to sink your teeth in and plan to stay indefinitely. We promise to give you whatever support you need. I know that there will be those doubters who think we made the wrong choice, but there will always be naysayers. We had discussed putting out a national search, but decided we wanted to stay with someone who knows exactly what he is dealing with. You are that person. You have had your finger on the pulse of this hospital for quite some time. Being the excellent diagnostician that you are, we predict that you can find the ills that are affecting our institution and do what is necessary to cure them. Sister Agnes has promised her support as well. In fact, she is the one who first mentioned you as a replacement. She has a very high regard for your abilities. Your only imperfection is that she has not converted you to Catholicism yet. But be sure, she has not given up trying," replied Mr. LeBlanc jokingly.

The board all laughed at this comment, but their eyes rested on Jeff. What was his decision?

"Let us hear what those ideas for the future of Charity involve," intoned Mr. LeBlanc.

"You may change your mind after hearing this," quipped Jeff. "There are several things lacking here that can greatly improve the quality of the hospital. First off, we need to develop a new surgical area, one that can be kept spotlessly clean and that has a viewing area so that the medical students can watch the procedures. Our pathology department needs to be expanded. This is an area where knowledge is growing rapidly. If we are to cure diseases and protect our patients from infections, we need to be able to investigate the causes of their diseases. We must get an X-ray machine; you know the Roentgen ray machine that actually allows you to see bones. Dr. Miles has been promising it for years now, but we are still without one. Our children should be in a separate facility. They should not be exposed to adult diseases and situations. I propose getting rid of all the wooden beds in the facility and replacing them with metal beds. The wood can hold germs and cannot be cleaned sufficiently. The nursing school is one of the best things to happen to our hospital. I can hardly wait for the first class to graduate, but we need more students enrolled. Sister Agnes is doing a wonderful job in training the young ladies, but if we had a home for the nurses I think we might attract more young ladies to go into training."

"Do you see why I thought for sure Jeff was the man for this job?" Mr. LeBlanc said to the rest of the board. "Jeff, your ideas are mind boggling. Apparently you have been thinking about these for some time. I dare say you even approached Dr. Miles about them in the past."

"Oh, yes. Dr. Miles was wonderful at making improvements. He cooperated in many ways. I can list the myriad of changes that have taken place since I first came here as a medical student. He heard all of my requests many times and simply responded 'All in good time, Jeff. Be patient. We will get there.' Well, perhaps this offer is my opportunity to see that we do get there. With great apprehension, I humbly accept your offer of the position of House Surgeon for the great Charity Hospital of Louisiana."

The room erupted in applause. Each member reached to shake Jeff's hand and congratulate him. Pats on the back emanated throughout the room. It was a very jovial gathering. At that moment, the door opened and Sister Agnes floated in. "I have been anxiously waiting outside in the hallway and I knew when I heard the excitement that Dr. Bloom had accepted the position. I am so glad that you took my advice, Mr. LeBlanc."

"Oh yes, Sister Agnes, we all wanted the best man for the job and I think we got him," responded Mr. LeBlanc.

"Indeed we did," remarked Sister Agnes. "We have just one little adjustment we need to make with him, but that will come with time." She smiled.

"Well, Jeff, this next week will be a whirlwind for you. The press will want to interview you. All of the staff will want to give you their input. City and state leaders will be calling on you making suggestions and, of course, offering you criticism. I think your hide may get a little tougher in the days to come," commented Mr. LeBlanc. "Once you get settled in to your new position I do want to discuss with you the suggestions you have. Of course, we cannot do it all at once, but I think we can start making inroads into advancing some of these initiatives. They all sound very reasonable to me."

"May I request that this announcement be kept under the cuff until after Dr. Miles' funeral tomorrow? I think it might be considered an affront to him and his family if we made this announcement today," said Jeff.

"See what a caring soul he is, Mr. LeBlanc!" declared Sister Agnes. "Always thinking about how his actions affect others. I shall have a very hard time keeping this to myself, but I shall. And will the rest of you?"

"Agreed, we will wait until day after tomorrow to make the announcement. However, Jeff, I think you ought to let your father know about your promotion. He should not hear about your new job from a bystander. I know he will be able to keep this under his hat although he probably will be busting with pride," quipped Mr. LeBlanc.

"I will go and see him as soon as I make my evening rounds. I do still have patients to tend. I am sure that the news will not travel that fast."

Jeff bid the committee a good afternoon as he departed to return to his patients. He stopped by his office before going on rounds to compose himself, and to let the full brunt of what had just happened settle in on him. How quickly your life can change! What was his dad going to say when he heard about this new position?

CHAPTER TEN

A New Job

"Dr. Bloom, I must meet with you at your earliest convenience," pressed Dr. Isadore Dyer, the professor of dermatology at the medical school.

"Certainly, Dr. Dyer, I will be glad to meet with you, but not until we have properly paid our respects to Dr. Miles. Would the day after tomorrow about three be soon enough?"

"I assume it will have to be, Doctor. I have heard rumors that I feel very sure are true about Dr. Miles' replacement. I hope you can confirm a few things for me."

"Well, rumors are just that. I will plan to see you day after tomorrow as soon as I finish my afternoon rounds. Shall we meet in my office?"

"That would be very good. Thank you, Dr. Bloom. This is of the utmost urgency."

"Well, I will deal with your urgency the best way I can."

Word was traveling rapidly throughout the community. Dr. Dyer was the fourth doctor to approach Jeff with an urgent matter. This job of house surgeon was going to be very stressful to put it mildly. That is what Pa had said when he met with him for dinner the evening before.

"Jeff, you have been making such a vonderful name for yourself as a surgeon and healer. Undertaking dis job will take you away from your patients, son. Are you sure you vant to move into managing such a huge facility as Charity?"

"Pa, I thought over the same things when they offered me the job. One of the things I loved about working with Dr. Miles is that he was eager to advance medicine at Charity. They could move someone into this position that is stuck in the old traditional ways, and refuses to allow us to pursue inventive new procedures. The Board of Directors was extremely supportive of some of the ideas I have been promoting. Even Sister Agnes is supporting me!"

"Vell, your mother vould be proud of you, God rest her soul."

"Well, you should be too. One of the reasons they chose me is because of my extensive training in economics. It seems my tenure in Vicksburg and in business is paying off after all. One of the big problems the hospital has is keeping the books in balance. It seems most doctors have trouble handling money. Thanks, Pa, for forcing me to learn about commerce. That training will indeed come in handy."

"I never expected it to pay off in that vay. I expected you vould be managing my company by now, but you had your mind set on medicine from a very young age. Luckily Louis and Arthur are doing a vonderful job with the business. It continues to prosper. They also have had some very innovative ideas about how it needs to change. We are no longer just selling lumber, but our inventory is now very broad. All these young people are not content with the vay things vere."

"Oh, Pa, think of how quickly the world is changing. Even you have put electricity into the house, and you now have indoor plumbing. Two very minor details that have really improved life, I would say. Before you know it, I am going to see you driving one of the newfangled horseless carriages they keep talking about."

"You vill never see me in one of dose things. Dat looks like a great way to keep you busy, repairing people after dey have been mangled in one of dose contraptions. I vill stick wit my horse and buggy. Dere is nowhere I have to be dat fast."

"I have not seen many in New Orleans yet, but I think they will be buzzing along our roadways before long. I think I would like to try one."

"Always Mr. Adventure! How is dat steam powered sailboat working?"

"Pa, it is great. The only problem is I do not get to take it out nearly often enough, and I am afraid this new position will give me even less free time."

"Jeff, I feel sure dat could be one of der problems of dis new position. I guess I vill be reading all about it in der morning papers."

"Actually, not tomorrow, Pa. I asked the board to keep this under their hat until after Dr.Miles' funeral tomorrow. The announcement will be made day after tomorrow. I wanted to make sure you were aware of it before hearing about it from strangers. Please do keep it to yourself for now."

"Of course, how thoughtful of you! Dr. Miles was a fine man. I plan to attend his funeral tomorrow also. I am sure dere will be quite a crowd."

"Yes, he was my hero. I hope I can continue to lead the hospital in the direction he had it moving. That is one of my greatest fears—being able to fill his shoes."

"Remember, Jeff, you will never be him. Vhat you need to strive for is to do der very best job you can. I have no doubt dat you will do an impressive job running dat hospital."

"I plan to put all I have into keeping Charity the most outstanding hospital in the south."

*　*　*

The funeral was attended by all the notables of the city. Even the governor was there. The eulogy expanded on what a loss to the city this was, and how a great man like Dr. Miles would be so difficult to replace. His vision and passion for improving medical care in New Orleans had been the reason the city's health had fared so well.

Jeff was very glad that his appointment had not been announced yet, otherwise everyone would have turned to look at him, wondering if he was capable of the job. He almost felt guilty that he could presume to accept this position. He felt a lot of eyes staring at him. Were the rumors spreading? He hoped to put Dr. Miles to rest in peace before all the chaos erupted. He knew there would be dissension. How could the board appoint someone as young as he to run this huge hospital? Well, he had a mighty job ahead of him. He had not slept a wink, tossing and turning and planning his strategy. But what an opportunity this would be for him! The world of medicine was changing so rapidly, and he wanted to be sure to stay in the forefront. He got up twice to look up articles in some of his medical journals. He made six different lists of his order of priorities. When he went to do his morning rounds, Sister Agnes had actually winked at him! How drastically life was changing.

Dr. Matas had stopped him in the hallway and shook his hand. How did he know? But he did, and apparently he approved. He got strange looks from many of the other doctors, but no one said anything directly. He knew that was coming. He wondered what Dr. Dyer's emergency was. He assumed he would learn soon enough.

Mr. LeBlanc stopped by Jeff's office early the next morning and mentioned that Dr. Parker and Dr. Fortier would serve as his assistant house surgeons. Dr. Matas had been appointed head of the surgery department. "Jeff, I need you to come to the board room at ten this morning for the official announcement. I know the press will have many questions for you."

"Mr. LeBlanc, apparently word has leaked, as I have gotten many strange looks lately. And if Sister Agnes does not stop winking at me, we will have a scandal erupting!"

"That would really spice up the rumor mill around here! I will see you at ten."

*　　*　　*

"As many of you know we recently lost our great leader, Dr. Albert B. Miles. Dr. Miles was a native of Alabama, attended schools in both Arkansas and Virginia, but received his Medical Doctor degree from the University of Louisiana. He had been House Surgeon at Charity since 1882, and during his tenure he completely changed Charity Hospital from a disastrous cesspool into a dynamic, successful hospital. He will be greatly missed," began Mr. LeBlanc at the press conference.

"However, we have chosen to replace him with his closest mentee. Dr. Jefferson Davis Bloom will be our new House Surgeon. As many of you know he is a native New Orleanian who graduated top of his class from Tulane Medical School. What many may not be aware of is that he also studied commerce in Vicksburg, Mississippi and was very successful in the business world before entering medical school. Medicine has long been Dr. Bloom's first love, as his father will attest. He has served as assistant to Dr. Miles for several years, and promises to continue to advance the progress of medicine here at Charity. Assisting Dr. Bloom will be Drs. Parker and Fortier, who will share those duties equally. Dr. Matas will assume the chair of the Department of Surgery. Are there any questions?" Mr. LeBlanc paused to see a few hands raised. "Yes, Mr. Jones of the Picayune?"

"Mr. LeBlanc, is not Dr. Bloom relatively young to be assuming such an important position?"

"Well, Mr. Jones, his experience and dedication override his chronological years. I think you will find he is very capable of handling the job. The board overwhelming chose him. Even Sister Agnes approves. Do you have any other questions?" No other hands were raised.

"Well, Dr. Bloom, let me give you an opportunity to speak to the reporters."

"Thank you, Mr. LeBlanc. Mr. Jones, I hope my youth will give me a little extra vim and vigor to achieve the monumental task that lies ahead. Since the war, the field of medicine has been changing drastically. Dr. Miles was a stalwart in pushing Charity forward. He encouraged all of the doctors on staff to thoroughly study the journals and attend professional meetings to stay up on the latest discoveries. Our staff has taken a lead in establishing new procedures that are now practiced throughout the world. However, we have a long way to go. When I accepted this position, I gave Mr. LeBlanc a list of the things I wanted to improve Charity, and that was just a starting point. Some of these are in the planning stages already. The bequest we received of $22,000 last month from the estate of Mr. Tommy Loflon will help in adding the space we need to serve our patients. At times we face tremendous overcrowding. I have many plans for this great institution, but before I list them publicly, I will make sure that the funding is available and that the board has the chance to approve them. They have promised me their full cooperation.

"Now if any of you would like to make a contribution to this great institution, Mr. LeBlanc will gladly accept them. And please do follow in Mr. Loflon's example, and keep us in your will. Unfortunately, most of these changes and upgrades are costly, but essential, to keeping Charity on top of the field of medicine. Thank you, gentlemen."

Several of the reporters stayed and asked a few questions, which Jeff, for the most part, was able to side step. Of course, they wanted to know what specific plans he had for the hospital, and as he said, that would come in time.

CHAPTER ELEVEN

A Leper Colony

"Dr. Dyer, please come in and have a seat. Now that the cat is out of the bag, please let me know how I can help you," smiled Jeff.

"Thank you for seeing me so soon after your appointment. I can only imagine the mountain of business you have before you, however, I need to make sure you are aware of something Dr. Miles and I had been working on, and hope to have your blessing to continue."

"Yes, please do let me know."

"As you know, as a part of my specialty in dermatology I have also specialized in the study of leprosy. Two years ago, the state legislature deemed that any person within the boundaries of Louisiana who suffers from leprosy must be confined to an institution or a hospital. Here in New Orleans, they are sent to the pest house. That is not a desirable situation, because in their already endangered health they are likely to contract numerous other diseases. We have been able to obtain an abandoned plantation about 80 miles upriver that could be used as a leper colony. It consists of 360 acres of land. The manor house was built in the 1850's under the direction of the esteemed New Orleans architect Henry Howard. As you probably know, he designed many of the prestigious plantation homes along the river like Belle Helene and Nottaway. It was originally owned by Mr. Robert Coleman Camp who served as a general for the Confederate Army and used to bring his troops from New Orleans to the plantation to rest and recuperate. He called it Woodlawn Plantation, although it is more commonly known as the Indian Point. Previously the site was used extensively by the Houma Indians for hunting and fishing. The manor house, although beautiful, is currently in a rundown condition and needs repairs, but there are seven former slave cabins that are habitable. It is currently owned by the heirs of Henry J. Budington, who have abandoned it completely as they now live in France. Dr. Miles and I have been arranging for provisions. Two of the dear sisters have volunteered their services, although the mother house has not given its full approval. I would arrange to visit on a regular basis to tend to their medical needs."

"Are you not afraid of contracting the disease?"

"Actually, Dr. Bloom, leprosy is not that contagious. Only a very small percentage of people are even susceptible to the disease. The only person we have on record locally as contracting the disease was Fr. Boblioi in 1879. He was the hospital chaplain and spent a lot of time in the leprosy ward. Most people actually acquire it as babies or very young children. We know that it is transmitted by a rod shaped bacterium, and can only be transferred by touch. I am very careful about not touching my patients. I have them apply the medicines and salves to themselves. You may have noticed the young boy who works at the fruit stand on Common Street just down from the hospital. He has had leprosy for many years now, and yet no one has contracted it from him. The horror of leprosy is how it eats away at your body. So many of the patients lose their fingers and toes, and are covered with ugly sores. One of the advantages of having them isolated is that in their own community they would no longer be subject to the cruelty of healthy people."

"What will you need from me?" asked Jeff.

"All the help you are willing to give. Dr. Miles kept a journal with the details of what he could send us. We expect to have the lepers themselves work at the colony to make it habitable and productive. We want it to be a place of refuge, not reproach, a place of treatment and research, not detention. It should be a place where these poor tormented souls can live in peace."

"Before I leave today, I am planning to pack up my office so that I can move into Dr. Miles'. One of the first things I will look for is his journal on the leper colony. It sounds like a wonderful idea to me, and I will indeed give you my blessing and support. Give me a few days to see what I can find, and we will meet again and try to finalize some details. We will probably simply pack his things and put them in storage. I plan to go through all of his journals, however, before anything is packed away."

"Thank you so much, Dr. Bloom. You have removed a huge burden from my heart. Could we possibly set our next meeting for a week from today? That should give you a little more time to settle into your new position."

"Good planning, Dr. Dyer. Who knows what other projects Dr. Miles had been working on? I feel sure you are the first of many. I will jot you down for next week at this same time."

"Good day, Dr. Bloom, and thank you."

Jeff wondered what would be next on his plate. After making the rounds of his patients, he returned to his office to pack. He was amazed at how much he had accumulated in such a few short years. So many journals had important studies cited. All had tags sticking out labeling them with their topic. He packed six boxes of medical books, and wondered where he would store all of this in his new office. Luckily patient files were kept in a general area and would not have to be moved. He had notes on cases he planned to publish in journals and share with other doctors. Publishing had become a keystone of the medical profession.

As he went into Dr. Miles' office, the first thing he noticed under the glass top of his desk was an article from the Times-Democrat written in 1892 scathing the hospital. Capt. F.S. Dugmore praised the medical staff and sisters, but hung the administration. He claimed that the general facilities were poor, bathroom facilities totally inadequate. Sixteen patients shared one or two makeshift lavatories. To get help at night, a patient had to bang on the wall to get the night watchman to assist him. Incoming patients were sometimes put to bed without even being examined. One example he cited was a man brought in on a Sunday night with a gunshot wound, who was not seen by a doctor until 8 the next morning. The man died at 9 a.m. When this article was published, Dr. Miles looked into all of the allegations and was striving to make sure such conditions were eradicated. The fact that it had such a prominent position on his desk indicated how seriously he had taken the affront. Jeff knew that the problems had not all been solved, and that they were now his.

Before even unpacking any of his things, Jeff knew he had to go through what Dr. Miles had pending. He methodically went from folder to folder and drawer to drawer making a list of pending projects. He then numbered them according to his priority. He cleared a file drawer and placed the folders in order of importance. He then made a second list of all the people he needed to talk with in order to accomplish each item.

One of the top priority projects included talking with the architect who was designing the new wing of the hospital that Mr. Loflon's bequest was funding. Now that he was in charge, Jeff wanted to be sure his input was heard. Secondly, he had to talk with Sister Agnes about the nursing school. He wanted to have his hands on it as firmly as he knew hers were. He also had to speak with the Board of Health and see what progress they had made in cleaning up some of the more disease prone areas of the city. Jeff firmly believed that filth contributed to disease, and there was a lot of filth to be cleaned up in the city. A new epidemic of yellow fever or small pox was not something he relished tackling. Then he had the maintenance people at the hospital. He wanted to set up a specific schedule of cleaning and have checklists in place to make sure they adhered to it. And then there was the staff. There would be a lot of changes under his leadership. Jeff wondered how they would be accepted.

He found the folder relating to the Leper Colony, and everything seemed to be in excellent order. One of the things he really liked about the idea was that the residents would be responsible for the upkeep of the facility. Everyone who lived there would have a job to do. Assignments, of course, would be relative to ability, but he knew this would give them more ownership in the place. The plans were to move a few residents there in November, and to gradually increase the number of patients as the facilities allowed. Dr. Miles had even sent a request to the Mother House of the Sisters requesting that several of the nuns be assigned to the leprosarium on a regular basis. So far, he had not gotten a response.

When Jeff glanced at his pocket watch, he was amazed that it was already two in the morning. He gathered a few things together and headed home for the evening. This would be the first of many long days.

CHAPTER TWELVE

Making Plans

"Dr. Bloom, it is my pleasure to meet with you again," said the architect. "I understand you have assumed the position of House Surgeon, so now you have the option of adjusting some of the plans for our new wing."

"Mr. Freret, it is indeed a pleasure to meet with you. I am a great admirer of your structures and know that you will produce the very best for us as well. Yes, I have looked over the plans that Dr. Miles had in his office, and there are a few adjustments I think we need to make. As you know, one of the biggest reasons for the addition was to increase the number of beds. However, there are two priorities that I feel also must be addressed. As I understand, the addition will be three stories. I would like to propose that we devote the bottom story to a state of the art surgery amphitheater, along with an expanded pathology department. There may be room there for a few offices as well, but that is secondary. We could convert some of the old surgeries into offices if necessary. The surgery theater should have at least four operating rooms and one must have a viewing area so that medical students can observe the operations. Also I want to remind you of the importance of cleanliness, which means you must arrange to have washstands available for each surgery, as well as washstands available in the wards. Lighting and ventilation in the operating rooms are also critical. The pathology department will need a dark room designed for our new X-ray machine which I plan to order forthwith. The top two floors would be divided into wards that could separate patients according to their diagnoses. In your plans, please be sure to arrange for a sufficient arrangement of lavatories for the patients. This has long been a problem in our current building.

"Fortunately, doctor, we are still in the planning stages and no actual construction has begun. We planned to break ground next month. Let us look over the blue prints that have been drawn up and see what adjustments you feel are necessary. Actually, Dr. Miles had made some of the same considerations. I think you, and several of the other doctors had given him your input."

"Indeed, Dr. Matas and I have been pouring over your plans and encouraging Dr. Miles to design it to our criteria. He always tried to be supportive of our requests, but now that I am in charge, I want to be certain that the design is to our utmost advantage."

The architect laid the blueprints on the table, and the next hour was spent making adjustments. Jeff called Dr. Matas to join them and give his input into the surgery wing. Mr. Freret had a tablet full of notes to use in his redesign. He promised to return within the week with the newly drawn plans. After the architect left, Rudy and Jeff sat down to discuss the progress that was being made.

"Jeff, I hear we have a staff meeting in the morning. All of the doctors who practice in the hospital have been required to attend. What is this all about?"

"Rudy, you know what a germaphobe I am. I am instituting new procedures that require all doctors to wash their hands before they touch any patient. They also will be required to wear gauze masks when dealing with open wounds. Instruments cannot be used on multiple patients without first washing them. I plan to cite many of the articles by Dr. Lister and Dr. Jenner that support these decisions. We need to lower the infection rates in our patients. I also plan to completely remodel the old hospital. I plan to get rid of every wooden bed and replace it with a metal bed. The metal ones can be properly cleaned, the wooden ones cannot. We have to find a way to install more lavatories on the wards. I have a meeting scheduled with the maintenance people this afternoon. They will be given new instructions on their cleaning procedures.

"Carbolic acid may be the new smell of Charity. These are some things I have been eager to see in place, and now I have the opportunity to make sure that they are. I may be one of the shortest lived House Surgeons in history, but I want to do this job right, and think these are important steps I need to take."

"Well, you know the doctors do not take well to being ordered around, but I do think many of them are aware of the problems and may welcome these new guidelines. I am assuming that you are also addressing the dear sisters and all the other clinical staff."

"Oh, yes. That will follow the doctors' meeting. I am meeting with Sister Agnes this afternoon to get her approval. Pray for me, Rudy," he chuckled.

"At least you know the wisdom of getting her on your side before you attempt changes. I hear that the sisters at Hotel Dieu are talking about bringing in some nurses from Boston to train their people on aseptics. They have been in contact with Carney Hospital which is also run by the Sisters of Charity. I do not know if they will be sisters or lay nurses, but you might ask Sister Agnes about that."

"Thank you for the information. That would be wonderful to actually have someone train all of our people. There is so much that I have only read about. I would love to talk to someone who has more experience on the subject. Please keep me informed on any other developments that you become aware of. I feel my new duties will keep me in a tailspin. I did not fully appreciate all that Dr. Miles did. I think about him often."

"You have only been on this job for three days now, Jeff. Things are bound to settle down. Dr. Miles was a good man, and I think he would approve of most of the things you are doing. By the way, I love the plans for the surgery amphitheater. What a change it will be from our current makeshift conditions!"

"I felt sure you wanted to give your input to the architect. You had some excellent ideas to add to the plans. Thank you for taking the time to meet with him."

"I might have barged in uninvited had I known this conference was taking place. Thank you for including me. I have surgery scheduled shortly. Let me go properly wash up before I begin," he said smiling.

"Rudy, be sure to check those fingernails."

It was good to have such a supportive friend on staff, especially one who was admired by so many. Dr. Matas had been making huge strides in his surgical techniques and was becoming world famous for some of the journal articles he had written.

Jeff decided that he needed to take a tour of the hospital from an observer's prospective. He brought with him a tablet, and started on the top floor. He interviewed patients and listened to their concerns. He took notes on deficiencies as he saw them. He spoke with the nurses and jotted down their complaints. He talked to relatives of patients. He walked through the surgery areas. He went through the outdoor clinic and made observations as though he had never been there before. In the past, he would rush to his station through a back door and avoid going into the waiting area. Today he stopped and asked patients for their suggestions for improvement. He decided he needed to do this on a regular basis—look at the hospital from a patient's point of view. It was an eye opener.

Immediately after lunch he met with the maintenance supervisors. He presented them with a list of required services, and a checklist that would be completed each week and turned in to him directly. He assured them that if it meant hiring additional staff to complete the tasks, that would be considered, but cleanliness was of utmost concern. All restrooms would be cleaned twice a day. All floors mopped once a day. When a patient was discharged, his bed was to be thoroughly wiped down and disinfected. Sheets would be changed on beds daily. He asked that the supervisors give him a list of who had been assigned to each job, so that he would know who was responsible for inefficiencies. He also wanted to commend those who were doing an excellent job. He noted that he had just toured the facilities and mentioned to them some of the appalling sights he had seen: unclean restrooms, overflowing wastebaskets, filth on the floors, dust an inch thick on some of the furniture. He asked that they be taken care of immediately.

The supervisors looked at each other, and nodded their agreement. They had the look of total surprise and amazement. Had he really taken the time to go check up on them? What was this new House Surgeon going to be like? They had all known Dr. Bloom to be a very mild mannered physician, who pretty much kept to his own affairs. He had never imposed himself on any of them. Charity was apparently in for a big change.

Jeff thought it had gone very well. He noticed them talking excitedly amongst themselves as they were leaving. It seems they were making plans for how they would implement these changes, or at least he hoped so. He would hate to have massive resignations from the maintenance department!

Next up was Sister Agnes. Jeff grabbed a cup of coffee to fortify himself for this meeting. He anticipated it would be one of the most stressful. Sister Agnes was on time for her appointment, of course. She was always punctual and would not tolerate tardiness from anyone else. She was almost bouncing as she came into his office.

"Oh, Dr. Bloom. How are your first days going? I can only imagine the stress you must be under. I have been praying for you. I know what a wonderful job you will do, but I know we all need the good Lord's help."

"Dear Sister Agnes, thank you for your prayers. They are badly needed. There are so many decisions to make, and I am trying not to step on too many toes as I make them. I am hoping you can help me."

"Gladly, my dear doctor, how can I be of assistance?"

"Tomorrow morning I am addressing all of the doctors who practice at Charity. You know that one of my big concerns has always been the spread of infections. I am putting in new guidelines that have to do with cleanliness. It is foolish of us to take germs from one patient and give them to another. That must be stopped."

"I agree wholeheartedly, but how can I help?"

"If we are requiring this of the doctors, it must also be required of all the staff. Just as the doctors will complain of it slowing them down, I am sure the nurses will complain doubly loudly. I need to have your full support in requiring this of all staff. Your nurses are your responsibility and they need to understand this directive is coming from both of us. Spread of contagions cannot be tolerated."

"I will proudly stand with you and emphasize that this directive is coming from both of us. I will make sure that the supervising nurses remind their aides to take the necessary measures to insure cleanliness. Now that was easy enough. What else is on your agenda?"

"You are a gem. Can you read minds, too?"

"No, doctor, but I just felt there must be more than this."

"Yes, I am very concerned about the nursing school. Now that I am the House Surgeon, I want to be the doctor in charge of it. I want to be able to walk in on classes and see what is going on there. I want to observe your students in their laboratories. I want to be able to discuss with them their ideas on health care."

"Dr. Bloom, I was going to suggest the exact same thing. That was on my list of things to talk to you about. I know that you are eager to have more trained nurses here in the hospital, as am I, and I think you should be certain that we are doing a good job of training them. Second problem solved! What is next?"

"Dr. Matas was telling me that the sisters at the Hotel Dieu are working to bring some nurses from Boston, experts in the latest sterilization techniques, to train their physicians and staff. I wondered if you had heard anything about that."

"I have heard rumors to that effect, but I do not think anything has been finalized. Would you like me to stick my nose into the matter?"

"Absolutely, and find out if they do have them coming, could we borrow them?"

"I will plant some seeds and see what I can find out. Is there anything else?"

"One more thing—you probably have heard that Dr. Dyer is planning to open a leper colony upriver. I know that Dr. Miles had written to your Mother House about providing sisters to care for the sick there, and wondered if they had contacted you."

"I have two sisters who have been nursing the leper patients in the pest house who would be very distressed if they were left behind when their patients leave. I have not heard from the Mother House on the matter, but I think we could possibly send these two with the patients even if we have not heard by that time. When do you think they would be departing? I think the idea is wonderful. Those poor people have been tortured for centuries. They would be so much happier if they had their own facilities where they would not be ridiculed and despised."

"The plans are still in process, but I anticipate their departure in the next few months. I still need to get back with Dr. Dyer and finalize some of the details. I am glad to hear that you are willing to send your sisters. I am assuming you anticipate that the Mother House will give its approval."

"I am sure they will eventually agree, but some decisions come very slowly from Evansville. This is just the kind of service St. Vincent de Paul would have approved of, and, after all, we are his daughters."

"I know Dr. Dyer will be delighted to hear that. Can you also help by making a list of the provisions you think they will need? Although we are starting with just a few patients, I anticipate the colony will grow rapidly once it is settled. Of course, we can always send more supplies, but I do want them to be as comfortable as possible."

"That is probably your easiest request. I will have one of my assistants come up with a list for you; in fact, I will have her start separating out the supplies from our stockpiles. Then we will know what additional materials need to be ordered."

"Oh, Sister, it has been a delight meeting with you. Now are there any special requests you have for me?"

"Oh yes, Dr. Bloom. Are you ready to convert yet, or do I need to spend many more hours on my knees praying for you."

"Well I hate to burden you and your knees, but I am still a faithful temple goer. My father has often wondered if you had put a spell on me to keep me here at Charity."

"I need to meet your father, or perhaps I need just to start praying for him, too. Please assure him that we use no witchcraft or Voodoo, only prayers to the same God you worship. We just have already received our Messiah and Savior. I would love for you to get to know Him as well."

"Perhaps we can do that another time, Sister. Thank you so much for all your help. Please plan to be at the staff meeting tomorrow morning. I need to have you stand beside me and confirm the changes we will implement."

"I will keep praying, but I will also be with you tomorrow. Have no fear. You are taking wonderful strides in the right direction. I think I will go over to Hotel Dieu this afternoon and find out what they are planning."

"Thank you again, Sister. See you tomorrow morning. I am anxious to hear what your spying report brings us," he chuckled.

Jeff was greatly relieved that their meeting had gone so well. He then left to take care of his rounds in the hospital. It would be good to get back to doing some doctoring. This decision making was really stressful, but he felt he was making progress. Perhaps he could even get home in time to share supper with Pa. Their time together had been very limited lately, and he did not want to lose his closeness with his father.

CHAPTER THIRTEEN

Meetings with Staff

DEAR DOCTORS,

PLEASE JOIN ME THURSDAY MORNING AT 10 A.M. IN THE CONFERENCE ROOM TO HELP DETERMINE THE FUTURE OF CHARITY HOSPITAL. BRING ALL OF YOUR HOPES, DREAMS, AND IDEAS WITH YOU. WE HAVE MANY DECISIONS TO MAKE.

DR. JEFF BLOOM

So read the note sent to every practicing physician in the hospital. Copies were also posted in the doctors' lounge. The hospital was abuzz with hushed conversations. Jeff found it ironic to see all the whispering taking place until he walked into a room and suddenly the conversations changed to the weather and everyone spoke in a normal tone again. He was determined that he was going to give all the doctors ownership in the changes he wanted to make in the hospital. He carefully prepared the message that he sent out. He did not want to appear weak or domineering, but he did want to make the invitation challenging enough so that most of the doctors would take time from their busy schedules to attend. The results were overwhelming. Over one hundred doctors packed into the conference room. Jeff had strategically placed a blackboard at the front of the room. The doctors signed in as they entered. At exactly 10 a.m. Jeff took the podium and began.

"It is with great humility that I accepted the position of House Surgeon when I knew the vast talent that existed in this hospital. That is why I called you together to help me find our direction. Having worked so closely with Dr. Miles over the last few years as assistant house surgeon, I am aware of some of the changes he had been working to accomplish. Since my appointment, I have been going through his files to determine the progress that has been made. Today I call on you to help me prioritize where we go from here. In my memo I asked you to bring with you your hopes, dreams and ideas, and my hope is that you have done your homework. What I would like you to do at this time is to break into groups of ten, discuss your ideas, and come back to me in fifteen minutes with an organized list of your top ten priorities for the hospital. I know how valuable your time is, so I implore you to save the congenial conversation until after our task is completed. Please select a spokesman for your group. We will reconvene in exactly 15 minutes," said Jeff as he checked his pocket watch. He turned from the group and sat at a nearby table and began to peruse a folder of papers.

The doctors stared at each other for a few seconds and then quickly formed clusters. The volume in the room was soon a roar, as you could hear men's animated voices expressing heartfelt opinions. At exactly 15 minutes, Jeff reconvened the meeting.

"If you have not gotten all ten ideas in place, we will go with your top priorities. I have asked my secretary, Miss Hebert, to come in and list your top ideas on the blackboard. What I would like each spokesman to do is to read off their number one priority. If that has already been stated, then please drop down to the second or third on your list, so that everyone has a contribution to make. Let us begin with the group to my left here in the front. We will proceed from group to group until everyone has spoken. Miss Hebert if you do not mind. Dr. Bradley, will you begin?"

The meeting proceeded in a very orderly manner with each group making suggestions. Many were amazed that so many groups had come up with the same priorities. When ten different suggestions were listed, Jeff stood again and said,

"Doctors, I think you have given me plenty to work on. Although I would love to say that I will have an open door policy, with patients coming in and out that is impossible. However, in the future, if you have suggestions, please submit them to me in a written form. Include your name so that I can get back to you if I have questions about your suggestion. I promise to take all of these ideas into consideration. I know there are some problems that are specific to different parts of the hospital, and I do not want anyone to be ignored. Now that you have seen the list, your recommendations for how these things can be implemented will be my next request. Remember we do have a budget. I have an appointment with Governor Murphy Foster to see if we can do something to improve that. He seems to be a very reasonable man, and I believe he thinks Charity Hospital is very important to our great state.

"The other good news is that some of these problems are already being addressed. Dr. Miles had the foresight to include several of these in his plans. As you know there is a new wing to be built onto the hospital. The plans will include a state of the art surgery amphitheater. But I do not want to promise anything until I am certain I can deliver, so I will refrain from getting ahead of myself. Please continue to send me your suggestions. Would the spokesperson for each group please give me the list that your team put together, so that I have a complete list of your ideas? I think our major list here on the board is where we need to start, but I hope we can accomplish the rest as well."

The list was exactly what Jeff would have made had he been working on his own.

1. Improve sanitation.
2. Better surgery facilities.
3. Find a new facility for the poor souls with leprosy.
4. Oversee the nursing school.
5. Get an X-ray machine for the hospital.
6. Find a way to curb infections from spreading from one patient to the next.
7. More patient beds.
8. Separate the children into another building.
9. Have a better system for cleaning surgery equipment.
10. Enlarge and improve the pathology department.

'Now the doctors have given me their okay to follow my dreams,' Jeff thought. 'Let us see if we can get the rest of the staff on board as well.'

A meeting with the nursing staff took place after lunch and proceeded in almost exactly the same way. There were a few variations in the order of the list, and the nurses were vehement about wanting the doctors to give them more liberty to treat patients as they had been trained. They felt the doctors did not give them the respect they deserved as nurses. They also wanted a home for the nurses that was not a part of the convent. Jeff soothed over that with the promise that as more registered nurses came to work at the hospital, the doctors would delight in being able to turn over some of their responsibilities to the nurses. As it was, the training of the nurses on staff was a great variable, and the doctors were unwilling to allow some of the nurses to make decisions that could end up costing someone his life. He would also look into a separate home for the nurses.

That evening Jeff went to a leisurely dinner at home with his father. He wanted to pick his mind about how to handle some of the more powerful people in the state, particularly the governor. After a delightful dinner, they relaxed over brandy and cigars, and Jeff broached the subject.

"Pa, what can you tell me about Murphy Foster? I am planning to meet with him day after tomorrow and I am trying to figure out the best way to get him on my side to help improve Charity."

"Vell, Jeff, you sure do not start vith der easy challenges. Murphy is one to be tackled head on for sure. If he is on your side, you vill be blessed, but if you irritate him in the least, you had better vatch out. He has been known to destroy people."

"Pa, how do you think I can go about getting him on my side? I know you have known him for years and have followed his politics carefully."

"First, I vould make sure you let him know dat you were delighted dat he is trying to outlaw der lottery. Dat is one of der most corrupt corporations to ever exist, and the sad ting is dat it plays on the hopes and dreams of the poorest of our citizens and strips dem of vhatever little excesses dey might have. Dat vill get you on his side quickly. You might even conjure up some stories of some patients you dealt vith who suffered greatly because dey had put all dey had into lottery tickets. I can remember vhen dey started it right after der war. It was intended to help rebuild dose areas of der state dat had been ravaged by der Yankees. Dey gave der Lottery Company a 25 year charter back in 1868 guaranteeing dey would have no competition. Now the Louisiana Lottery is popular all over der nation vith more people outside der state gambling in it than inside der state. Der legislature has tried to repeal der charter, but der company has learned quickly who to bribe in order to keep it going. Dey keep renewing its charter. It is making some people a lot of money. All der other state lotteries ver banned back in '78, but ours has kept on filling der pockets of its managers. Dere is talk dat Congress is getting ready to ban der passing of lottery tickets across state lines. Now dat ours is der only one operating in der nation, probably 90% of its supporters are out of state. Dat vould really help curb it. Dere are rumors that der corruption in der lottery company is monumental."

"Maybe I should look into getting the Lottery Company to contribute to the support of the hospital," Jeff quipped.

"You vould really be playing vit fire, Jeff. Keep your nose clean. I predict dose folks in der Lottery Company have a good chance of ending up vith Col. James up at Angola. I hear dat is not a place you vant to spend much time visiting. In fact, dat may be a topic to bring up also. I hear Murphy is being harassed by a lot of do-gooders who tink dose convicts up dere should be treated nicely. Dey tink dey should just be able to sit around and enjoy life.

Humph! I hear Col. James runs a really tight ship up dere. He does not mess around vit dem. But I also heard a rumor dat he is not in der best of health. I hear his son is taking over a lot of the running of der operations. Murphy gets along really vell with Col. James. He believes prisoners should vork to earn deir keep. Dere is quite a huge farming operation going on dere now. Dat is probably der only place in der Old South vhere slavery is not dead. He works dose prisoners hard.

"Murphy is basically an old country boy. He grew up in Franklin, a little town vest of Morgan City, and he studied at Washington and Lee in Virginia, but came back to Tulane to get his law degree. One of der big things he has done since he von office two years ago was to set up refugee camps after der floods last year. Make sure he knows you are a Democrat. He vill not have much to do vit you if you are not. I tink having der name Jefferson Davis vill not hurt you at all—he is a big supporter of der Jim Crow laws separating der coloreds from der vhites. In fact, I think he just got back from Washington vere our laws were being challenged in the Supreme Court. Vhen are you meeting vit him?"

"I have scheduled a meeting Saturday morning. I have met with all of the staff and had them draw up a list of priorities for changes at the hospital. Their list was identical to the list I had made before I met with them, but now they all have ownership in the changes we will start making. Of course, they all cost money. It is going to be quite a challenge to take the hospital into the direction it needs to go in the new century. So many improvements are being made in medicine. I am very lucky to have doctors on staff who are eager to learn about advancements and even experiment to make some of their own.

"First thing I want to order is a new X-ray machine. Pa, can you believe it actually takes a picture of your bones! You can see inside somebody! I had been harping on Dr. Miles for years to get one. Now that I am in charge it will be one of the first things I will order."

"Jeff, your mother vould be so proud of you. It is a shame she never got der chance to see you grow into der fine young man you have become. But now tell me, where is your Mrs. Bloom? You need a wife and children to make your life complete. I know I do. After your mother died giving birth to Hannah, I struggled for two years on my own. But I am so glad that I met my own Hannah and she vas villing to take care of me and my children. Having a vife makes all the difference. Vitout her I vould not have young Arthur. It is time you settle into dis vonderful new position and find der right young Jewish lady who can produce bountiful offspring."

"Pa, you never quit," laughed Jeff. "You are probably right, but I do not think you would be happy if I married the wrong girl and ended up miserable. I have been looking for Mrs. Bloom since I was fifteen, but just have not run into her yet. I will let you know as soon as I do."

"Now dat you have such a prestigious position I vould expect the ladies vould be banging on your door. You are der most eligible bachelor in town vithout a doubt."

"That will probably explain the invitations I have received in the last few days. They have been incredible. Unfortunately, if I attended all of those social functions I would not have time to do my new job. I am struggling now to see my patients. I have been going through all of Dr. Miles' papers to see exactly what he had already begun. I do not want to step on toes of people who have already committed to doing things for the hospital, but there are many things I have to get moving. Pa, thanks for all your insight into how to deal with the governor. You have been a huge help. I have a little reading to do before I turn in for the evening, so if you will excuse me I will be heading home."

"Jeff, anytime I can be of assistance, you know I am eager to help you. Get a good night's rest. Hope you vill come by for a visit again soon. Shalom."

"Bye, Pa."

CHAPTER FOURTEEN

Becoming a Nurse

"Mary Rose, cover those curls. You are going to put our patients in shock when they see that bright red hair," shouted Sister Ann. "If you are going to be a nurse, you have got to stop smiling."

"I will try, Sister Ann, but it will not be easy," replied Mary Rose.

In 1863, Andrew Carney gave a gift of $75,000 to the Daughters of Charity to establish a hospital in Boston. It was the first Catholic hospital in New England, and was staffed by four physicians, two lay people and two sisters. Since then it had grown to have outpatient clinics in two adjacent buildings. The need for staff was great, and as Mary Rose had grown up in the orphanage run by the dear sisters, she had been strongly encouraged to become a nurse. It was actually something Mary Rose loved doing. She could meet so many people and help all of them. She seemed to have quite a knack for making them feel better.

Mary Rose had helped out in the hospital since her early teen years, but when Carney Hospital opened a nursing school she was admitted to one of its first classes. Desirable applicants were between the ages of twenty-five to thirty, and Mary Rose had just turned twenty, but, to her great delight, her application was accepted. The application stated that it expected nurses in training to be sober, honest, truthful, trustworthy, punctual, quiet, orderly, clean, neat, patient, kind and cheerful. Some of those would be a stretch for her. The kind and cheerful came naturally, but the sober and quiet she would have to work on. All applicants were subjected to a one month trial to determine if they would be worthy of the training. Once admitted they had to sign an agreement to remain at the school for two years and to conform to all of the rules. According to the application, the instruction included:

- The dressing of blisters, burns, sores and wounds, and applying of fomentations, poultices and minor dressings.
- The applying of leeches, and subsequent treatment.
- The administering of enemas.
- The applying of friction to the body and extremities in the best method.
- The managing of helpless patients in bed, in moving, changing clothing, giving baths, keeping patients warm or cool, preventing and dressing bed sores, managing position, and in feeding.
- The making of bandages and rollers, and bandaging.
- The making of beds and changing sheets with patients in bed.
- The cooking, preparing, and serving of food and delicacies for the sick.

Additionally they were expected to clean the rooms and all utensils, keep the rooms aired and at a comfortable temperature. They would also be required to observe the sick accurately in regard to the state of secretions, expectorations, pulse, breathing, skin, temperature, eruptions, sleep, appetite, effect of diet or of stimulants and medicine; and manage convalescents.

As a nursing student they would be paid ten dollars per year the first year, and $14 per year the second, which was to cover clothing and personal expenses. Room and board were automatically included, because they were required to live at the hospital. Their education was considered full equivalent for their services. They worked on the wards daily as assistant nurses with lectures, demonstrations, and exams interspersed as needed.

One of the most exciting facets of being a part of the Carney Hospital was that it was on the cutting edge of medicine, because they had adopted the revolutionary recommendations of Dr. Joseph Lister. In the past, almost 50% of all surgery patients died from infection. Dr. Lister required surgeons to wash their hands as they went from patient to patient. He separated the patients according to the diseases they had. Originally Dr. Lister insisted on spraying everything with carbolic acid to kill bacteria. Carbolic acid had many uses, such as preserving railway tracks and the wood on ships. It also cured cattle of certain infections. But there was a problem. The carbolic acid was so potent it tended to harm the patients and physicians as well. Lister had been very successful in keeping infections down in his clinics, but the caustic spray would bleach out and numb the skin. Fingernails would crack and peel. Even the lungs became sore after breathing the air treated with it. Luckily, by this time, Lister had found that boracic acid worked equally well on the bacteria, and was much gentler on the humans. Sterilized surgical gloves and masks were used. All dressings were sterilized as well. The results were that death due to infections had been markedly reduced.

Sterilization was one of the most important duties of the new nursing students. Surgical garb was not just washed, but was boiled, as were all the dressing. Cleanliness was insisted upon. A nursing student could be dismissed from the school at any time, and having unclean hands or nails was one of the most common reasons for dismissal.

Mary Rose loved being a nurse. For the first time she was able to meet people from all over the world. Her patients would thrill her with their stories of places they had been. She was a great listener, and her patients loved having such an attentive audience. The dear sisters had tried to convince her to become a Daughter of Charity, but she knew that was not her destiny. She had places to go and see. She wanted the freedom to travel. She dreamed of traveling to foreign shores to help soldiers in battle, or perhaps to go to England to meet the formidable Dr. Lister himself. And, besides, if she became a nun she would have to completely hide her beautiful red curls. She remembered how much her father had loved them. It was one of the only things she remembered about her father.

She quickly became a favorite with the patients, although the administration was not always amused with her antics. It seemed she always got extra duties because she had been caught doing something she should not have been doing, like singing to a patient or telling them a rousing tale. Mary Rose always performed her duties with intensity, but she also loved to have a good time, and she had a knack for mixing the two. Her best friend, Mary Ellen Faircloth, was of the same nature, and together they posed a formidable challenge for the dear sisters.

Chapter Fifteen

Sister Agnes

"Dr. Bloom, I hope you have been able to locate all the information about our new leper colony," said Dr. Dyer as he shook hands with Jeff.

"Dr. Dyer, one thing I have to be very thankful for is how well organized Dr. Miles was. I have a folder here that seems to have all the information in it that he had been accumulating. It seems you had proposed moving the lepers there in just a few months. Tell me what progress you have made."

"Well, Dr. Bloom, I have had quite a bit of difficulty finding any captain who is willing to board lepers on his boat. It would have to be a sizeable boat, because we also want to bring all the provisions we would need with us. The cabins and manor house all need repair, which the lepers themselves will do, but they will need material to accomplish it. Although we plan to plant gardens and raise animals on the property, to begin we will need to bring with us all the food we need for the first few months. I am also trying to round up a cow or two and some chickens. We are like pioneers setting out in the wilderness."

"How will you get supplies?" asked Jeff.

"Baton Rouge is only twenty miles upriver. Once we get set up, we will be able to have some supplies delivered to us. There is a very small farming community called Carville nearby, but from what I hear they are not very happy about our coming, and I do not expect we can count on help from the locals. Luckily there is a good bit of farming equipment on the property which we will put to good use. As soon as we get settled, we hope to start our winter gardens."

"How long does it take to get there by boat?"

"Depending on the river's current, anywhere from six to twelve hours."

"Dr. Dyer, how long do you plan to stay there?"

"I hope to get them all settled in before I come back to the city. It will probably take about a week. I plan to go back every week or so to treat them and tend their needs. I want to make sure they have the supplies they need before I go and leave them stranded."

"I can understand that. How many are you anticipating taking to the new colony with you?"

"I have twelve who are in good enough health who are eager to go. I want to make sure the ones I take can help build the colony. Once we get things settled down, we can bring some of the sicker patients."

"Have you made any provisions for nursing care?"

"I was going to talk to you about that today. Would you address the Daughters of Charity and ask if they would be willing to undertake this assignment as one of their missions? I have a couple of sisters who are going with us originally to get the patients settled, but the Mother House has to approve their appointment, and the Mother House does not act quickly on most things."

"I spoke with Sister Agnes about this, and she feels you will have a hard time leaving the two sisters behind who have been caring for your patients. Although it is not official, she sees no reason that the Mother House would not approve their appointment to the Leper Colony. She has also been encouraging the Mother House to approve it. I would think that the dear sisters would consider this quite a challenge. It has to be presented to them in the right way, and Sister Agnes is a gem at doing that, but I will also draft a letter of request to the Mother House.

"As you may know, I am quite a sailor myself. I would like to be able to visit the colony and see how it progresses. Would that be a problem if I took it on myself to sail upriver occasionally and check things out?"

"Dr. Bloom, I think they would love to have visitors like you as often as they can get them. But let me warn you, the people of New Orleans may not accept you back as readily if they know you have been consorting with lepers. My social life has dwindled to almost non-existent. People are so prejudiced. That is probably the one thing the Bible has done that is not good—instilled in good people a deadly fear of contact with lepers. They do not want any part of you if they know you have been around lepers."

"I will also look into my contacts and see if we can find a suitable boat. Is there a docking facility at the compound?"

"It is pretty dilapidated too, but it will do for now. That is another thing we will have to repair. I think boats would be willing to drop off supplies on our dock, if they did not have to make contact with anyone in the colony. We could assure them that we will spray our money down with Carbolic Acid before giving it to them," he said with a chuckle.

"You are a good man, Dr. Dyer. I will get back to you after I talk with Sister Agnes, and also will let you know about a boat. I would offer my sailboat, but it certainly is not large enough for all the cargo you will need to bring."

"Thank you, Dr. Bloom. Any and all help is greatly appreciated. You should hear how the inmates are talking about their paradise!"

"Let us hope they still feel that way once they have moved in. I think it will be a splendid paradise once you get things in order."

"I think it is an ideal location and will give the patients a lot of privacy. There are many problems yet to be resolved, but I think we are on the way."

*   *   *

"Sister Agnes, it is so good of you to come. Your wonderful counsel is desperately needed by this poor doctor. There are so many facets of this hospital that I was unaware existed. I have learned more in the last few days than all the time I was in medical school," Jeff laughed.

"Well, Dr. Bloom, I will gladly come to your aid. First of all, may I suggest that you go ahead and convert to Catholicism? That will definitely get you started in the right direction." Sister Agnes smiled as she waited for Jeff's reaction.

"Thank you, Sister, for thinking I am worthy, but at this time I chose to remain Jewish. I know you are praying for me, and I need all the prayers I can get.

"There are a number of items on my agenda that whenever I address them, your name keeps popping up as being the solution. Let us start with the nursing school. I have a list of doctors who would like to serve on the board of directors. They were complaining that they wanted to be certain that the school is being properly run, so I suggested that the best way for them to ascertain that was to have them accept a position on the board. I would like to serve as chairman of the board. That way I can help you keep them in line. If they are on the board, they are less likely to be critical of how things are run. Here is a list of their names, and I would suggest that you call a meeting of the board for some time in the next few weeks."

"They say the best way to take care of your critics is to give them ownership in what you are doing. You are a wise man, Dr. Bloom. I will be glad to accept these nominees for the board, and I will check the calendar for when our first board meeting will be held. That was easy. What is next?"

"Dr. Dyer would love to have the two sisters who have worked closely with the lepers move to the leprosarium on a permanent basis. Perhaps we could just keep this under the cuff until we get official permission from the Mother House. Is that agreeable?"

"Well, Dr. Bloom, I think St. Vincent would approve. It is a shame how often bureaucracy slows down helping the needy."

"We will be sending more than ample provisions for their care, and will continue to supply their needs as necessary. Dr. Dyer will visit the facility every two weeks to check on the status of the patients and prescribe medications as needed."

"When will they actually be moving to the plantation?"

"We hope to get them moved sometime in November. Having two sisters with them would be a great comfort for them."

"I understand that the plantation is in dire need of repair!"

"That is the first item on the list of things to do there—repairing the structures. The sisters would be staying in the manor house and the patients would be occupying the old slave quarters. We plan to separate the patients by gender and race, of course. Since the sisters know most of these patients well, I do not think they would be fearful of them."

"My sisters will be dancing with joy knowing they will be going to 'paradise' with their patients."

"We will plan the movement of the healthier patients soon, so they can get started with the building repairs."

"I will send another letter to the Mother House, hurrying them to approve the appointment, and I will consider the best approach. So many changes! I think the leper colony is a wonderful idea. I have seen that pest house and it is abominable. Now, what is next?"

"One of the greatest concerns that our staff has brought to my attention is the spread of infection from one patient to the next. I am working on a memo to all staff that will require the washing of hands before touching any new patient. I also plan to meet with housekeeping to see about better cleaning of linens and bathroom facilities. We need to do a better job of cleaning surgical instruments as well. Do you have any ideas on how else we can get this under control?"

"I was planning to mention this to you. I spoke to Sister Mariana at Hotel Dieu and, as you know, she is trying to get trained nurses from Carney Hospital in Boston to come to New Orleans to instruct their doctors and nurses in the germ theory as espoused by Dr. Lister. Carney is well known for the remarkable job it has done in lowering the number of deaths from infections.

"The whole idea is in the preliminary stages, but yes I do think we could get some benefit from this as well. In the meantime, please do submit that memo about hand washing. We are providing the Octagon soap you recommended at every station. I will also talk to the janitorial staff about cleanliness being next to godliness! We will begin soaking all of the surgical tools in carbolic acid. It is just so hard on your hands and nose!"

"Sister, as you know I read everything in print about changes in medical practice. They are considering using other disinfectants that might be milder but still kills the germs. In fact, we have a group of medical school students working on that right now. Hopefully we will get some results soon. In the meantime, carbolic acid is the choice. Please do keep me informed about the nurses from Carney."

"Glad to help in any way I can. Do not forget I am praying for you to convert. Prayers are powerful things, my son. Do not be surprised when the spirit suddenly moves you."

"Yes, dear sister, I will be waiting for the movement. Pray for me when I meet with Governor Foster tomorrow. That will probably be my most intimidating meeting so far in my career as House Surgeon. I hope he looks kindly on us."

"Oh, Governor Foster has been very good to Charity Hospital. Would you like me to come with you to the meeting? I have met with him several times and he has always been very pleasant. Are you trying to get money from him?"

"We are definitely underfunded by the state and need additional assistance. You are a very productive fundraiser. Are you willing to share any secrets?"

"Now, Dr. Bloom, you do not think I manipulate my donors, do you? But I have always found that first you have to make the donor believe that you are meeting with them because you want to help them. Then you work it around so it is their idea to help you out by donating to your cause. It works like a charm! I hope that tip helps you. Is this your first venture into fund raising?"

"Never did I think this would be a part of my job as a doctor! Luckily I have some experience in commerce, but I always hated the part of asking for money. I guess I had best get used to it. This hospital costs a lot to run."

"You will do just fine, Dr. Bloom. And I will add that to my list of things to pray about for you."

"Thank you again, Sister. Please feel free to meet with me whenever the need arises. I appreciate your wise counsel and devout prayers—whatever it takes to make Charity into a better hospital."

*   *   *

"To vhat do I owe another visit from der famous Dr. Bloom? I have been reading a lot about you in der papers lately. Vould you care to join me for dinner? Cook always overdoes, so I am sure dere will be plenty. I tink she might be feeding her whole family off our leftovers."

"Good to see you again, Pa, and dinner sounds wonderful. I do miss Dulcie's wonderful meals. Somehow the hospital food just does not compare.

"I have come to see you on a matter of business, however, and this has to be kept very confidential. In just a few months we are planning to move our patients with leprosy upriver to Indian Point. Dr. Myles and Dr. Dyer had secured a lease on the plantation, and I have been arranging a lot of the details. One of the biggest problems has been trying to find a captain who will bring our cargo upriver. They are so afraid that their boat will be quarantined after carrying lepers, or that no one will be willing to come aboard after that. Being a man who does a lot of shipping on the river, I knew I could come to you for advice. Not only would we have the patients, but we would also have a large quantity of supplies as well. It would take a fairly large vessel."

"You do get yourself into some hassles, Jeff. Let me tink on dat for a while and see vhat I can do to help you. Vhat exactly are you planning to do wit dem at Indian Point?"

"Well, the old Woodlawn plantation is there and there is a manor house and slave cabins that, although in need of repair, are habitable. We are planning on making it a community where the lepers can be self-supportive and live in peace and harmony. They will be raising their own crops and some livestock as well. They are so abused in the city it is sad to see, and the pest house they live in is deplorable. Indian Point is a grand location for them. It is 360 acres of land surrounded on three sides by water. There is a boat landing on the river, which also needs repair. We are only sending the healthier patients in the beginning, so they can get on with the repairs, and the rest will follow. Two years ago, the legislature required that anyone diagnosed with leprosy must be confined to a hospital or sanitarium, and many of them have gone into hiding and are getting no treatment at all. At least here they would have a nice place to live, and could get good treatment."

"How many patients vill be going?"

"According to Dr. Dyer, there should be less than twelve going in the beginning. Dr. Dyer will be accompanying them as well as two of the sisters. We are enlisting the aid of the Daughters of Charity to take this on as a new mission. You know how much good work they do around the world. They are perfectly suited to take on this new challenge. We just have to convince them of it!"

"I have an idea how we could send all dis upriver, and fairly inexpensively. I have several barges dat belong to me. If we loaded der patients and der supplies on a barge, I feel sure I could get one of der tug captains to push der barge up der river. He vould not have to come in contact with your patients at all."

"That does not sound very comfortable, Pa, but it definitely has possibilities."

"To further comfort der tug captain, I would suggest dat we board der patients and leave der city during der night, so dat fewer people are aware of vhat is happening.

"Ve can set up beds and chairs on der barge, and perhaps even surround dem vit der cargo to take der chill river vind off der patients. How much cargo are you planning to send?"

"My list is growing daily. I have acquired 80 beds as well as the linens that will be needed. I also have other furniture and all the food they should need for the first month. We can fill a barge!"

"I will have my men load der barge during der day before you leave, and der patients will have to unload once you get to Indian Point. How many miles upriver is it?"

"It is about 80 miles. I plan to sail up this weekend to get an idea. It should take about eight hours to get there. I may have to use my steam engine to aid the sails. The current will make coming back much swifter—taking less than half the time. I may send a crew of workers up earlier to repair the docking facilities. That should not be hard to get laborers to do that when they have no idea they are working for lepers. I will have to get on that project soon."

"A stable dock vould certainly expedite unloading, as vell as delivering supplies in der future.

"Vell, here comes cook with our dinner. It is time to end der shop talk and enjoy the wonderful roast beef. Dulcie, it looks like you must have known Jeff was coming for dinner, because you prepared his favorite foods."

"Master Bloom, thars no way I could have read his mine, and you knows it takes more than a few minutes to cook up my delicious roast beef. Master Jeff, I got those potatoes and beans you love too. But save room for the pecan pie I have cooking right now. I did slap that together once I saw Master Jeff coming at supper time. I knows he don't get good food like dis anywheres else but home."

"Dulcie, you have outdone yourself again. Thank you so much for preparing such a feast for me."

CHAPTER SIXTEEN

The Governor

"Governor Foster, thank you so much for allowing me to meet with you this morning. I hear it is a time for celebration."

"Indeed, Dr. Bloom. I returned from Washington, D.C. recently and have been tending to much business in New Orleans before heading back to Baton Rouge, so this was an ideal time for us to become better acquainted.

"As you obviously know, Louisiana just won a huge victory in the Supreme Court. Of all the nerve of that uppity darky wanting to ride in the same coach as us white folks! The Negroes have a perfectly good coach of their own to ride. Luckily the Court upheld our Jim Crow laws for separate but equal services. Imagine the can of worms that would have opened if they had required us to mix the races together! We would have darkies in every restaurant, theater, probably even in our schools. I cannot imagine it.

"Now if I can just chase those scalawags that run the lottery out of town, but that is a whole other battle I have to fight. Tell me how are things going at Charity? I was saddened to learn of Dr. Miles' untimely death, but he spoke of you frequently, whenever he was not raving about the miracles Dr. Matas was performing. He was always eager for medicine to progress so that more lives could be saved. He believed that you and Dr. Matas were going to make that happen. I hear the new wing is scheduled to break ground soon."

"Hopefully that will take place soon. I have been meeting with the architect and making decisions about exactly how it will be organized. One of the things in the plans is the new state of the art surgery amphitheater. I am hoping the board will agree to name it after Dr. Miles—it was his dream."

"I do not think you will have a problem selling that idea to the board. They will unanimously approve It. What else will be included?"

"Of course, there will be many additional patient beds. The new wards will have ample restroom facilities as well. Charity has always needed more room, and we need to remodel the old wards to add restrooms. That was sorely overlooked in the building of the hospital. The other feature the doctors are extremely excited about is the new pathology lab. We believe it is the key to finding the cure for so many diseases. One thing we badly need to add is what they call an X-Ray machine. It shoots roentgen rays through the body and allows the film to photograph the skeleton. It will be critical in diagnosing broken bones, and assuring that we are putting people back together the way the Lord meant them to be! It is very expensive and not quite in our budget, but it is something we desperately need to add."

"Let me write that down, and I will see to it that the Legislature adds that to your budget. Send me a memo telling me exactly how much it costs. I agree it is needed. And what else is happening?"

"You probably know that Dr. Miles and Dr. Dyer had leased the Woodlawn Plantation at Indian Point as our new Leper Colony. It is located about 80 miles upriver from New Orleans, and we are hoping to relocate our first group of lepers there shortly. Their living conditions at the pest house are not fit for dogs, and it is unfair that they are condemned to such dreadful circumstances. By getting them away from the city, they can hopefully have a very quiet and peaceful existence in their own little community. I know the patients are very excited about the possibilities. The manor house and slave quarters are in need of repair, so the first group going will be the healthier of our patients who can work to repair the facilities. Then we can send the less healthy ones. I am working to get the good Daughters of Charity to accept this as their newest mission. This is still on the hush-hush. You know how frightened people are of lepers!"

"Oh, yes. No one wants them in their community. I cannot imagine what that pest house is like. Dr. Miles had cleared the lease of the plantation with me some time ago. I think it is a wonderful idea. As I understand, they will be able to raise crops and livestock as well. Perhaps they can become at least partly self-sufficient."

"Not only that, but it is so important that they have jobs to do so they can feel they have value. Everyone needs to have a reason to get up in the morning."

"Well, Dr. Bloom, are you totally overwhelmed with your new job?"

"Actually, Governor, I have gotten so much support from everyone that it is going smoother than I ever imagined. The first day, my head was spinning and I was having trouble figuring out which way to go. Day by day it is coming together. Dr. Miles was very well organized and kept copious notes on every facet of the hospital. He had a filing system with everything in its place. The staff has been extremely cooperative, and Sister Agnes is an angel.

She wanted to come with me to meet with you. She thought I might need her guidance," Jeff smiled.

"She is indeed a good person to have on your side, but, Dr. Bloom, I think you are very capable of handling these meetings on your own. It has been a pleasure to meet you and I look forward to your memo about the, what is it, X-ray machine? Please do not hesitate to let me know of any other ways I can be of assistance. As governor, I am here to serve the people of Louisiana. Call on me frequently. I want to be proud of our great Charity Hospital, and make it a standard for all the other states to emulate."

"Thank you, Governor. I look forward to working with you."

* * *

Jeff left the meeting totally elated. The governor was such a delightful gentleman! He was going to get his X-ray machine! He approved everything Jeff had done so far. What a beautiful day it was!

Since it was early Saturday, Jeff decided to take his boat out for a visit to Indian Point. He would dock it and assess the property. Sailing was a very relaxing way to spend a day, and Jeff loved taking his boat, the *Miss Lillian*, out on his own. He stopped at a local market and grabbed some provisions and headed to the Yacht Club where he harbored his boat. Before long he was making his way through Lake Maurepas and then on to the Mississippi River. He knew this would also be a good time to think about and plan his strategies. He had been comparing and dreaming about X-ray machines for so long, he knew exactly what he wanted to order. 'I wonder if I can just go ahead and order it Monday, or whether I need to wait to get approval from the legislature,' Jeff thought. 'I had better play it safe and wait for their approval. I know it will take months to get it after it has been ordered, and I do not want to make enemies with the legislators by stepping on their toes. Anyway the building is not going to be ready for months so I would not have a place to put it if it came in early.'

There was a good southerly wind pushing Jeff's boat quickly up the river. This late in the summer, the river current was not as strong as it was in the spring. The trip took only five hours. Jeff moored his boat on what remained of the landing, and made notes on what he planned to have built. He then disembarked and walked over the levee to see what there was to see. The manor house was massive. It reminded him of several of the other plantations he had visited. It had six huge brick columns across the front on the bottom floor supporting a second floor veranda overlooking the river. The veranda had lovely Corinthian columns extending up to the roof. He could envision the patients sitting in their rocking chairs enjoying an afternoon breeze.

There was obvious roof damage and the place was in dire need of paint. 'Those things can be repaired,' he thought. Again he added to his notes the materials he thought were needed—shingles, paint, flooring material, sand paper, nails, etc. He then walked over to the slave quarters. There were seven small one room buildings, each had a fireplace, and there was one outhouse to service all of them. 'We need to build a proper cistern to provide water and a cesspool to take care of sewage. In fact, a proper bathroom would be appropriate if people were actually going to live in these cabins. Actually, we will need at least two—one for the whites and one for the coloreds. I would not want to upset ole Jim Crow.' He added that to his notes. As he was finishing his rounds of the property, he was suddenly overwhelmed with mosquitoes. 'Mosquito netting,' he added to his list. He boarded *Miss Lillian* and headed back downriver. 'That had better be a big barge,' Jeff thought.

*   *   *

Jeff joined his dad at temple the next morning. His Pa was surprised to see him there. The congregation enthusiastically congratulated Jeff on his appointment as House Surgeon. Several young ladies made a special point of speaking to him and wishing him well. His dad took great pleasure in seeing all the young ladies flocking around Jeff after temple.

"Come home for dinner, Jeff," Pa invited. "If you vould like, you could invite one of your lady friends as vell."

"Thanks, Pa, it will be my pleasure, but I will pass on bringing a lady friend," Jeff replied. "I wanted to tell you about my meeting with Governor Foster. I am thoroughly enchanted with the man. He seems to really have the interests of the state at heart."

"He does seem to be a very good man. I voted for him in der last election. I vill bet you did not even take der time to vote, did you?"

"You are right again, but I can see how that will have to change. Apparently I will be knee deep in politics from now on. If I expect to get things done, I will have to have the support of not only the governor, but all the legislators as well. That is something I never thought of as being important. Times have changed with my new position.

"But the governor approved everything I told him I had been doing and he even said he would have the legislature allocate funds for the X-ray machine we need so desperately. He also said just to let him know what else I needed, and he would be glad to help me get it."

"Oh, Jeff, you have a lot to learn about politicians. I am glad you have started off on the right foot vit the governor, and I hope dat continues. Please understand dat all politicians are great at telling you vatever dey tink you want to hear. Do not believe it all!"

"I am not that naïve, Pa, but I was impressed with how friendly and helpful he seemed to be. I expected him to be arrogant and pretentious. After all, he went to Washington and Lee University."

"And den Tulane, just like you. He actually is just an ole country boy. Probably did not vear shoes most of der time growing up, until his father sent him off to school. Although he has a proper mansion near der capital in Baton Rouge, he spends most of his time over at his plantation near Franklin. He loves to hunt and fish. No, I vould never describe him as being arrogant, dat is, unless you get on his wrong side. It looks as though he is going to put an end to the Louisiana Lottery. Dat took quite a lot of doing. People have been trying to shut it down since der end of der war."

"Dulcie put another plate on for Jeff. He looks mighty hungry today," shouted Isaac into the kitchen as they entered his home. Isaac's second wife, Hannah, welcomed Jeff with a big hug. The big house was always too quiet, and Isaac reveled in having one of his children home again.

Jeff and his Pa settled into the big chairs in the parlor. "Vell, Jeff, I saw all dose young ladies hanging on your every vord. Surely you have found one worthy of sharing your life?"

"Not yet, Pa, and I have been looking. I have met many delightful young ladies, but they are all missing that extra something I think I need in a wife. She needs to be someone who understands the importance of medicine and how much it means to me. Most of them are downright flighty, worrying about the newest chapeau, or something equally unimportant."

"You have not started dating that Sister Agnes, have you? She has quite a 'chapeau,'" Isaac smiled.

"Sister Agnes is an angel, but she is not available at this time. She has come to my aid so many times since I have been at the hospital, and she is such an intelligent person. I love teasing around with her. Just this week, I gave her a list of assignments to make my transition easier and she accepted them all as if they were a gift! I would love to find someone like Sister, but not quite so religious, if you know what I mean," Jeff chuckled.

"I took the *Miss Lillian* up to Indian Point yesterday and surveyed the property. Can you recommend a crew I could send up there to build a proper dock for us? I would also like to have a cistern and cesspool installed before the patients arrive. I do not think it would be advisable to let the crew know what the future of the plantation is. They might balk at the idea of helping lepers."

"Jeff, I have a crew of five men who could probably do dat for you in just a few days. Dey are hard workers, and love a challenge. Vy not let dem repair der roof of der manor house vhile dey are dere? I hate to tink of some of dose poor guys who are missing fingers or toes trying to climb on der roof and repair dose shingles. Ve can load all der equipment on one of der small barges and a tug and send dem up dere. Had I known you ver going up dere yesterday, I vould have gone vit you. If you order der supplies tomorrow and have dem delivered to my pier, I vill have der men ready to go by Tuesday. Dey will plan to camp dere until dey complete der repairs. I vill just pay dem through my company so you do not have to vorry about der cost. Consider it a gift!"

"Oh, Pa, that would be wonderful! Like I was telling Governor Foster yesterday, so many people have come to my aid it has made this job much easier. I have already made some sketches of the dock, and have a good idea of the lumber needed. I will get busy ordering everything first thing in the morning. I am assuming I can get the lumber from you, at a good price, of course," smiled Jeff.

"Of course, Jeff, but you do need to order der cistern and der cesspool and der shingles. Bring by your sketches in der morning. My men vill have a good idea of vhat additional supplies dey need and deir provisions. Perhaps ve can sail up next Saturday and see how it is going?"

"Pa, you are the best! That sounds grand."

"Dinner ought to be ready by now. Dulcie, vhere is dat wonderful meal I have been smelling? Jeff and I are wasting away. Jeff, let us go into der dining room making a racket and perhaps she will get der idea."

They enjoyed a delightful meal together. Jeff departed to rewrite the list of materials he would order first thing Monday morning. Everything was coming together beautifully.

CHAPTER SEVENTEEN

Moving to Carville

"Pa, thank you so much for providing this barge. As you can see, it appears to be full of supplies. There is a void in the center where we will be setting up chairs and beds for our patients. We are only taking seven patients this trip: five men and two women. Sister Agnes insists on going with us to make sure her sisters will be cared for properly. The two volunteer sisters, Dr. Myers and I will make the first trip with them," said Jeff.

"I am so glad you prepared der place for dem before dey arrived. Der dock is now in excellent shape and should be easy enough to unload der supplies. You have even provided a wagon and dray horse dat vill be helpful in getting der supplies over to der plantation house. Der roof no longer leaks although dere is considerable damage inside der manor house. Der cistern and cesspool are functioning, as vell as der old vell. With as many people as you plan to house dere, you vill need more vater dan a cistern can provide. Once der patients get settled, ve need to send dem some chickens and cows . . ."

"Pa, you are really getting involved in this!"

"I am so glad you took me dere to look over der facilities. I have always felt so badly for dose poor lepers. Dey had no cure and no future. Vhat a pitiful way to spend your life, literally wasting away. Now you are giving dem hope. Dere may still be no cure, but at least dey can have a good life. I still do not vant to get too close to any of dem, but I vill be glad to help provide dem vit basic needs. Der good Lord has blessed me in so many vays, dis is one vay I can pay back."

"Thanks, Pa. I do hope you understand that you will get no public recognition for all you are doing. I plan to keep my name out of this entirely. The chance of catching leprosy from one of them is minimal, but I understand if you want to keep your distance. If my patients knew that I was associating with lepers, I would no longer have a practice. I think it is best if we keep your name out as well."

"I understand completely. So you are planning to launch at 11 tonight?"

"Yes, we will bring the patients over and get them hidden on the barge and then take off. It should be a full moon so piloting along the river should not be a problem. I am glad you have provided us with one of your most able tug captains."

"I did have to twist his arm considerably, but he is a good man and you can depend on him to get you dere safely. His orders are to remain at Indian Point until everything is unloaded and moved over to der manor house. He vill give you an additional six hours to see dat all are settled in, but den he vill be returning to New Orleans. Hopefully, you vill be on board, and should be back by tomorrow evening."

"Excellent. Sister Agnes will be returning with me as well. I plan to sail back up this weekend and tow a smaller boat with me for the use of Dr. Dyer and the sisters. We hope to be able to move more patients up soon. The Mother House has not approved the sisters going as of yet, but we hope to get approval soon. That is why she is insisting on going on this trip."

"How many beds are you bringing up there? It looks like a lot of beds."

"I had access to 80 beds. We are converting all the beds at the hospital to metal beds, so we had all of these wooden beds that we were going to give away. Wooden beds could fester germs from one patient to the next in the hospital, but the patients at Indian Point will have their same bed for a very long time, so that should not be a problem. We will need all eighty there before long. Once this is set up, lepers from all over the south will be coming. Dr. Dyer keeps insisting that it is to be 'a place of refuge, not reproach, a place of treatment and research, not detention.' He is adamant that his patients will receive the tranquility they deserve."

"If I were a little younger, I vould go vit you dis evening, but I tink my aching bones vould get der best of me in der night air. All you vould do is hear me complaining, and you surely do not need dat."

"Pa, you have already helped us so much. I do not know how I can thank you."

"Well, Godspeed. I will be tinking about you on your great adventure. I hope all goes vell."

"Thanks again, Pa. Do not fret all night. We are going to have a wondrous adventure!"

*　*　*

The ambulance brought the patients to the dock in the quiet of the night. They loaded their few belongings on the barge and found a comfortable spot to rest. Sister Agnes and the two volunteer sisters chose chairs for the journey. There is no way a Daughter of Charity would be caught lying down in public! Jeff hustled about, talking with the captain of the tug, and assuring that everything was secure. The barge pulled away at 10:30, a bit earlier than planned. Everything was going beautifully, even the weather was cooperating. There was a pleasant breeze that helped chase the mosquitoes.

"Well, Sister Agnes, this will be a night we will remember for a long time. I hope you took the opportunity to rest a little this afternoon. I doubt we get much rest on this journey. With this good weather, I think God is blessing us on this endeavor."

"Yes, Dr. Bloom, I do believe the good Lord has given us His blessing. If you do not mind, the sisters and I would like to begin our journey with a prayer. You are welcome to join us as are any of the patients."

"I would love to join you, and I think most of the patients will too. This is quite a new beginning for them, and I know they would want the Lord to go with them."

Sister Agnes gathered the group together and led them in a spontaneous prayer. The sisters then separated themselves and began to pray the rosary. They continued praying the rosary repeatedly throughout the night. The quiet drone of their prayers mixed with the sounds of the river, the tug's motor, the water lapping the edge of the barge, the crickets and frogs calling out their songs, and an occasional owl hooting its delight.

Jeff and Dr. Dyer settled in for the journey. "This is not as bad as I had imagined," said Dr. Dyer. "It was so good of your father to provide the barge and tug and so many of the materials. He is a good man."

"He sailed upriver with me when we were first planning how to transport the supplies and patients. He even sent a crew of his men to do many of the repairs, to make it a little easier on us. He has been making lists of all the other things he wants to send: chickens, cows, you name it. He, like so many, has a great fear of getting too close to the lepers, but he does want to help them."

"You know I have been working with the lepers for twenty years now, and I do not know of anyone who actually contracted the disease from one of them. One of the things I hope we can do at Indian Point is to isolate the germ that causes leprosy. Once we learn that, we may be able to provide a cure. Having a small lab that I can use exclusively for that study will really help."

"Those supplies are not on board yet, but I think we need to add that to our list. I really think there would be many people like my pa who would be willing to contribute goods and money to this project, as long as they do not have to come in contact with the patients. You may want to get a committee together that would be willing to work on that."

"I have had many people indicate just that. They look upon these poor people and are thankful they have not been afflicted, and would like to help. Once they know we are moving them out of the city, they probably will be eager to donate to make the new leper colony successful!"

"Sister Agnes taught me that just a few weeks ago. If you want people to help you, you have to make them think of how it is helping them to help you! She is one smart woman. It has worked every time so far."

"She is a gem. I could not believe she insisted on coming with us, but she was adamant that she could not allow two of her sisters to go off without verifying their safety. I may ask her to head my committee."

"That would be a wise move, Dr. Dyer."

The journey upriver passed peacefully. The moonlight helped the tug captain maneuver over the ever changing sand bars. The two doctors dozed in their chairs, while the sisters kept their vigilant watch over their charges.

Just as the sun was rising, they heard the captain shout: "Land Ho! We are arriving at Indian Point and I need some help down there."

Jeff jumped up, rubbing his eyes, and immediately went to tie the barge to the dock. Dr. Dyer was close behind.

"I am not much of a sailor, but I do know how to follow directions. Jeff, just tell me what to do."

"Go to the aft, er rear, of the barge and take the rope that is there and climb onto the dock with it. Whatever you do, do not let go of the rope. Wrap it around that post, and it will make it easier to hold. I will come tie it off." Jeff was already on the dock with the bow rope. The tug was maneuvering to the opposite side of the dock. After Jeff adeptly tied his rope, he relieved Dr. Dyer and tied off the aft rope as well.

"Dr. Bloom, this is a nice new dock. I do not remember seeing it on my trips upriver."

"Yes, Captain, we just rebuilt this so that it would be easier to unload our cargo. Hopefully ships will be willing to stop and drop off supplies for us in the future, without having someone make a special run just for the hospital."

"As long as they do not have to deal with your patients, I do not see why not. Like I said, this is a very nice dock. If you have your patients go ashore with a load, I will have my men unload the barge for you. We have the wagon and horse loaded for the first run, which you could take with you. The rest will be piled on the dock. Once your patients unload the supplies in the wagon, they can bring it back for the next load."

"The men will be glad to help you, Captain."

"No, thank you. We want to keep our distance. We will unload everything on to the dock and then go onboard the tug and take a little siesta. It has been a long night, and I understand you want to make sure everyone is settled before our return."

"I would prefer that, as would Sister Agnes. We will be returning with you to New Orleans."

"If everyone would grab their personal belongings, let us head ashore to your new home," Jeff called to the patients. He hitched up the horse to the wagon and drove it over the levee himself.

As soon as they had vacated the barge, the captain and his crew made short work of emptying the barge of its cargo. The dock was piled high with supplies and beds. As the sun was rising, they retired to the tug for a much needed nap.

It took twelve trips with the wagon full and everyone carrying all they could carry before all the supplies were on the porch of the manor house. The sisters and the patients were eager to tour their new surroundings. The patients would be staying in the slave quarters, men in one cabin and women in the other. They picked out the ones they thought were in the best condition and moved beds into each. All of the food supplies were moved to the kitchen of the manor house. Extra beds, linens, bandages and miscellaneous supplies were stored in the former library.

"I think this would make an excellent laboratory one day," Dr. Dyer said of the library. "I have selected a room I will be using while I am staying here, and the sisters have chosen theirs as well. We have moved beds into each, but today will be a good day to use a broom and mop and get busy cleaning. I am glad the roof was repaired and we have water available. Your father's crew did an admirable job."

"They did what they were asked to do. As you settle in, let us make a list of the things you need. I will be returning this weekend and could bring some supplies with me. I will have the sisters and the women patients sort the foodstuffs and make a list also. We probably should go through the medicines we brought and see what is lacking."

The women were already cleaning the kitchen area. There was a good supply of pots and pans, as well as dishes and flatware already there, but all needed washing. The cupboards were huge, but they had some unwanted residents living in them which had to be removed before anything could be stored.

"Cleanliness is next to godliness," spouted Sister Agnes as she took a broom to a mouse. "We are not sharing these facilities with vermin. You will have to find a new home."

"Only Sister Agnes would counsel the mice as she chases them out of the kitchen," smiled Dr. Dyer. "Apparently some of God's creatures have found this to be a very pleasant home. I hope our patients do also."

"Mouse traps are the first thing on my list. There are some newfangled ones that do not hurt the mouse. You could use the mice in some of your experiments. Let me add cages to my list. Putting them to the use of science is a much better alternative than just killing them. I feel sure they will keep returning if we just shove them out the door. Sister Agnes does not need to know," smiled Jeff.

"I do not think the sisters will mind at all, and I think the cooks will be delighted to help me catch them. They seem to have a good handle on the kitchen, let us go survey the rest of the manor house and see how many patients we can house here. We will have only the sickest ones who need constant care here. The others will live in the cabins. We may need to build a lot more cabins."

"I agree. I think you would want to keep the manor house for the sisters and visiting doctors, and this is where the patients would come for treatments. The dining room is suitable for the colony now, but it will have to be enlarged as well."

"Our two women patients are excellent cooks, which is one reason we brought them. As hard as our men are going to be working, they will need proper nourishment."

After touring the rooms of the manor house, the doctors walked over to the barn to see what equipment was there. There were rakes and shovels, hoes and plows stored in the barn. Provisions had been made for the horse, and there was a chicken coop that only needed minor repair.

"Apparently when the former owners decided to give up the plantation, they just left and did not bother to move anything but the furniture out. Jeff, how about bringing some seeds for a winter garden? I am no expert on what you should plant in November, but I am sure there are some things we could start now, perhaps sweet potatoes and onions, maybe some greens. Check with someone who would know and let us see about getting our farm started. I think that would be wonderful therapy for our patients."

After surveying the facilities and making lists of needed provisions, Sister Agnes and Jeff boarded the tug for the trip home. Jeff took two chairs and placed them on the back of the tug so they could wave to the patients as they left. Sister Agnes actually dozed part of the way back, but Jeff hardly noticed because he was doing the same.

CHAPTER EIGHTEEN

The New Wing

Work was finally complete on the new wing. Not only did it add 200 extra beds to the hospital, it also provided that wonderful surgery amphitheater and the greatly enlarged pathology lab. One room of the lab was a dark room devoted to the much desired X-ray machine. The company that made the machine sent a technician with the machine to train the people who would be using it. Jeff was the first in line to receive the training.

"Show me one more time exactly how to place a person with a broken humerus on the table so that we can see exactly how it needs to be set," Jeff requested.

"Actually, it is best if you X-ray the patient before you cast the arm and afterwards to make sure you have it in the best position to heal. The first picture will show you the severity of the break so that you are better able to manipulate it back into position. The second picture will confirm that you have done that," responded the technician.

The technician remained in the hospital for two weeks explaining the process to any staff interested in using the equipment. However, Jeff had other plans. He made sure that four staff members were very knowledgeable, and was going to require them to do all of the actual X-rays. One person would always be on duty. He did not want all of those doctors and nurses using this very expensive piece of equipment. Too many people using it would almost definitely destroy the machine, whereas if he had four specialists working the machine, they could take much better care of it. He wanted all of the doctors on staff to be aware of how it worked, but he knew letting all of them use it would be a fatal error. He would announce that after they had taken the time to be trained.

"Jeff, I cannot tell you how wonderful our new surgery wing is," exclaimed Dr. Matas. "Dr. Miles would be so proud to have the amphitheater named after him. It is a masterpiece. I know he is smiling. The medical students can watch the procedures and the professors can discuss what is going on in the gallery. It is a wonderful teaching tool, and the lighting and ventilation are excellent. I think our success rate with surgeries is going to improve dramatically." Rudy not only was the chief of surgery, but also taught surgery in the medical school.

"I did my first operation here last week, and I agree it is a huge improvement over our old facilities. I think we thought everything through before we had the architects complete the design. The gallery will allow our students to watch the procedures and learn from the practicing surgeons. I think our graduates will be much better prepared. But I also want to commend you on the wonderful new procedures you have developed. I am getting letter after letter praising your journal articles explaining what you have learned and sharing it with the world. You are going to be very famous if you keep this up," smiled Jeff.

"Luckily I do not have to tell them about the ones that fail," quipped Rudy.

"Most of those patients probably would not have made it anyway. Hundreds of lives are being saved because of your ingenious procedures. I especially am impressed with the work you have done on aortic aneurisms. That is brilliant!

"Rudy, the next thing we need to work on is getting a separate facility for the children. I have been talking with Mrs. Deborah Milliken. She is willing to help us, and I do believe she is capable of making a considerable contribution. She is extremely interested in helping the children of our city. Would you mind seeking her out and perhaps pushing her a little too?"

"I am going to a dinner party at her home next week, and I am sure I can slip it into the conversation. Perhaps we need to get Sister Agnes on board as well?" suggested Rudy.

"Sister has a way of getting people to give their all for a just cause. You know that the children have always been very special to me. I almost left Charity back in '89, when I was offered the position as head of pediatrics at the New Orleans Poly Clinic. I would love to have a hospital built just for children that would keep them away from all these dread adult diseases."

"I will stoke your fire for you, Jeff. I agree it would be a wonderful idea. I am glad you did not leave Charity. That was back in the days when we were making a list of all the utensils needed for each surgery, so that the nurses could have them clean and ready for us to use. I am surprised with all that drudgery going on that you did not go over to the Poly Clinic. Life would have been much simpler there."

"Simple, yes, but boring as well. Life is never boring at Charity. You will recall that I spent two years as assistant house surgeon at Touro. Touro is a fine institution, but it is only one tenth the size of Charity."

"Jeff, I hear you have been doing a lot of solo sailing. The talk is all over the hospital about how every other weekend you disappear aboard *the Lillian* and take off for who knows where. That is definitely unlike you, especially with all that is going on at the hospital."

"Rudy, this is in strictest confidence. I have been going up to the Leper Home to check on how things are going there, and bringing patients with me. That is top secret—no one is to know about it. I would be banned if people knew I was spending so much time with lepers."

"I knew something was up. It was so unlike you just to go off and have fun. How are things going at the Leper Home? How many patients are there now?"

"Well, Rudy, if you are not afraid to be around the lepers you can come and see for yourself. I am helping Dr. Dyer by checking the patients over for diseases other than leprosy. The colony is growing continually, and they have started a farming operation as well. The patients are delighted to have a place of their own. Most of them miss their families, but they are making new 'families' now. We have added five more cabins for them. The sisters finally got approval from the Mother House, so there are more of them treating patients as well.

"What I have been doing, is keeping my boat at the yacht club as always, but I do not bring the patients there. We have found an old camp on the lake with a decent dock, and I meet them there to take them to Carville. I will be taking four more patients up this Saturday. I plan to leave at 5 A.M. so that I can pick them up about 5:30. It is actually easier to get there going up Bayou Manchac than going against the current of the river. But remember everything must be kept top secret. I usually return on Sunday. I am glad to hear that people think I am out having a good time. They probably think I have a lady friend I am meeting!"

"I have heard suggestions of that, as well, and I assume your father would be especially pleased. I have heard him giving you a hard time about producing some offspring."

"Last weekend, when I was at the old house, Hannah, my sister, came over with her four year old, Edgar. It seems he was not doing well, and she wanted me to check him out. I gave her the same instructions I give most of my mothers: Make sure he is getting a lot of fruits and vegetables; outdoor play is essential to good health; do not let him stay cooped up in a dark room; drink lots of fresh milk and orange juice. Avoid any canned foods, but only feed him fresh foods. Hannah had been keeping him locked up in the house and feeding him nothing but soup and crackers. I told her 'Go for a walk with him every morning. Take him to the playground. There is nothing wrong with that child that a little fresh air and fresh food won't fix.' She had him on a steady dose of castor oil which I told her to stop immediately. She was afraid his bowels were not moving fast enough. That is such a common mistake so many mothers make—every child's bowels move at their own speed. Do not mess with nature! Let it take its own course. And then when the bowels moved too much she would dose him with paregoric. Paregoric is a dangerous medicine. Mothers should not be allowed to have access to it!'

"How is the youngster now?"

"Rudy, I do not know if my sister took my advice or not. I have not talked to her since we had our chat, and she went away furious, still believing that castor oil and paregoric were wonder drugs. Mothers should be trained before they are allowed to have children!"

"Well, Jeff, mothers have been managing quite successfully all these years."

"But they did not have access to castor oil and paregoric! It is no wonder that we get so many youngsters in the hospital that are dehydrated. Some are even addicted to the paregoric. That is a very sad situation. It is so much easier for children to become addicted, and so much harder to get them off of it."

"Not little Edgar?"

"There is not a chance of that yet. I am so glad that she brought him over and sought my advice. I hope I scared her into stopping the medicines. Drugs are wonderful if properly used, but it is so easy to misuse and abuse them. That was a huge problem when I was at Touro—the men who were dependent on opium, and their main source of it was paregoric. I told her about how they actually stop breathing, and how hard it is to keep them alive. You might remember my telling you about using the bellows apparatus when I first returned to Charity. It was from that idea that you developed your fancy pump that we now put so many of our patients on when we do surgery."

"I remember it well. It was indeed an inspiration. You had the original idea of pumping patient's lungs to keep them alive. It does work well.

"I am going to have to refuse your kind invitation to go sailing this weekend. My new bride demands my attention on weekends, but do have a good trip."

*   *   *

"Michel, it is good to run into you today. I was wondering if you would like to go sailing again. I am heading up to the Leper Home at Indian Point, and would love to have another doctor along to see the patients. You might learn a little something extra on the way."

"Have you arranged for a couple of beautiful young ladies to go with us?"

"Actually, two of our patients are young ladies. It is most unusual for women to suffer from leprosy, but we have two who are eager to join the colony, but I do not think you will want to fraternize too closely with them. We actually need to get more women in the colony. They are thinking of allowing some non-patients to move in with their spouses. That is probably the biggest sacrifice the patients have—giving up their families."

"I can imagine. Then you will have children there also, and that means starting a school, and adding teachers. The colony could grow dramatically."

"Although I have been bringing patients to the colony on a regular basis, it seems many are finding their way on their own. It is the only facility of its kind in the country, and is getting quite a reputation for how idyllic it is for lepers. Dr. Dyer was really inspired when he came up with this idea, and is doing a great job with improving the conditions and the care being given. We hope to add a resident doctor soon. Would you be interested in the job, Michel?"

"Oh, I do not believe I would. I plan to move back to my hometown next summer and hang out my shingle there, but I am always eager to increase my doctoring skills. What time shall I meet you?"

"I will pick you up in my carriage about 4:30. The grooms are used to me leaving my rig at the yacht club early in the morning. Dress as though we were just going yachting—no white coat. You may want to bring your bag along. Who knows, you may get to practice your skills a little while we are there!"

"Sounds like the makings of an interesting weekend. See you then."

* * *

"Sister Agnes, I have a new project for you to work on for me!"

"Dr. Bloom, what are you up to now? I have been talking with the sisters at Hotel Dieu and they are still begging Carney Hospital to send them some nurses. What is this new project?"

"I have been talking with Mrs. Deborah Milliken about building a facility just for the children. She seems to be very interested in funding it, but I could use a little help pushing her in the right direction. I have already talked with Dr. Matas about encouraging her. I know she thinks he is wonderful, and will do almost anything he asks. I know you have great success as well at encouraging patrons to assist you in your endeavors. If you happen to be around Mrs. Milliken, would you mind putting in a good word for The Milliken Hospital for Children?"

"I know that has been one of your goals for many years. Now I have a project I hope you can help me with. The sisters at the Leper Colony have converted one of the slave cabins into a chapel, but it is sorely in need of an organ. I know that you do not want anyone to know how involved you have been with the day-to-day operation of the facility, but I thought you might be willing to have your name on a donation. Do you have an organ at your synagogue?"

"Actually, all the chanting at the synagogue is done a capella—no organ is needed. I thought you Catholics did that also. Exactly how much does an organ cost?"

"I knew that would be the deciding factor. I spoke with Philip Werlein just yesterday, and he is willing to sell us a nice chapel organ for just $150. It is fairly plain and does not have a lot of decorative carvings on the case, but the sound is excellent. It would suit our chapel beautifully, and would make the dear sisters ecstatic. Sister Ruth loves to play the organ and has sorely missed her music. I am sure that the patients would also greatly benefit from the glorious hymns."

"Well, consider it a donation. I shall go down in history as the first Jewish doctor contributing an organ to a Catholic chapel. Make sure my name is on it. I want to be remembered for something at the Leper Colony. I have carefully kept my name out of everything else about it."

"I understand completely. I will talk to Mr. Werlein about shipping it for us as well. I will assure him that they can simply leave it on the dock, and the residents will move it to the chapel. You are a good man, Dr. Bloom. If only I could convince you that you should become a Catholic."

"Not yet, Sister, but do keep me in your prayers. Running this hospital takes more than I ever imagined."

CHAPTER NINETEEN

The Arrival

Hotel Dieu in New Orleans had been sending requests for nurses to train their surgeons and nurses in the aseptic practices of Dr. Lister for several years. Carney Hospital had become famous for its attention to these details, and since Hotel Dieu was staffed by the Daughters of Charity, the connection was automatic. In the fall of 1895, the administration knew exactly who they should send.

It was like God had been listening to all of Mary Rose's prayers. Not only would she experience a whole new world, her best friend would be coming with her. The fear of the unknown was tempered by the fact that she would still be working with the dear Daughters of Charity and knew that she would be cared for appropriately. She quickly accepted the offer, and had to twist Mary Ellen's arm a little to get her to agree as well.

They packed all their belongings and boarded the southbound train, ready for adventure. This would be Mary Rose's first train ride since that fateful trip with her sister from Philadelphia. At least this time she would have a lot more freedom to meet people and enjoy the ride. They would actually go to the dining car for meals. They could go to the club car during the day and visit with other travelers. Sister John would never have allowed such. Mary Ellen had never been on a train, so Mary Rose convinced her that she could show her the ropes. After all, she had done it before. She did not mention that she was only five at the time.

The porter escorted them to their quarters, a comfortable cabin they would share. It had one small sofa, which would convert to a bed, and there was another overhead that would be pulled down for the second bunk. Mary Rose wanted the top bunk. Mary Ellen readily agreed. The journey would take about four days with one long stop in Atlanta, where they could disembark and walk around downtown Atlanta. Mary Rose wanted to see as much as she could see. She planned to keep the window shades up the whole trip, except perhaps at night while they were sleeping. Mary Rose did not remember clearly what their quarters were like on her first trip, but she knew this had to be much nicer. The restroom facilities were at the end of the car. That is one thing she did remember—making her sister walk her to the restroom every hour or so just so she could see something other than the insides of their compartment.

Three of the sisters went with them to see them off and bid them a fond farewell. Sister John, of course, was among them. As they boarded the train, there were some tears and promises to visit each other in the future. Mary Rose waved perhaps too gleefully from the window of her cabin as the train pulled from the station. She had never experienced such a feeling of freedom in her life. She wondered where this adventure might take her. She had seen pictures of New Orleans, and had heard horror stories as well. It definitely would be different from Boston. She knew there were problems with sanitation, and that diseases such as yellow fever and malaria had fostered epidemics in the past. However, it rarely snowed, which is something Mary Rose would not miss one bit.

The first hour, Mary Rose stayed with Mary Ellen in their compartment arranging and rearranging their belongings. There was not much room to work, so it was critical to place things in their optimal location. They sat and watched the landscape go by and, both of them being city girls, saw venues they had only seen in books. The acres and acres of farmland, miles and miles of forests, small towns where they stopped briefly to pick up or unload passengers passed quickly by their window. Finally Mary Rose said, "It is time to go exploring. I do not plan to spend this whole trip cooped up in this little compartment. I wonder what else is on this train."

So the two young girls gathered their handbags and exited their compartment. The aisle was extremely narrow, and it took a while to get the hang of walking with the movement of the train. They giggled quite a bit making their way down one car after another. The conductor had told them that the club car and the dining car were to the rear of the train only followed by the caboose. The club car was full of people drinking liquor and playing cards. This is not what Mary Rose had anticipated. Several of the men looked them over, and even made rude comments as they walked through. They quickly exited to the dining car. The steward told them that luncheon would be served starting at 11:30, but they could order tea if they would like. They both took a table and ordered tea and biscuits. They had both been too excited to eat any breakfast before they left, and a little snack was definitely in order. They were the only ones in the car other than the steward.

As they enjoyed their snack, an elderly couple, Mr. and Mrs. Dreyfus, entered the dining car and took a table across the aisle from them. They also ordered tea and biscuits, and as soon as the steward left, Mary Rose struck up a conversation. Mary Rose quickly learned that they were also headed to New Orleans. They had been summering in upper New York State and were returning home now that fall had arrived. As much as they disliked the hot humid summers, they equally abhorred being snowbound for days at a time. Since Mr. Dreyfus had qualified staff to run his business for him, he annually spent the summer months near Albany. That way they enjoyed the best of both worlds.

At that point, the inquisition began with Mary Rose and Mary Ellen asking them a myriad of questions. "Is it true that raw sewage runs through the streets?" "Does the whole city reek of decay?" "Are there really people who have black skin?" "Is the carnival as wild and sinful as we have heard?" "Does everyone sleep under mosquito netting?" And on, and on, and on.

Soon the lunch crowd started making their way into the car. Mary Rose could hardly believe so much time had passed and they had learned so much about their destination. The Dreyfus' rose to leave and said they would take their lunch later. Mary Rose decided this couple would be good escorts for their trip back through the club car, so they also decided to leave. Her intuitions were correct. The crowd was still drinking and gambling, but not a crude word or indecent look passed their way. That was a relief. Apparently the club car would not be the place to pass the journey.

When the girls returned to their compartment, Mary Rose took out her journal and began to write down all she had learned from the Dreyfus'. Apparently he had a merchandising establishment on Royal Street which is in the French Quarter. They had both lived in New Orleans all of their lives, and seemed to delight in diminishing some of the horror stories they had been told. Mary Ellen was greatly comforted by learning that New Orleans was quite a civilized place with an opera and a university and a well-established social scene. The Dreyfus' even invited them to come to tea once they settled into their new routine. Mary Rose hoped that all of the people in New Orleans were as nice as the Dreyfuses.

About an hour later, the girls decided they were ready for lunch. They walked slowly through the cars hoping they could find others headed into the dining car with them. This became their procedure for every meal—they would not pass through the club car unescorted. It seemed to be easy enough to tag along behind someone else headed in that direction.

The jaunt through Atlanta was exciting. The train arrived at 10 a.m. and would be at the station until 3. It seemed silly to stay on board when they had the opportunity to see Atlanta. The weather was beautiful, and so was the city. They walked towards the downtown area and studied the windows in all the stores along the way. They spotted a café with umbrellas over tables and decided that would be a perfect spot for lunch. They noticed how well dressed the women were, with hats and gloves. It had already gotten chilly in Boston, but it was perfect in Atlanta, in fact the wool dresses they wore seemed a bit stifling. The maître de sat them at a table where they could watch the people as they walked past. The lunch took much longer than they had anticipated, because they did much more looking than eating. When they finished they walked down Peachtree Street and were taken back by the huge plate glass windows in front of the largest department store they had ever seen, M. Rich and Brothers. It was four stories high and seemed to take up most of the block.

"I have never had a store bought dress," said Mary Rose. "I think it is time."

"I have always made my own dresses, Mary Rose. I never even thought about buying one!"

"Well, if we are going to make an impression on the people of New Orleans we need to be properly dressed. Not only do we need new dresses, but I think a new hat would also be appropriate for our arrival. Let us see what we can find."

The girls were overwhelmed with what they found. Mary Rose purchased two new dresses with hats and purses to coordinate. Mary Ellen was much more conservative and only bought one dress, but did find two hats she could not choose between so bought both.

"I wonder if New Orleans has stores like this?"

"Boston probably does, we just have never been in one," joked Mary Ellen.

They gathered their purchases and hurried back to the train station just in time to board.

"Oh, Mary Ellen, look how much fun we are having already. I think this is an omen of the wonderful life ahead of us."

"I sure hope so. Just think we will be in New Orleans tomorrow morning. Do you think the sisters will be there to meet us at the train?"

"There will be someone there to meet us; I am not sure who it will be. How else would we know where to go or how to get there? I trust they will take care of us. And we will be the most stunning young ladies arriving from Boston. We will just knock them off their heels."

* * *

Little sleep took place in their compartment that night. The train was scheduled to arrive around ten in the morning. The girls packed and repacked their belongings. They tried on each other's new dresses and hats, and decided they could share them. That way their new purchases could go much farther. Both girls were about the same size, but Mary Ellen had dark hair and brown eyes as compared to Mary Rose's red hair and green eyes. They made sure the dresses they bought were dark cottons, appropriate for fall and winter, and not nearly as hot as the woolen ones they had brought with them.

Their excitement grew as they passed through piney woods and more piney woods, interspersed with a swamp every so often. The train traveled so fast that you could not see many of the animals. The girls looked hard for the much talked about alligators that supposedly dominated the wetlands. In Boston, the leaves had already started changing color, but everything here was so green and there were wild flowers everywhere.

"What a beautiful place! Look at the grey beards all the trees are wearing. How strange is that?" asked Mary Rose.

"That must be Spanish moss. I read about it in one of the books on Louisiana. The locals actually use it to stuff mattresses and furniture, and even as poultices for wounds. It apparently does not hurt the trees it grows on, but it certainly gives them a strange appearance," responded Mary Ellen.

"Can you believe all of the flowers? I think we have reached the Garden of Eden."

"Mary Rose, I am not sure this is a Biblical paradise quite yet. We should get to know the place a little better before we make such assertions. After all, did Eden have alligators and snakes?"

"Look at those red trees! They look like they live in water, but they have their roots coming up out of the water. There is very strange vegetation here!"

"That must be the cypress trees. My book said it has needles like a pine tree and its seeds are in cones, but it is not an evergreen and turns bright red before it drops its needles. They call them bald cypress tress because they are naked half the year."

*   *   *

The girls had been primping since daybreak. Each had on a new dress and bonnet. They were eager to see who was to meet them when they arrived at the train station at the foot of Canal Street. As they exited their car, they saw a tall black man holding a sign with their names on it. He was the blackest person they had ever seen, and he was huge! How did he get their names? The girls gave each other questioning glances and then decided to ask the porter's assistance.

"Sir, that huge Negro has a sign with our names on it. What are we supposed to do? Is it safe to talk to him?" asked Mary Rose.

"Yes, ma'am, that's Big Fred. He is one of our most reliable carriage drivers. Someone must have sent him to pick you up. I am sure he did not write your names, and he is trying hard to pick you out of the crowd. I will go with you and introduce you."

"Thank you, sir. Will he be able to take our luggage as well?"

"Of course, he will. Just follow me. Big Fred, you must have been sent to pick up these two young ladies."

"Yessuh, I is lookin' for Miz Wenban and Miz Faircloth. I tinks that's what ma sign says. Is you da two new nurses for da hospital?"

"Indeed we are, but we expected some of the sisters would come to greet us. Why are they not with you?"

"T'day bees All Saints Day, and dey is all at da graveyards cleanin' and puttin' flowers on da graves. Dat's a tradition heah. Dey was torn 'tween meetin' youz and takin' care of der kinfolks, and de kinfolks won. Dey knew I could takes good cares of youz, and dey should be back at de hospital before weez gets back. We'll pass a graveyard on de way over so ya'll can see how pretty dey be!"

The girls looked at each other, questioning the safety of going with Big Fred. Decidedly this was their only option. "Will you please see to our bags?" asked Mary Rose.

"Yessum, I was just getting to dat. Just point 'em out to me and weez be on our way."

The girls showed them their bags and were amazed at how much Big Fred could carry. They followed him to a nice black carriage drawn by a beautiful black horse. He placed all the luggage in the back of the carriage, assisted the ladies in getting into their seats, and then climbed up on top and gave the reins a pop while saying "Hold your head up high, Nellie. We is carryin' two boodiful young ladies t'day."

"Well, so much for impressing people as we got off the train! I have never seen anyone so big or so black in all my life," whispered Mary Rose. "I guess we did impress him! Here is another first. I will have to remember to put that in my journal tonight."

As they passed the cemetery, the girls noticed that all the tombs were above ground. Crowds of people were milling around, admiring their own work as well as that of others. They seemed to have tables set up with food on them.

"Sir, is this really a cemetery? Why are the graves built above ground?" asked Mary Rose.

"Nawlins is wet! If we putz our people in de ground dey would floatz back up and tell us to tries again. White folk's been buryin der people like dis forevuh. Some of deez "hotels" costs dem a fortune. Wish I had dat kind of money."

Saint Louis Cemetery

"Mary Ellen, I think we will have to learn a new language as well. I hope the doctors and nurses are easier to understand. I expect we will have patients who speak this way, however."

"It is all a part of the adventure," Mary Ellen smiled.

As they drove into the driveway of the hospital, they could see the dear sisters standing in the portico awaiting their arrival.

"I am so sorry we could not meet you personally, but we knew that Big Fred would take good care of you."

"Once we got over the initial shock, he was wonderful. He even explained about where you were and your local custom of decorating graves on All Saints Day. We passed one of your unusual cemeteries on the way here. There seemed to be people having a party there!"

"You will find we have a lot of customs that may seem strange. They say the people here are always looking for a reason to celebrate, even if it means going to the graveyard to have a party. People pack picnics and spend the day visiting with relatives and friends. All Saints Day is quite a big to do!" said Sister Mariana, the head of the hospital.

"We are delighted to have you come and help us make Hotel Dieu a sanctuary for the sick and injured. We are eager to learn all you can teach us.

In fact, Sister Agnes from Charity has been after me to get you to go help them as well. We will worry about that once we have gotten Hotel Dieu up to standards. I am sure you are exhausted from your journeys. I will have Big Fred take your luggage to your quarters. Lunch will be sent in to you so you will have some time to unpack and relax before supper. The dinner bell rings promptly at six. You will meet some of your colleagues tonight, but I look forward to introducing you to the entire staff in the morning."

The girls followed Big Fred as he once again grabbed their luggage and seemed to know exactly where to go. Once he got to the door of the dormitory he dropped all the bags and said: "I is so sorry, but dey don't let me go in dere. Dis is as far as I can takes yo bags. No mens goes in dere."

The sisters who were with them each grabbed a bag and entered the dormitory. The girls thanked Big Fred for his services and Mary Rose tried to give him a small tip.

"Oh no, Miz Wenban, I don't wants none of yo money. Maybe one day you be takin care of me. Da sistaz pays me to drive ma buggy. It's been ma pleasure introducing you to Nawlins," he said with a big grin that stretched from ear to ear.

"I will have to remember to call on you whenever I need a carriage. Thank you so much," said Mary Rose. She reached out to shake his hand, but he quickly turned and left. "I guess that is something ladies do not do around here."

They took their hat boxes and headed into the dormitory.

*   *   *

The dorm room they would share was relatively small, but comfortable. Each had her own bed and desk. There was a small chiffarobe, which seemed to be ample for their belongings. They spent the afternoon unpacking and settling into their new surroundings. Several nurses stopped by to welcome them. At exactly six the dinner bell chimed and the girls followed the rest of the nurses to the dining room. Once all were seated, Sister Mariana called everyone to order by saying grace. She introduced Mary Rose and Mary Ellen to the other diners. She gave them such a wonderful introduction it was embarrassing. Apparently few of the other "nurses" had actually completed nursing school, but had been trained on the job, so to speak. Once Sister Mariana left the room a number of Negro waitresses brought food to their tables. Each table sat eight, and there seemed to be five tables, although only two of the tables were occupied.

"Are there usually more people here?" asked Mary Rose of the nearest diner.

"Oh, yes. So many of the girls have gone home for All Saints Day, and some are on duty in the hospital. Of course, the sisters eat in their private quarters. You probably know they are not allowed to eat in public."

"I have lived with the Daughters of Charity since I was orphaned. In fact, my oldest sister is one of them. I know them well. It is just that everything here seems to be so different. It may take me a while to learn all the strange customs and practices you have. Would you be my mentor and help me adapt?"

"I would be honored. I am Jane Calhoun. I was born and raised in New Orleans and hope you will come to love it as much as I do. I am looking forward to learning all you have come to teach us as well."

"I will be delighted to have you as my first new friend in New Orleans. It has already been quite an adventure, and I am sure the surprises will continue. I look forward to sharing with you my training from Carney. It may be quite an adjustment for you too."

"If we are going to save lives, we must adjust. Our rate of infections is spiraling out of control. You seem to be the answer and we are all eager to learn."

"We were advised that you were suffering some major problems in that area, and I do think if everyone is willing to cooperate we can get it under control. Mary Ellen and I are scheduled to meet with all of you tomorrow to explain the regimens that we will put into place. We will also try to explain why each of these procedures is necessary. We have cut infections at Carney to almost non-existent."

"I cannot wait to hear how you will help us work miracles."

"It all goes to the things Dr. Lister has been discovering. He is changing all we know about medicine. I would love to someday meet him in person. He must be an amazing man."

CHAPTER TWENTY

Hotel Dieu

"Mary Ellen, I think our first chore would be to survey the hospital and see what changes need to be made. We certainly do not want to offend someone if they are already using correct procedure."

"What a good plan, Mary Rose. Shall we ask someone to give us a tour of the hospital. I will bring notebook and pencil in hand and see what needs correcting. Perhaps they are doing a better job than we thought."

"Sister Mariana, we had hoped that we could begin this morning with a tour of the facilities. We would like to see exactly where improvements need to be made to eliminate some of the infections."

"Oh, no, my dear Nurse Wenban. We have the doctors scheduled to meet with you at 9 a.m. You are to give them your demands, or suggestions, for how our surgery can be improved."

"But how can we do that, if we have not seen the surgery? Doctors can be a mean lot if you get on their wrong side, and we certainly do not want to do that. We need them to cooperate with us if we are going to be successful. Perhaps you could introduce us to the doctors this morning and ask them to welcome us into their treatments. I would much rather make suggestions one on one with a doctor than issue decrees. I hope you have refreshments planned for the meeting. Refreshments always put doctors in a better mood. I am sure they are not delighted to be pulled from their busy schedules to meet the new Yankee nurses who are going to start telling them what to do. You do understand my point of view?"

"Oh, Mary Rose, you are wise beyond your years. Doctors never like to be told what to do. What a grand idea. I will introduce you to the doctors and give them your credentials and ask them to cooperate with you so that you can get the nursing staff to improve. We will not even suggest that the doctors need improvement! And yes, we have refreshments prepared. You will find that you will rarely attend any function in New Orleans that does not provide food. Eating is a major pastime here."

"Sister Mariana, I think we will get a much better response that way. Approximately how many doctors will be in attendance this morning?"

"I am hoping we will have twenty, but it could be more. There are actually thirty doctors who practice at the hospital, but, as you suggested, some of them are way too busy to take time out to meet with a couple of "Yankee" nurses, as you described yourself. There are ten on staff who practice exclusively at Hotel Dieu and they will all be in attendance, but the others are at liberty to choose whether it is important enough for them to come. Sister Agnes, who runs the huge Charity Hospital has begged me to let some of her staff come as well. The House Surgeon and his assistants will be here, as they are eager to find ways to lower the infection rate at their huge hospital. Charity is about five times the size of Hotel Dieu, and, as you might assume from its name, it treats all of the indigents of the region. It is also run by the Daughters of Charity, so how could I refuse? Once you meet Sister Agnes you will understand how hard it is to refuse her anything. She is a dynamo."

"The food here is quite different from what we are used to in Boston. I hope my digestive system can adapt. We are used to eating a lot of seafood, but dinner last night was truly unique. The other diners told me it was something called Shrimp Creole. It was delicious, and then for breakfast we had something called grits which I had never even heard of before."

"There will be some adjustments for you, my dear girls. New Orleans cuisine is very different from Boston or anywhere else in the world. I hope you come to love it. Most people do. We do have about an hour before the meeting begins, if you would like, I could give you an abbreviated tour of our facilities."

"That would be grand, Sister Mariana. I am a little nervous about our meeting this morning and know my nerves will only get worse if I just sit around thinking about it."

"Nurse Wenban, you just need to turn on that Irish charm and you will have the doctors eating out of your hand. Smile a lot and let them know that you are here to help them. I am sure they will love you. Perhaps we should start our tour at the surgery wing."

As the doctors filled the assembly hall, Mary Rose and Mary Ellen got more and more nervous. Apparently the doctors had heard that they were going to be given new orders by these upstart Yankee nurses, and were most agitated at the very idea. There were probably fifty doctors in the audience, all with grim, unfriendly faces. It was a very hostile environment. Even the Café Au Lait and croissants could not soften them up.

"Mary Rose, you will have to do most of the talking. I am so nervous I am having trouble keeping my knees from shaking."

"Have you ever seen so many mean looking men? I wonder what they were told to expect. I am glad I have a podium to help support me. Remember to smile, Mary Ellen. You have a beautiful smile. We just have to win them over. First impressions are so important."

"I wish I could have worn one of my cute new hats instead of my nurse's cap. Remember, that was how we were going to impress the people of New Orleans."

"Now, now, we must be professional. Just imagine you are wearing a jaunty little hat. Which one would you have chosen to wear, the black one or the red one?"

"It would be the red one! I feel better already. You have such a knack for making people more comfortable. Am I not ravishing in my jaunty red hat?"

"You are indeed, but I think it is the smile beneath the hat that is making you look so beautiful. We are here to win these doctors over to our side, so just keep on smiling."

Sister Mariana stepped to the podium and asked the doctors to join her in a prayer. The doctors took their seats after the prayer, and she began her address:

"Thank you so much for coming to Hotel Dieu this morning. I am delighted and overwhelmed by how many of you are here. Obviously you are all interested in improving medicine in New Orleans. Several months ago, I contacted the Daughters of Charity who run the Carney Hospital in Boston. Carney has been able to lower the infection rate of their patients after surgery to a mere 15%, whereas ours is closer to 75%. I asked them to share with me how they have been able to accomplish such remarkable results, and they said it was all to the credit of their nursing staff. Their nurses have all been trained in the Lister technique which eliminates as many germs as possible. I then boldly asked if they would be willing to send us some of their nurses to train our staff, and was delighted when they replied that they had two volunteers who would be willing to come to New Orleans and help us improve our patient care. Today I am delighted to introduce to you the two volunteers. This is Nurse Mary Rose Wenban and this is Nurse Mary Ellen Faircloth. They are both graduates of the Carney School of Nursing in Boston and have received abundant training in what is known as Aseptic Practices. I know many of you have read in the journals about the Lister Germ Theory and how Dr. Lister has been researching ways to prevent infections, and now we have two experts who can help us actually use these techniques. They are not here to reprimand you, but to help us correct and improve our practices. They will be observing throughout the hospital and making recommendations. Please make them feel welcome. Remember they have sacrificed a lot to come and help us.

"Nurse Wenban, would you be willing to say a few words?"

"Sister Mariana and honored physicians and staff, it is my privilege to come to New Orleans and help bring your Hotel Dieu to the standards we hold at Carney Hospital. Not that Carney Hospital is perfect; after all, it does not serve grits for breakfast!" This comment got chuckles from all of the doctors. The mood had changed.

"At Carney we found that just small changes in routine would make a huge difference on whether patients became infected or not. What Nurse Faircloth and I hope to do is to identify the ways we can help you keep your patients safe. As you are well aware, medical care has been changing drastically. I know many of you are pioneers in improving medical care. We are here to help, but we can only do so with your help. Most of the changes will take place with the nursing staff. The nurses will be responsible for assuring the cleanliness of all the equipment you use. We look forward to working with you to bring quality care to all of your patients."

As the doctors filed out of the room, the doctors from Charity came over to meet Mary Rose and Mary Ellen.

"Nurse Wenban, I am Dr. Jeff Bloom, House Surgeon at Charity Hospital. The other doctors and I are anxious to hear what changes you are making. We would also like to improve the care we are giving our patients. I would like to have the privilege of staying in touch with you and asking you to keep me informed on how you are changing things. Once you get things settled at Hotel Dieu, I would be honored to have you visit Charity and look over our proceedings as well."

"Dr. Bloom, I am honored by your invitation. At this time, however, my hands will be quite full with Hotel Dieu. Perhaps in a month or so Nurse Faircloth and I could visit your hospital and make some recommendations, with Sister Mariana's permission, of course."

"It would be my honor." The intensity of her green eyes threw him off guard. "Perhaps in the interim I could take you to dinner in one of our fine restaurants?" he stammered.

"Dr. Bloom, I did not know that Southern gentlemen were so forward!" said Mary Rose blushing. "How dare you even suggest such!"

She turned from him and struck up an immediate conversation with Sister Mariana. They walked off together to sister's office, leaving Jeff with his mouth ajar.

'Who is this woman?' Jeff thought. 'I have never met anyone like her. Is her hair really that red and curly? And those eyes are so intense; I thought she was staring right through to my soul. Who is she to suggest that I am forward! She obviously knows who I am. What an interesting creature!'

Jeff returned to his hospital, but his thoughts kept returning to the red-headed whirlwind he had met in the meeting. He asked Sister Agnes what she knew about her, and sadly got very little information that he did not already have. Knowing Sister Agnes, he expected she would find out additional facts and get back to him, especially if she knew his interest was piqued, and that he was intrigued by a good Irish Catholic girl! She already had the match set.

Later that day, Mary Rose and Mary Ellen were evaluating their meeting.

"Can you believe that fresh Dr. Bloom? He asked me to dinner with him!" exclaimed Mary Rose.

"And what did you respond? He is the House Surgeon at Charity."

"I do not care what kind of a big shot he thinks he is, can you imagine his audacity? I told him I thought he was being much too forward. He must think we are here to find mates. There were enough men in Boston after my hand, I certainly did not come here looking for a husband. Or maybe he thought I was just an easy woman! You know I heard in some areas they equate nurses with women of ill repute."

"Oh, Mary Rose, you do go on. He probably wants to learn from you and thought he might extend a social invitation to encourage you to help his hospital also. I do not think you look or act like any of those street walking women we had as patients at Carney Hospital."

"Well, it will be a long time before I am willing to accept any invitations from him. Do you know he is Jewish? I have never met anyone who does not believe in Christ our Savior. What kind of person can he be? Did you notice those beady eyes behind his rimless glasses and that bushy mustache?"

"He is probably a very dedicated and educated doctor. He was just being friendly. Perhaps next time we should not smile so much. Keep a stern face at all times."

"You are asking me not to smile. You sound like old Sister Matthew. She was always after me to stop smiling. I have always found it so much nicer to be around smiling faces than old grumpy geese."

"Then, just take it as it is—a kind dinner invitation to a stranger in the city. You are making a mountain out of a mole hill. I feel sure we will get to know Dr. Bloom much better in the future, and then you can decide about his intentions.

"Well, beside your incident with Dr. Bloom, how do you think the meeting went?"

"I am sorry, Mary Ellen. He just upset me so much! I had heard that southern men were such gentlemen. He really took me by surprise. Other than the incident with Dr. Bloom, I was very happy with our meeting. I do not think we offended anyone, and I think all the doctors will welcome us to oversee what their nurses are doing, and how teaching the nurses will help their patients. We will see their attitude towards us once we get on the wards."

"Mary Rose, you did a great job in addressing the group. I think I would have died had Sister Mariana called on me! You acted as though you spoke to large groups all the time. I was so proud of you."

"Oh, you are such a ninny. You could have done equally well. Next time I will let you address the group."

"Not I, Mary Rose. I was so nervous just being there I thought I might take sick. You will have to be the speaker for us."

"Well, let us go stick our noses into the business of this hospital and see what needs changing. Come, Mary Ellen, we have a big job to do and lives may depend on us."

CHAPTER TWENTY-ONE

Testy Operations

"Nurse Wenban, it is so nice to see you again," greeted Jeff.

"Dr. Bloom, I am here to assist you in surgery. I understand that you are especially talented with repairing knife wounds, and this patient insisted on having you treat him. Do you come to Hotel Dieu often?"

"Actually, I am on staff here as well as at Touro, but my commitments at Charity are so vast that I rarely have a chance to work at other hospitals. This patient happens to be the son of an employee of my father whom I have known since I was a boy. When his family requested my help, I could not refuse. I am delighted to have a chance to see what it is like to practice under your stringent requirements. Please direct me as to the normal procedure."

"First, you must scrub your hands and arms up to your elbows, and then I will place the rubber gloves on you. The sterilized surgical gown is hanging next to the washstand. I will assist you in putting that on next. All of the instruments you will be using have also been sterilized, and are protected by a sterile drape. The patient is already sedated and ready for you."

"Exactly how do you go about sterilizing everything?"

"While you begin scrubbing, I will try to give you a brief overview. Basically, we boil everything. The clothing, the instruments, even your gloves have been boiled. The gloves do not last very long, but it is far better than not protecting the patient. After you have washed and have put on the gloves, I will place the sterilized mask over your nose and mouth. In that way, your germs remain your own, and if you are bringing some from another patient, they will not have the privilege of relocating in our patient."

"You have given up the carbolic acid?"

"Carney found that breathing the acid was extremely dangerous, and boiling produced an even better level of sterility."

"And the soap you use?"

"We rely on the Octagon soap. I am sure you have read about it in the literature. It has proven to be the most effective."

"It is the only soap we use at Charity. I agree it has helped greatly in reducing the spread of germs."

"We also use it in washing all of the linens. We simply put a bar in a huge vat of water, add the linens and boil everything for fifteen minutes. It not only kills the germs, but is excellent in getting linens white. We then rinse them and hang them on a line inside the hospital. We have clothes lines all around the boiler room. It takes a little longer to dry, but it eliminates the problem of bird droppings and dust."

"Well, Nurse Wenban, am I clean enough?"

"Yes, Doctor, but please do not touch anything but the patient and the utensils now that we have your gloves and mask in place."

"Yes, Ma'am, I will try to do my best. Let us go see if we can repair the damage done to that poor youth. Do you know how he was injured?"

"Dr. Bloom, I do not get into the gossip that surrounds each patient. I only know that he received a severe stab wound to his abdomen, and there may be some internal organ damage."

Jeff thought, 'Did this impudent nurse just chastise him? What is this world coming to?'

"Of course, Nurse Wenban, we would not want to gossip. I will get the facts from the family later. But I am still anxious for you to come to Charity and share your expertise with us. We have been making great strides, but I know there are still problems that should be addressed. Please consider sharing your knowledge with us. We have some of the latest equipment at Charity as well. We recently completed our surgery amphitheater which has all the latest in electrical equipment. We also have a Roentgen ray machine. Just yesterday I took an x-ray of a young man's whose foot had a bullet wound, but we could not find the bullet. I did not want to tear up any more of his foot than necessary, and the skiagraph showed me exactly where the bullet had lodged. It made the surgery much simpler."

"Thank you, Dr. Bloom, I am sure there are wonderful things to see at your hospital and for your confidence in me. I will speak with Sister Mariana and Mary Ellen and see if we can accommodate you sometime soon."

As Jeff left the hospital, he could not get Nurse Wenban off his mind. 'She has got to be the most unfriendly person I have ever met. Why am I so eager to impress her?'

*   *   *

"Mrs. Milliken, I am so delighted to see you. How can I help you?" asked Jeff.

"Dear Dr. Bloom, after careful consideration I would very much like to sponsor the building of a hospital devoted to children. My late departed husband left me with more money than I can ever spend, and our biggest heartache was that our only child, Fannie Allen, drowned while we were on vacation in Maine. We talked about doing this many times while Richard was still with me. If I can help others prevent such sadness, I want to do just that. Dr. Matas and Sister Agnes have been encouraging me to make this dedication to the hospital, and after talking with my attorneys and financial advisors, I have decided to move forward."

"Mrs. Milliken, I cannot tell you how happy you have made me! I have watched these poor darlings amidst every hooligan imaginable, and thought, 'if only we could separate them from the adult population.' Now we will be able to do that. What I propose to do is to build a separate building next to the present hospital. It would have the proximity to all of the resources of the hospital, but away from the detritus. Young children who are hospitalized have enough to deal with without being exposed to adult problems as well. I propose we name it 'The Richard Allen Milliken Memorial Hospital for Children.' I think Mr. Milliken would be proud to have his name on such a worthwhile endeavor."

"Dr. Bloom, as you know, I lost poor Richard just last year when he was struck by a trolley on St. Charles Avenue. It was such a sudden and tragic accident, and I have had great difficulty dealing with my grief. We shared the grief when we lost little Fannie Allen, but now I need to find a way to cope with my latest loss." She paused to wipe a tear from her eye. "I was talking with William Morris, the architect, about the possible design for the hospital. I met with him while I was in Baltimore visiting relatives. He cheered me greatly with his wonderful ideas. He suggested we have a very happy central rotunda, one that will give the children and adults great delight. Mr. Morris suggested we have Tiffany design four glorious stained glass windows representing the seasons. It would bring beauty and light into the center of the building. I had mentioned to him how much I loved fountains, and thought we could incorporate a water feature there also. I would like for you to meet with Mr. Morris at your earliest convenience about the planning of the rest of the hospital. You have a much better idea of how it should be set up than do I, and I know Mr. Morris is anxious to get your input."

"I have not had the pleasure of working with Mr. Morris in the past, but I have been a great admirer of his work. He has a reputation for incorporating great beauty into his designs. Such a rotunda would be a very 'happy place' in a hospital. I think it is a wonderful idea."

"Had he the time, he would have preferred to design the windows himself, but that is just impossible now, and Tiffany does beautiful work as well. I will let him know that you are anxious to meet with him, and we will arrange an appointment at a mutually convenient time."

"Thank you so much, Mrs. Milliken. It will be wonderful to work with such an incredible architect to design a place to heal our little ones. Thank you for being so generous."

CHAPTER TWENTY-TWO

Yellow Jack

In August of 1897, a much more serious problem faced the physicians of New Orleans. A young boy had taken ill with a mysterious fever. The doctor in charge, Dr. Sidney Theard reported to the Board of Health that he diagnosed the boy with yellow fever. He had just returned from vacationing in Ocean Springs, Mississippi. A committee of physicians was called in about the diagnosis. They determined that it was not yellow fever, but dengue fever which had symptoms very similar to the saffron scourge. On September 6, the boy died and his autopsy showed it was definitely yellow fever.

Yellow jack, as it was commonly called, had a history of epidemics in New Orleans. The last serious one was ten years earlier when 686 cases were reported and 193 deaths occurred. The cause of the disease was in question. Many doctors and health officials thought it was caused by breathing unclean air. New Orleans had been working to clean up all the sewers and canals to prevent the spread of other diseases such as typhoid and malaria as well. Whenever a yellow fever epidemic occurred, the wealthy residents evacuated the city as soon as word came out that it was present. Only the poor or encumbered remained. The city would be quarantined and all business would come to a screeching halt, including the port of New Orleans. It created a financial disaster. A declaration of yellow fever was not something to take lightly.

An embargo was placed on Ocean Springs and all coastal areas west of Mobile, but New Orleans was not included. The medical society met on September 7 due to great public demand that some action be taken. There was huge controversy among the doctors as to what should be done, however a majority of those present chose to put the matter into the hands of the Board of Health.

On September 22, a member of the society, Dr. Joseph Lovell, died of fever after he treated some children who had been in Ocean Springs. Other cases had also been identified.

"Jeff, what are you going to do about the number of cases of the fever?" asked Rudy Matas. "The pest house is already filled past capacity. Even though most cases have not been diagnosed as yellow fever, we still must keep them away from our other patients. We need another asylum for strictly yellow fever patients."

"Rudy, I have been looking into the matter seriously. I have talked with the mayor and we have leased the Beauregard school over on Canal and St. Patrick streets. I have workmen there working to convert it to a pest house strictly for fever patients."

"When will it be ready? We are past having a need for it."

"Sister Agnes and I are going over this afternoon to determine the status of the efforts and see if we cannot start sending patients there tomorrow."

*   *   *

That afternoon Jeff, Sister Agnes and several of the nuns were touring the facility. Workmen were removing the school desks and replacing them with beds. A crowd of several hundred residents surrounded the school and prevented the workmen from doing their job. They heckled both the workmen and the sisters, and had prepared a noose that they declared was the perfect size for Jeff's neck!

"Sister Agnes, this is a very dangerous situation. I need to get you and your sisters away from here and get the authorities to come dismiss this crowd."

"Jeff, I have a better idea. Follow me."

Sister Agnes then ordered her sisters to surround Jeff. She knew he was the one in most danger of being hurt by the protestors. She led the circle out of the building and warned the angry crowd that one of these days they might need her help. They left the premises unharmed.

"Thank you, Sister Agnes, for saving my hide. Fear is a dreadful motivator of people's actions and I know that crowd is just afraid. We have to reassure them that we are not bringing patients here to give them and their families the fever."

*   *   *

That night some hooligans set fire to the outer building. As the firemen were putting out the blaze, their hoses were cut allowing two of the smaller structures to be totally consumed in flames. The police intervened and were able to save the main building. The next morning, the mayor arranged for a large crew of workmen to begin repair, and work proceeded night and day. In the forty-eight hours of constant work, six buildings were constructed in addition to the main house for the patients: quarters for the sisters and nurses; dining room, kitchen and pantry; doctors' and male nurses' quarters; a dead house; and a lodge house for entry.

In this last building was a fumigation room. The doctors, upon their arrival, would disrobe and put on a germ-proof gown. After visiting the patients they would undergo a course of fumigation before they could don their street clothes. The fumigation room is constantly filled with formaldehyde. All clothing and personal effects of any patient brought into the building enter through this room. Before a cured patient is released, he also must be completely disinfected. According to a newspaper release, when a patient leaves the pest house: "he is as free from germs as is the purest lily that ever rested on the bosom of a fair communicant at Easter time." Over 200 patients were housed at the school for several months. Usually upon their release they would ride the Canal Street trolley to their home.

Repeatedly the press assured the residents that the germs from the patients in the pest house could not contaminate them, and that it was not yellow fever.

In October, Dr. H.A. Veazie presented a paper on Aestivo-Autumnal Fever to the medical society. He had treated a lot of yellow fever patients during the epidemic ten years before. He says this disease is characterized by a parasite that gets into the blood. How it gets there is a mystery. It could be by breathing it in, or eating something that contains it or by an insect bite. The disease most prevalent in the city is affecting only the weak, but yellow fever attacks the strong and healthy too. Also he said that this disease is responding to quinine, which yellow fever does not. Dr. Veazie was determined that this disease was not yellow fever. Jeff concurred.

The battle with the mysterious illness continued on for the next two years. Some doctors were certain it was yellow fever and even attempted to have the medical society charged with murder for refusing to quarantine the city. Despite the fact that doctors declared there was no yellow fever in the city, the public records in 1897 listed 298 deaths due to yellow fever.

The smell of burning sulfur filled the air. By setting barrels afire, the smoke supposedly helped kill the mosquitoes. Many of the residents worried that the horrific odor would do harm to them as well.

CHAPTER TWENTY-THREE

The Visit

"Nurse Wenban and Nurse Faircloth, I am so glad we could finally get you to visit us at Charity. It has only taken me five years to get you here! Sister Agnes wanted to do the honors of taking you on a tour of our facility, and I would like to meet with you after you complete your walk around. Please do take some notes on improvements you feel we should make. I hope you are suitably impressed with our new surgery amphitheater. It is state of the art. And Sister Agnes, be sure to take them into the pathology lab to see our X-ray machine."

"Dr. Bloom, I promise to show them all of your gadgets," smiled Sister Agnes.

"Actually, Dr. Bloom, we had an X-ray machine for several years at Carney. I am surprised that it has taken you so long to get one. It definitely aids in diagnosing injuries and helping repair the damage," quipped Mary Rose.

"Well, it does sometimes take us a little longer to catch up, but we are definitely making great strides. Please plan to join me for lunch in my office after your tour."

As they start out on their tour, Mary Rose shakes her head and exclaims, "I do declare, that is the most forward man I have ever met. And to think he is a doctor. He should have better manners. Sister, is it because he is Jewish?"

"Oh, Nurse Wenban, he is one of the nicest men and most devoted doctors you will ever meet. He, however, is extremely busy and does occasionally cut corners. I know how anxious he has been to get you to come and observe his hospital and make some suggestions for improvement. He kept asking me to beg Carney to send us some nurses also. I know he meant only the most generous appreciation in inviting you to lunch today."

"Well, Sister, the first time I met him he invited me to dinner. What do you make of that?"

"As I said, he has wanted to improve Charity's infection rate since he came here as a medical student. He has seen you and Nurse Faircloth as an answer to a long standing prayer and has been eager to get your input on what he has failed to see and do. Please do not consider his invitation as an affront. I am certain he has only the highest regard for both of you.

"Once we have completed the tour of the hospital, I want to take you next door to the new Milliken Children's Hospital. It is nearing completion and will be a delightful place for youngsters to come to heal. The young ones are Dr. Bloom's favorites. He has been teaching pediatrics in the medical school for some time now, and is so anxious to get this new facility operating so we can move the children out of the big hospital. Mrs. Milliken has been extremely generous in her donation to build the hospital, but I think her admiration for both Dr. Bloom and Dr. Matas have inspired her to really build something she will be proud to bear her late husband's name."

"There has been quite a lot of chatter about the beautiful stained glass windows," piped in Mary Ellen.

"Only the best—Tiffany made them and they are huge: four feet by ten feet each. They ended up only doing three of the seasons: summer, winter, and spring. I guess they decided that fall is such a short season here it almost goes unnoticed. And you should see the darling fountain in the center of the rotunda. It has a statue of a young boy holding up his boot, but his boot has holes in it and the water is dripping through. I am sure it will delight all of the children. I know it makes me smile every time I see it."

"It sounds delightful, but first let us see this surgery amphitheater I have been hearing so much about," directed Mary Rose.

After the tour, Sister Agnes and the nurses walked back to Dr. Bloom's office.

"Thank you so much, Sister Agnes. You have an enormous hospital here, and you are certainly doing the Lord's work in caring for the needy and indigent. It is hard to imagine that there are so many of them here," said Mary Ellen.

"New Orleans has a large port, and many of our patients are seamen who have traveled from afar. They bring with them all manner of illness. We also draw from all the rural areas surrounding the city. One of the problems is that often it is too late when some of the patients are finally brought to us, and there is little we can do. Of course, another large segment of our population is the party goers who have too much to drink and end up shooting and stabbing each other. We get way too many of them. They say that the doctors who work here have the broadest aspect of medicine found anywhere, mainly because they have had to treat such a wide variety of illnesses.

"You know we also have pest houses which we service, as well as the leper colony upriver. We just got the leper colony started when Dr. Bloom took over as house surgeon. It was one of his first big projects. But there have been many to follow," cited Sister Agnes.

"Well, Sister Agnes, you certainly are a champion of Dr. Bloom!" quipped Mary Rose.

"Actually, Nurse Wenban, I cannot say enough good things about him. Once you get to know him a little better, you may come to appreciate what an outstanding individual he is.

"Let me tell you about our leper colony. It is an old deserted plantation that was leased from the owner's descendants. It began with just the huge manor house and seven slave cabins, along with a few outbuildings for the animals and equipment. It is growing by leaps and bounds. Our colony draws lepers from all over the United States now. It is intended to be a place where they can live and mend in peace without the ridicule and abuse they get from the general public. There also is a tremendous amount of research going on there, and hopefully they will come up with a cure for that dread disease soon. Dr. Bloom has been very generous in supplying it with everything they could possibly need. He even personally donated an organ for the chapel."

"Is not Dr. Bloom Jewish?" declared Mary Rose.

"Much to my distress, he is still Jewish, but I am working on him. I simply told him the organ was needed, and he felt that it could not come from hospital funds, so he made the donation himself. It really brightened the lives of all the residents to have beautiful music in the chapel.

"Well, here we are back at Dr. Bloom's office. Let us go in and you can give him a full report on the changes you think we should make here at Charity. Please say a few nice things as well, Nurse Wenban. That poor man works so hard, he needs a little encouragement!" teased Sister Agnes.

"I will try, Sister Agnes, but it will not come naturally! I tend to be very honest."

* * *

"Well did you see our X-ray machine? Did you have such a fine one at Carney?"

"Oh, Dr. Bloom, it is state of the art, and much nicer than the one we had," replied Mary Ellen. "And the surgery amphitheater is an ideal arrangement. I know your doctors are delighted to have such a facility. But I really love the new children's hospital. Those windows took my breath away. And the fountain is too cute!"

"Nurse Faircloth, you are too kind. Those windows are dramatic! I cannot take any credit for them, but I am delighted to be able to enjoy them too. Mrs. Milliken insisted on making the rotunda a fun place to be. She knows how stressful hospitals can be, and if something can be added to bring beauty and cheer to a place, she insisted on doing so. You do not want to know  the cost of Tiffany designing and creating such masterpieces. I probably would have chosen to put the extra money into medical equipment, but Mrs. Milliken was not to be argued with. She had those windows ordered before we had finished designing the hospital! I hope you can meet her someday. She is truly a lovely lady."

"She must be to give so much to the children of the city. I would love to make her acquaintance."

"And Nurse Wenban, what did you think of our institution?"

"Well, Doctor Bloom, it certainly is big! I can understand why you are so enamored with your new surgery wing, it does seem to be most modern," responded Mary Rose.

"I am hoping you have some suggestions for us," added Jeff.

"Indeed I do. I have made a list of infractions that should not be tolerated in a modern hospital. Perhaps we should go over these one at a time."

Jeff was taken aback by the brashness. It was like she had stabbed him. "Please have a seat and let us go over your list. I will see to the corrections immediately."

"I am anxious to see these also," added Sister Agnes. "My staff will probably be involved in many of the corrections."

Mary Rose pulled out her three page list of violations which ranged anywhere from a spot of blood on the surgery floor, to soiled linen in the corner of a patient's room. She also cited incidences where equipment that should have been sterilized was open to the air. She went on and on, Jeff making careful note of each item, his cheeks getting redder and redder as they went down the list.

"Nurse Wenban, you have opened my eyes. These infractions are things I never would have noticed had you not pointed them out to me. I will get with my staff this afternoon and see if we cannot eliminate each and every one. Most are minor violations that can easily be addressed."

"Dr. Bloom, each of these is critical to keeping your hospital sanitary. It is so often the tiniest infraction that could bring infection to a patient. You do realize that we did not go into every ward. I am sure there are more problems that we did not observe. I am hoping that you and your staff will go through the hospital on a regular basis and correct these inefficiencies."

"Indeed we shall. Right, Sister Agnes?"

"Of course, Dr. Bloom, I will address this to the other sisters at lunch today. I understand you are having lunch brought in for yourself and the nurses."

"Yes, the trays should be arriving shortly. Dr. Alfred Danna, one of my assistant house surgeon, plans to join us as well. I thought he would enjoy our discussion."

"Oh, I know he will," quipped Sister as she left the office.

"Ladies, please come in to the conference room where our lunch will be served shortly. Ah, here is Dr. Danna now. Dr. Danna, may I introduce the two nurses I have told you so much about? This is Nurse Wenban and this is Nurse Faircloth. They have been on a tour of Charity this morning and have a list of violations that should be corrected. I knew you would take great interest in this as well, but let us not ruin our appetite. The cafeteria staff has just brought in our dinners. I took the liberty of asking the dietitian to choose for all of us. I hope her choices will be to your satisfaction."

The conference room table was appointed with linens and fine china. Cafeteria staff stood in the background, ready to serve.

"Nurse Faircloth, may I do the honors?" asked Dr. Danna as he pulled out a chair for Mary Ellen.

"Thank you, Dr. Danna," Mary Ellen smiled as she took her seat.

"I am anxious to hear what you and Nurse Wenban found at Charity today," added Alfred.

"Actually, if we compare what we found at Charity to what we saw at Hotel Dieu when we first arrived, Charity would receive a B-. Hotel Dieu got a D-, but we have been making great improvements," said Mary Ellen.

"Some of the doctors at Hotel Dieu were still using sea sponges!" exclaimed Mary Ellen.

"Oh, it was not long ago that we were as well. When Dr. Bloom returned to us from Touro it was one of the first changes he implemented, although he was just an assistant house surgeon then. He insisted that the sterilized gauze be used instead. He is also the one who put that horrid Octagon soap all over the hospital, and had us washing our hands a hundred times a day. Jeff had an uncanny ability to convince Dr. Miles to make many changes and believe they were his own ideas, but I knew better," smiled Alfred.

"Dr. Miles was a staunch supporter of all the changes we made. The changes had to come from him, or you know the doctors would never have gone along with them. As nurses, you probably know how hardheaded doctors can be. They do not like to take directions, and they certainly would not have taken them from me at that time," said Jeff defending himself. "In fact, that is one of the reasons I accepted this position. Much as I miss having as much patient time, I know I can make a difference by improving the patient conditions here. Dr. Danna has been my partner in sneaking changes into the system. We have convinced a lot of doctors to change their ways."

"Sister Agnes was going on and on about the leper colony you started. It sounds very interesting. Can you tell us more about it?" asked Mary Ellen.

"I wish I could take credit for the Louisiana Home for Lepers, but I just happened to come in at the time everything was in place for it to happen. Dr. Miles and Dr. Dyer had already done most of the groundwork. I just finished what they started. It is doing beautifully, I must add."

"Jeff, you are too modest. Among the things he did was send a work crew to the plantation to get things repaired so they could move in. And this was a crew that worked for his father, so Charity did not have to pay for it. And they could not find a boat to take the first residents there, so Jeff arranged for a barge that happens to belong to his father that took all of their equipment and furnishings as well as the patients to the plantation," added Alfred.

"Tell me more about how things are going there now," pleaded Mary Ellen.

"The residents have done wonders with the place. They have gardens growing most of the vegetables they need, chicken coops for their eggs and chickens, cows provide their milk and meat needs. They have been doing a lot of building to make room for the many patients who continue to show up at their doors. The good Daughters of Charity have accepted it as their own mission and have several sisters ministering to the sick."

"How are you getting supplies to them?" asked Mary Rose.

"Most people are unwilling to actually come in contact with the lepers. They have an irrational fear of catching the disease. So we have worked out a deal that supplies are delivered to the dock, and the money for the supplies is paid by the hospital here so that the boat captain does not have to talk or meet with any of the lepers. One of the first things we had to do was repair the dock. Pa and I sailed up there a couple of months before the first patients were brought, and he immediately offered to send his crew to make some necessary repairs. There is a nice dock there now."

"Well, Doctor Bloom, do you go up there often to check on the status of the colony?" asked Mary Rose.

At this, Jeff blushed a brilliant red. "Officially, no," replied Jeff.

"But unofficially?" pursued Mary Rose.

"In the strictest of confidence, not to be shared with anyone outside this room, I do sail up every other weekend to check on the patients and make sure all is going well. If word of this were to leak out around the city, I would no longer be able to treat patients or participate in social activities. Everyone at the yacht club assumes I am just enjoying a quiet weekend on the lake. I would like for it to remain that way."

"Dr. Bloom is there some way we could go with you?" asked Mary Ellen. "I would love to see such a remarkable establishment. I understand there is even a chapel."

"We sneak priests in from neighboring parishes to hold services whenever possible. The sisters insisted on it. Once the colony becomes big enough, they would love to have a priest assigned to them on a full time basis. Right now it is hit or miss.

"Would you really be interested in going there? I am planning to go this weekend and would be glad to take you along. It will all be very proper, of course. I usually leave very early in the morning on Saturday, and return Sunday evening. I am sure the sisters would love to have two nurses help them see to their patients. Perhaps you could give them suggestions on the aseptics of their care as well."

"Oh, Mary Ellen, what are you getting us in for?" quizzed Mary Rose.

"Mary Rose, you were the one looking for excitement! Remember? I cannot imagine anything quite so exciting that we have done so far. I am sure we will be in the capable hands of Dr. Bloom, and the dear sisters will look out for us once we arrive. It sounds like an enchanting weekend to me. Are you suddenly becoming afraid to try something that promises to be memorable?"

"Dr. Danna, have you been there as well?" asked Mary Rose.

"Jeff has shanghaied me on several occasions. It is an enchanting experience. Jeff, perhaps I should go with you as well. You are not scheduled to bring any new patients with you, are you?"

"Not at this time, but you know *Miss Lillian* could well hold more than just the four of us. I am trying to teach Alfred how to sail. Have either of you ladies been sailing before?"

"*Miss Lillian*?" asked Mary Rose.

"That is the name of my boat. It was so named before I got her and it seems to suit her well."

"Most people would refer to *Miss Lillian* as a yacht, but Jeff keeps referring to it as his little sailboat. She is beautiful and well fitted, and Jeff is a master yachtsman," added Alfred. "You would not have any fear of your safety unless a hurricane came along, and this is not hurricane season. And you will have two of the best doctors in the city at your command should something go wrong."

"How will we explain our absence to Sister Mariana and the other nurses?" asked Mary Ellen.

"Perhaps you could suggest to them that you are going to go advise another hospital?" responded Alfred. "That would not be lying. You could say that the hospital wanted to keep it confidential and that you really could not say any more about it. Tell them we are escorting you. They know that Jeff and I are gentlemen who can be trusted. Jeff, this sounds like it could really be a fun weekend."

"It definitely will be memorable. Well, ladies, what do you say?" asked Jeff.

"If I were to ask Sister John, do you know what she would tell me, Mary Ellen?"

"Sister John would tell you that you are looking to get into mischief again, and there is no way she would approve of such an adventure, which means we have to do it! Right?"

"I have been giving my biological sister, Sister John, fits since she became my guardian many years ago. She always gave me wonderful advice which I usually refused to take. You are right, Mary Ellen, this is too grand an opportunity for adventure. We came to New Orleans to see the world, and mostly we have seen the inside of a hospital. Yes, Dr. Bloom, we would be delighted to join you on a sail to the Louisiana Leper Home this Saturday. At what time should we expect your carriage?"

"Dr. Danna and I will be at the nurses' home to get you about 5:30 Saturday morning. We can have breakfast on the boat. Pack lightly. It will indeed be quite different from my usual trips to Carville! I will tell Sister Agnes what we are doing and she can assure Sister Mariana that you are in good hands without giving anything away."

CHAPTER TWENTY-FOUR

The Voyage

"Mary Ellen, did we make a bad decision? I am so nervous about going on this trip with the good doctors. I have never done anything like this in my life!"

"Mary Rose, remember we wanted adventure and now we are going to get some. I cannot believe I have to talk you into this. You are usually the one who is eager to seek the unexplored. And what is there to worry about. We are going with the two most handsome and eligible bachelors in New Orleans, not to mention that they are both renowned doctors. And not only that, we did not even have to explain it to Sister Mariana. Apparently Sister Agnes spoke with her about it and told her how helpful we could be to this "mystery" hospital."

"It does seem Sister Mariana was eager for us to go. She said something about how I will learn to appreciate what a fine man Dr. Bloom is, and come to admire him. I know that came from Sister Agnes. She could not say enough good things about Dr. Bloom, but I believe there is a very small chance of that happening. He has shown me too much of his rude side. The only reason I agreed was because that delightful Dr. Danna was coming also. He is such a gentleman."

"Oh, Mary Rose, he is a delightful distraction! And did you notice the other nurses when they were told of our 'adventure.' They were pea green with envy—every one of them. They would have jumped at a chance to take our place. We are going to have a grand weekend!"

"If Sister John knew what I was doing this weekend she would wear out her rosary beads. It is best she not know."

"I imagine she is wearing them out anyway, not knowing what you are doing. She was beside herself when you told her you were accepting the offer to go to New Orleans."

"She has been very good to me, and I should not take such delight in stressing her so much. I hope one day she will be proud of me. She always tried to squelch my enthusiasm for everything. She is still hoping that I will become a sister."

"I know there will never be a Sister Mary Rose. Imagine having to cover your beautiful hair in one of those awful habits!"

"This hair has gotten me into more trouble for as long as I can remember. My father loved it, but he was a very colorful gentleman. I wish I could remember more about him. I do remember on our trip to Boston after my parents died, Sister John made me put on my bonnet every time we went to the restroom on the train ride. She was afraid I would attract too much attention. Well, I attracted attention with or without the bonnet!"

"Here is the carriage now. My stomach is turning upside down I am so nervous."

"Calm down, Mary Rose. Do you want Dr. Bloom to think you are anxious?"

"I must take a deep breath and steady my nerves. No, I want to appear as cool and collected as I possibly can. I could not bear for him to know how exciting this adventure is going to be for me."

"Good morning, ladies. I am so glad to see you are ready to travel. Let me grab your satchels for you," said the gallant Dr. Danna smiling.

"Oh, we would not keep two eminent doctors waiting," smiled Mary Ellen back. "I think that is a cardinal sin of nursing."

"Good morning, ladies. It looks like we will have a beautiful day for our journey," smiled Jeff. "Let me help you into the carriage."

"It does appear that the good Lord is smiling on us from above. I hope he continues to bless our endeavors this weekend," smiled Mary Rose as she climbed into the carriage. She had already decided she was going to mention God whenever possible. It was well known how hard Sister Agnes was working on Jeff's conversion. Perhaps she could assist the process. Having been raised by the sisters, she was well aware of the lingo.

"Indeed, it does look like we have found His favor," Jeff retorted with a twinkle in his eye. "I hope this hour is not too early for you ladies."

"Well, I hardly slept a wink anyway, so I was glad when the hour to get up arrived," quipped Mary Ellen. "This promises to be a very exciting day."

"To add to our excitement, we have three extra passengers meeting us at our secret dock. They will become new residents of the colony, and have come all the way from Florida. It is rare that I do not have a few stowaways on my journeys to the colony."

"Leprosy is one of the diseases we did not see in Boston. It seems to be more prevalent in the warmer climates. I am eager to learn more about the disease. Are you sure we will not be endangering our health by being on board with lepers?' asked Mary Rose.

"Only a very small percentage of people are even susceptible to the bacillus that causes the illness and almost all of them are men and very young. I would not have suggested this trip if I thought you were in any danger. We think it is transmitted by touch, so I would avoid touching the patients, just as a caution. I have not seen these patients yet, and they may have some horrifying features because of the disease. You do know how it eats away at body parts, especially the extremities. Please do your best not to stare at their wounds. Most lepers are very aware of the stares. It makes them feel uncomfortable."

"But, of course, Dr. Bloom. We are professional nurses after all," quipped Mary Rose tartly.

"I wanted to warn you because you will see some horrific deformities this weekend, and thought a little preparation was in order. You will find they are all beautiful people once you get to know them. I did not mean to undermine your professionalism."

"Thank you, Dr. Bloom, for the warning. I can remember seeing pictures of lepers in our nursing textbooks, and they were very unsettling. I do believe that Miss Faircloth and I will not embarrass you or the lepers."

"I am sorry if I offended you, but I felt it necessary to mention the warnings in advance. The leper colony has been specifically designed to give these poor wretches a place where they will not be pitied or looked down on. That is one of their guarantees."

"Oh, Dr. Bloom, you are so kind to forewarn us. Sometimes these things can take even the most experienced nurse by surprise. I can remember one patient that made me cry every time I looked at him, he was in such pitiful condition, and that was from an accident, not a disease like leprosy," added Mary Ellen.

"Dr. Danna, do you like to travel?" asked Mary Rose, changing the subject.

"No, I am not the traveler. Jeff is. He has been visiting hospitals all over the northeast trying to find ways to improve ours. That is how he spends his vacations, when he is not sailing up to the leper colony."

The chatter continued as they rode to the lake where the boat was moored. "This is our local yacht club," said Jeff. "I keep my boat here because

I can leave my horse and carriage with the grooms. They are used to me coming and going at all hours, and they take excellent care of my horse."

"And the yacht club has lovely parties as well," added Alfred.

"Alfred is the party goer," smiled Jeff. "He probably attends more parties here than I do and he is not a member!"

"Jeff does not have time for many parties. He rarely gets his nose out of the hospital," teased Alfred. "I am glad I am just his assistant."

"Well, let us get on board and underway," said Jeff quickly changing the subject.

"This is *Miss Lillian*?" asked Mary Rose with a shocked expression.

"Indeed, this is Jeff's little sailboat. Oh, by the way, if the wind is still, there is a steam engine we can use to get to our destination. It comes in very handy going upriver."

"She is beautiful, Dr. Bloom," said Mary Ellen. "I have never been on a yacht before. This is far more than I expected."

"It looks as though you could live on board," said Mary Rose.

"There are bunks for four below, as well as a head and a galley. I have often dreamt of taking *Miss Lillian* on a cruise to Cuba, but I have yet to find anyone willing to go with me. She is a beauty!" remarked Jeff. You could see the love in his eyes.

"She is a beauty," agreed Mary Rose. "I am eager to see her interior."

"Have either of you ever been sailing before?" asked Jeff.

"This is a first for both of us," said Mary Rose. "It was part of the reason Mary Ellen was so excited about coming."

"And you too. Admit it, Mary Rose."

"Yes, I have been looking forward to this also. I love to experience the things I have only read about. This is also far better than anything I had ever imagined."

"Just take a seat over there and Alfred and I will get her underway. We will have lots of time to chat once we get sailing. Alfred has become quite an able first mate."

In just a few minutes, Jeff had them sailing out into the lake. "After we pick up our special cargo, we will go up through Lake Maurepas and then through Bayou Manchac and it will take us to the leper colony without having to fight the river current. There is a camp on the shore of the lake where we will stop to pick up our new patients."

The lake was calm and the journey to the camp took only a few minutes. The patients brought with them considerable luggage which was loaded first. The last of the patients was brought out in a wheel chair after everything else had been stored. This patient had to be lifted onto the boat and then the wheel chair was brought on board. It was obvious that not only had this patient lost his right leg from the knee down, he also was missing several fingers on each hand.

Mary Ellen and Mary Rose introduced themselves to the patients and tried to make them comfortable. There was a bench that surrounded the rear of the boat, and they all found their spot for the journey. After Alfred untied the mooring, Jeff masterfully took the boat back into the lake and then on its course. The wheel house was situated in the center of the boat, so that the captain could easily converse with all of the travelers.

"Miss Faircloth would you like to steer the boat for a while?" asked Jeff.

"Do I dare? Will you show me how?"

"Of course, once we are in the lake it is a fairly simple procedure. Do you see that lighthouse far in the distance?"

"Yes, I do."

"Just aim the boat in that direction. Do not make any sudden turns, but do keep your hands on the wheel at all times. I will be nearby if you need assistance. We are fortunate to have a nice breeze this morning so we should not need to run our engines. It is so peaceful when we can rely on the wind."

Jeff watched her steer the boat for a few minutes and then pulled out a table and a picnic basket and proceeded to set up breakfast. Biscuits, pastrami, jelly, hot coffee in a thermos, orange juice, and all the plates, glasses and tableware needed.

"What a lovely feast," said Alfred. "It looks like you visited your father's cook again."

"Dulcie loves to prepare picnic baskets and is totally delighted whenever I ask her to prepare one for me. Pa does not always let her know how much he appreciates all she does for him, but I sure let her know. She has been working for Pa for as long as I can remember. She knows only too well my favorite foods. That is why we have biscuits. She knows how much I love her biscuits. Please help yourselves. There should be plenty to go around."

"Let me take over the steering so you can enjoy a little breakfast. I tease everyone I bring sailing with me that they have to work for their keep. It will be Miss Wenban's turn next."

The patients insisted that the doctors and nurses help themselves first, and then they also enjoyed the breakfast. One of the lepers doted over the severely handicapped one, preparing his food and actually feeding him. After lunch, the ladies started to pack up the leftovers, but Jeff stopped them.

"Is there some leftover pastrami?"

"Yes, there are a few pieces," responded Mary Rose.

"Well, we can put them to good use." He put Alfred on the wheel to guide the boat and pulled out two fishing poles. He baited each with a piece of pastrami and then handed one to each of the ladies and instructed them to hang it over the side of the boat and see if they could not catch their lunch. He told them that when they felt a bite, just pull up on the pole and then reel in their catch. Within minutes each had hooked a fish, which Jeff helped them pull on board and release from the hook.

"I thought I had caught a whale," said Mary Rose. "That fish was pulling so hard on my pole, I was totally surprised when the fish was only a foot long. What kind of fish is that?"

"That is what is called a catfish, and they are fun to catch. You notice its long whiskers. They do not have scales like most fish, but they do have sharp barbs on their fins so you have to be very careful when you handle them. There is nothing better when they are fried.

"Miss Faircloth brought in a flounder. These are strange because they are so flat. They lie on the floor of the lake and both eyes are on their top side. Again, they are very good when fried. Let me rebait your hooks and see what else you can bring in."

Lake Pontchartrain is brackish, which means it is a mixture of salt and fresh water, and a wide variety of fish can survive in the lake. As they moved through Manchac, the water became mostly fresh, which made the type of fish being caught more limited. However, the fishing continued through the morning, with excitement coming with each new catch. When they ran out of sausage, the ladies were glad to take a break and enjoy the scenery. Alfred and Jeff took turns pointing out the various birds and animals they sighted. As they went through Manchac they sighted raccoons and deer as well as a few alligators sunning on the shore.

CHAPTER TWENTY-FIVE

Carville

The strong breeze made the journey shorter than usual and they pulled up at the dock of the leper colony at noon. Jeff handed the fish to one of the lepers who came out to greet them and asked him to take them to the cook to prepare them for their lunch. They helped the patients disembark, and watched as Jeff tied up his sails and secured the boat. Then they all headed across the levee to survey the colony.

Jeff introduced the nurses to the sisters who immediately took them under their wing. Jeff and Alfred headed over to the main house to see what they had in store for them. Luckily it appeared that there were no catastrophes that had to be attended, which meant no surgeries would be needed, but all the patients wanted to see a doctor. They scheduled appointments for that afternoon, and headed towards the dining room. There they found Mary Rose and Mary Ellen enjoying their catch.

"This is the best fish I have ever eaten in all my life!" exclaimed Mary Ellen.

"There is nothing like fresh fish fried by someone who knows how to cook it," remarked Alfred. "I hope you saved some for us."

"There is still plenty for you and Dr. Bloom. They also are feeding us something called hush puppies, and they fried the vegetables as well. I think they called this okra," said Mary Rose. "I have eaten more strange foods since I arrived in Louisiana, and it all surely tastes good. So different from what we ate in Boston."

"I imagine your digestive tract has been in shock since you came here. I hope it has agreed with you," said Jeff.

"Oh, yes, it definitely has agreed. I may have to get all new clothes soon it has agreed so well," smiled Mary Ellen.

"Alfred and I will be seeing the patients this afternoon. We would love for you to assist us. You will not need to touch any patients, just provide us with the necessary equipment as we ask for it. After lunch we will go over to the manor house and make sure all the utensils and bandages are properly prepared."

"We would be glad to assist you however we can," said Mary Rose. "That is what we came to do—help. The sisters have already shown us our room and helped us settle our things. We are at your service. Today has already been such a delightful experience. I hope we can repay you by being the best assistants you have ever had."

"When I come here, I usually have to do everything myself. With both Alfred and I seeing patients and having your excellent assistance, I am sure the rounds will go quickly this afternoon, and we will have a chance to survey the property. There is a horse and buggy that we can take to see the progress that has been made, and what has yet to be conquered. The acreage here is beautiful."

"But work always comes first, of course."

Both nurses nodded their agreement, and then headed off to the manor house to arrange the supplies. They were pleased to see the degree of sterilization that was already in place. They spoke with the sisters who cared for the patients on a daily basis, and set up examining rooms for each of the doctors. The doctors arrived soon after, and then the patients started lining up. Word had spread quickly through the compound that these two exceptional physicians were at their disposal. Dr. Dyer cared for them on a weekly basis, but his specialty was dermatology. These two doctors could cure anything, or so they believed.

When the last patient was seen, the doctors scrubbed up again, and asked to have the horse and buggy brought around. The foursome boarded the carriage, and Jeff took them on a tour of the property. There was a huge garden growing near the compound and several of the residents could be seen working the fields. Jeff identified each of the crops being grown, and all of it was intended to be used as food for the people of the colony. There was a cleared pasture where several cows grazed peacefully. Pigs wallowed in the mud of their sty. The chicken coop had been doubled in size and the birds could be seen pecking away at the ground outside. They passed a small cemetery under some giant pecan trees for those who had not survived. Their last stop was the slave quarters that had been converted to homes for the patients. They had freshened and painted them and had planted flower gardens all around the porches. One of the cabins had been turned into a chapel. New cabins were under construction.

"This is amazing. They all look so happy," said Mary Rose.

"Their only complaint is that they had to leave their own families behind. They would love to bring their families here to live with them. Of course, then we need to think about schools for the young ones, and who knows what else," added Jeff.

He steered the carriage up the levee, and they watched the magnificent sunset over the river. "This property used to be hunting and fishing grounds for one of the Indian tribes. They believed that every evening you should throw all of your troubles into the sun, and watch them disappear beyond the horizon. Our residents have found that is a wonderfully calming practice. These people are the happiest I have ever seen them, and I am hoping that soon we could move families in as well. We simply do not have the buildings available for them yet. New patients arrive almost daily. Word of this heavenly place for lepers has spread quickly across the United States."

As Jeff swatted a mosquito, he turned the carriage towards the manor house. "That is one of the problems here, the mosquitoes like it too. Let us get back to the manor house. I want to show you the lab before supper."

Dr. Dyer had set up his lab in the former library and had cages of mice, armadillos, and rabbits. "One of the things Dr. Dyer has found is that the armadillos seem to be more susceptible to leprosy than either mice or rabbits. I think he also tested raccoons, opossums and bats. Luckily it is easy to catch all of our test subjects on the property.

"Here is a slide of the leprosy bacteria. If you look through this microscope you can see their rod shaped structure. Have no fear; the bacteria have been killed so they cannot infect you."

"Does he think he can actually find a cure for this dread disease?" asked Mary Rose.

"He is determined that if he does not, he will make great strides so that whomever follows him will. He is also working on ways to treat the illness and minimize the damage it does to the body. As you have seen the deformities it causes are devastating."

"I think that is why it surprised me how happy they seem to be," said Mary Rose. "I do not know how I could possibly handle such horror."

"They are all very religious. I would like for you to join us at chapel in the morning. They put their trust in God to help them get through it."

"You attend the chapel here?" asked Mary Rose.

"Please do not tell my Pa, but yes I do. It does my heart good to see them rejoicing in their faith in God to show them their way," said Jeff smiling.

"It sounds like Sister Agnes is making progress," quipped Alfred.

"Not exactly, I still go to temple at home, but I do accept their need to worship God in their way. It gives them great strength."

"I would love to attend their chapel in the morning. Does a priest come every Sunday?" asked Mary Ellen.

"We are lucky to get one most Sundays. Mass is scheduled for 10:30 tomorrow, but it depends on when the traveling priest can get here. Most of the priests have their home churches where they say Mass first and then come here. It is a bit of an inconvenience for the colonists, because they fast from all food and drink from midnight until after Mass. So no breakfast will be served in the morning, but there will be a delightful brunch immediately following Mass. We will plan to leave after brunch so that we can get back to the city at a reasonable time. Going down river is usually much faster."

"I expect they will serve us a hearty supper tonight!" chimed in Mary Ellen. "Is that the bell I hear ringing now?"

"Indeed. We should head over to the dining room. They are very excited about having guests in the compound, and I am sure they have prepared something special for you."

Roast chicken, sweet potatoes, mustard greens and cornbread composed the evening menu, along with fresh pecan pie for dessert.

After supper, the colonists rearranged the dining hall into an auditorium where they put on a show for their guests. They portrayed Longfellow's story of Evangeline and her lover Gabriel—French Canadians who were expelled from Canada and relocated in southwest Louisiana. The lovers were separated during their journey and Evangeline spent the rest of her life looking for Gabriel.

A musical sing along followed with all of the residents taking part.

"It is hard to believe that this is a leper colony!" sighed Mary Ellen.

"They decided they needed to have a culture evening. They have been putting this play together for weeks. They were really excited that you all are here and their play was ready to perform. They do have some sort of activity every Saturday evening. Sometimes it is a dance. Those in wheel chairs dance in their chairs. It is something to see."

When they arose in the morning, Mary Ellen and Mary Rose decided to go for a walk on the levee to watch the river and discuss all they had seen.

"I think Dr. Danna is charming," smiled Mary Ellen.

"Yes, he is," agreed Mary Rose. "But I am beginning to see why Sister Agnes is so fond of Dr. Bloom. He does so many wonderful things, but fails to take any credit for them. He is a very modest gentleman."

"I wish I had brought my bird book with me. I do not think I have ever seen so many different birds. Look at those beautiful tall white ones standing on the bank of the river. And see the beautiful green ones over there. And is that a red headed woodpecker flying near the manor house? I guess we could count one hundred different species."

"And to think if we were still in Boston, most of the birds would still be in the south where they had flown for the winter. It would still be bleak and desolate, and yet Louisiana is totally green. I do love it here."

They headed to the chapel when they heard the singing. It seems the residents gather well before the priest is expected, to practice all of the songs they will sing during the Mass. Many of them thanked Jeff for the wonderful organ, and told him how much it added to their *joie de vivre*. The priest arrived a little after ten, and, although he kept a distance from all of the patients, you could tell that he really cared for them. The Mass was uplifting and the singing increased in volume with each hymn. The final hymn had the whole chapel reverberating with the joyous harmonies. As they left the chapel the hymn kept playing in Mary Rose's head.

Brunch consisted of pancakes with strawberries and blueberries, bacon and sausage, scrambled eggs, garlic cheese grits, Café au Lait, and a choice of juices. Everything but the coffee had been produced on the plantation. They thanked their hosts for their generous hospitality, bid them a fond adieu, and promised to return again. They boarded the Lillian and headed down river.

"Well, what do you think of our little colony?" asked Jeff.

"It is remarkable. You have created a peaceful home for these poor wretches, and, as you said, although their bodies may be repulsive, they are the sweetest souls ever. My heart goes out to every one of them," sighed Mary Rose. "How long ago did the first patients come here?"

"We brought the first group here about seven years ago," answered Jeff.

"I am amazed at how much of their own food they are producing!" said Mary Ellen. "They seem to take so much pride in their community. And at the Mass this morning, I felt like I was surrounded by angels."

"They do rely on their faith. I guess the Bible talks so much about lepers, that they feel God must know them very well," cited Alfred.

"It must be dreadful to be diagnosed with such an awful disease, and know that you will just waste away. I do hope a cure is found soon," said Mary Ellen.

The sail home was uneventful and filled with small talk. Once they arrived at the yacht club, Jeff offered to take them in for supper.

"Are we dressed appropriately, after a day at sea?" asked Mary Rose.

"Remember this is a yacht club. Most of the people inside will have just come in from sailing as well. This is probably something else that you have never experienced. I understood you were the one seeking adventures, Miss Wenban. Is Miss Faircloth the real daredevil?" teased Jeff.

"Apparently she is becoming such," chuckled Mary Rose. "Yes, here is another first to add to my diary. I would be honored to dine with you at the yacht club, sir."

The yacht club is a three story building that sits on a point that juts into the lake. The dining room had walls of windows so that the view of the lake was magnificent.

"We can watch the sun set again this evening, but from a very different view. Be sure to throw all of your worries and cares into the fiery orb, so you can have a very peaceful evening," reminded Jeff.

"I shall do just that. What a wonderful way to end a delightful weekend. Thank you so much for allowing us to come with you," said Mary Ellen.

"You made the weekend much easier on us. Our rounds went quickly, and I noticed that you gave the sisters a few pointers on sanitation. The residents could not have been more excited about having two beautiful guests in their midst," chided Alfred. "Perhaps we can do it again sometime."

After supper, Jeff and Alfred escorted the ladies back to their residence and bid them a good evening.

"Well, Jeff, I did not think that Miss Wenban would ever warm up, but you really charmed her. I think she will not think you are so rude anymore now that she knows you better."

"I hope not. She is such an intelligent and attractive young lady. I would really like to get to know her much better. I know I have never seen hair quite that color."

"Jeff, I have never heard you talk about any girl like that before. Oh, I think Cupid may be shooting some of his arrows around."

"Please, do not go that far, but I definitely am interested in her. She is so level headed and sensible, too. I have never met a girl like her."

"Sister Agnes is going to be so happy to hear about this! Jeff is interested in a Catholic girl. She has been praying for just that to happen."

"Alfred, she had better hear nothing of the kind. Do you understand?"

"Oh, I think she will be figuring it out on her own, I will not have to say a word."

"I know that religion will be a huge impediment to our relationship. My Pa would just go into apoplexy if he heard I was interested in a Catholic girl. He has been trying to set me up with a good Jewish girl since I was eighteen."

"And I can imagine it works for her family as well. Imagine a girl raised by the Daughters of Charity marrying a Jew who does not even believe in Jesus Christ!"

"Alfred, I think you are way ahead of yourself. I do not have the time or energy to get involved with someone. You know how much time I spend at the hospital. And when I get home I am devoted to reading all the journals on changes in the medical field. There is no time for a family. I rarely get by Pa's to visit him."

"That can change, my dear boy. When Cupid does his thing all sorts of changes take place. I have seen it happen too many times."

"Please keep all this nonsense to yourself. It was a very pleasant weekend, but you must be exhausted which would explain all this crazy talk. I will drop you at your home before I head back to the hospital just to make sure there are no problems there."

"I am glad I am just your assistant. I can go home and get a good night's rest, while you may be nestled in the arms of that megalith of a hospital until the wee hours of the morning. I hope all is well and you can go home soon."

CHAPTER TWENTY-SIX

The Carnival Ball

"Mary Rose, are you excited? I cannot imagine actually going to one of the balls. We have heard so much about them!" whispered Mary Ellen.

"Yes, dear, as you can tell I am beside myself. Will you help me do my hair up in a fancy style, rather than the sensible bun I wear every day in the hospital? Perhaps we could have ringlets falling down the sides. And then help me get into the beautiful green satin gown you talked me into spending a fortune on."

"Oh! This dress matches your eyes perfectly. Dr. Bloom will not be able to take his eyes off of you. This will be a night you will always remember!"

"I imagine it will, and I am adding another first to my list. I hear these Mardi Gras balls are fabulous. I only wish you were coming with me. We were to share all of these new adventures."

"Unfortunately I do not have someone smitten by me as you do. Every time I see Dr. Bloom's dewy eyes looking at you, I want to weep with joy and jealousy. I am not sure which is the stronger emotion."

"You are so silly. Dr. Bloom and I just have so much in common that we have developed a strong friendship. I am sure it will not go any farther than that."

"After he sees you floating down the stairs in that magnificent dress he will be hooked forever. He will not have a chance. Let me get busy on your updo. It could take me a while to get all those curls in just the right place. I hope we have enough pins to hold it. I would hate for it to collapse after the first dance!"

"It is so exciting! My heart is beating so fast, just thinking about how glorious it will be."

"I think it is Dr. Bloom that is making your heart race, you silly goose."

"Well, I do so enjoy his company, and each time we go out he makes sure it is something I have never done before. Last week we went on a tour of the St. Louis cemetery. You remember we saw them decorating the graves on our first day in New Orleans. This time we were trying to determine the cause of death of each of the residents. The first people were buried there over a century ago. We passed by the tomb of the famous voodoo queen, Marie Laveau. People still leave her gifts, and tradition says to protect yourself from the *gris gris* you must mark her grave with a red X. It was eerie. We went through both the Catholic and the Protestant sections of the cemetery. All the famous people from New Orleans are there in their private hotels. It was ever so interesting."

"And did you put your X on the grave?"

"Of course, as I said a prayer for the repose of her soul, but my X looks more like a cross."

"Mary Rose, you are one of a kind! What did Dr. Bloom think of your cross?"

"I think he thought it was an X. Anyway he did not comment on it, he just chuckled. He is such a nice man. How could I have thought such bad things about him when we first met?"

"Well I am glad you have changed your opinion of him. Think of all the fun you would be missing if you still thought so poorly of him. Hand me the hairpins as I try to manipulate this mane."

"It is a bit unruly, and there is an awfully lot of it. However, you are so good at getting things under control, I have faith you will manage my hair as well. I will be your nurse as you doctor my hair. Forceps?"

"No forceps necessary, but hairpins aplenty. Just keep handing them to me. I will let you know when we have stabilized the patient."

Mary Ellen worked on the auburn tresses, pinning and curling as she went. One of the other nurses brought a beautiful rhinestone barrette to hold the top in place.

"I wish my dear father could see me! He would be so proud of me. His Irish Rose is off to the ball with Prince Charming."

"I am sure he is looking down and smiling. I hope he keeps a watchful eye on that good doctor who is escorting you. I am glad he is an honorable man, because you, no doubt, will be the belle of the ball."

"I will tell you all about it in the morning." When Mary Ellen had declared the surgery a success, Mary Rose put on her gown, and pinched her cheeks to make them rosy. "I wish I had a little lip rouge to warm the color of my lips," she sighed.

"You are beautiful. You do not need to paint yourself up like those trashy women we see in the hospital."

Just then, one of the nurses knocked on the door to let Mary Rose know that her escort for the evening had arrived. All of the nurses came out of their rooms to admire their glamorous coworker, and a little envy seemed to tingle in all the well wishes.

When Jeff caught his first sight of her descending the stairs, it took his breath away. "Oh my, I am going to have to be very diligent this evening. I can already imagine how many call-outs you will be receiving. I am glad I can sign your card for the very first dance. You are so beautiful!"

Mary Rose looked to the floor to try to cover her blushing cheeks. There was no need to pinch them to make them rosy. She took Jeff's hand as he led her to the carriage.

"I feel like Cinderella, looking for my fairy godmother. Will all this disappear at midnight?"

"Cinderella you are not, but the most beautiful princess in the world. I plan to keep you out well past midnight, so you can be assured you will not have dreamt our evening. There is a breakfast after the dance which my sister Hannah is hosting at her new home. I can hardly wait for you to meet her."

They boarded the carriage and the driver took them to the French Opera House. After escorting Mary Rose to her reserved seat, Jeff introduced her to his sister, Hannah. He then disappeared.

"Where have all the men gone?" asked Mary Rose.

"Oh that is part of the tradition of the balls. The men go behind stage and will reemerge in costume and mask so that you cannot tell who is who? They will introduce the court of debutantes and then put on what is called The Tableau, a brief skit usually about something in Greek history. Since this is the Proteus ball, you would expect most of them to appear to be sea creatures, but the program says that the theme of the ball this year is Flora's Feast. I wonder what that is? After the tableau, the call-out dances begin. There are twelve call-out dances and after each dance the krewe member gives his dancing partner a gift. You can never be sure with whom you are dancing. Some of the members are so secretive they will not even talk to you while they are dancing with you. It is great fun to try to make them give up their identity."

"What a magical event this is! How do you know if you are to be danced with? I would hate to just sit here all the evening and watch everyone else dance."

"The men backstage are arranging it now. They are trading names with their krewe members to make sure everyone's card is filled. Before each dance, the ushers will call out your name to come and meet your partner. I feel sure Jeff will not have any problem finding volunteers to dance with you!"

"Some of these will be complete strangers?"

"They will seem like that for certain. Many will be men that you may have met before. One I am sure you will dance with is my husband, Maurice. I will see if I can spot him during the tableau and point him out to you. We can both see if we can guess who Jeff is. You may spot some of the doctors. Many of the doctors and board members of the hospital are krewe members.

"After the call-out dances, the krewe members go backstage and return in their formal attire and the dancing continues, only this time you are aware of who your partner is. The ball itself ends at midnight. I certainly hope Jeff told you about the breakfast I have prepared for after the ball. I have invited about fifty couples to my home to continue the celebration. It often goes until the wee hours of the morning. I certainly hope you are free from duties tomorrow."

"I thought this would be a very late evening and arranged to be off in the morning. You must have a very large home that you can invite one hundred people in for breakfast!"

"Maurice insisted that we build a new home a bit farther upriver on St. Charles Avenue from our first home. It is so big that I get lost in it sometimes. Luckily I have wonderful help that maintains it for me. The cooks have been preparing this breakfast for the last week. We moved in just a few months ago and this will be my first major party. I am eager to show it off."

"I look forward to seeing it as well. It is so kind of you to include me in your party."

"Jeff would not have heard of anything else. He has done nothing but talk about this wonderful nurse he has been seeing. Apparently you have enraptured him."

"Dr. Bloom and I are just good friends. We have many interests in common, both being in the medical field and so obsessed with sanitation. I think you may be seeing more to our relationship than actually exists."

"Well, I noticed the look in his eye when he brought you to your seat and introduced me to you. I have never seen him with a grin quite so wide. He apparently is enjoying your 'friendship'. Here comes the orchestra. It should not be long before the merriment begins."

The orchestra began to play and the captain of the ball came onto the stage. He wore an elaborate costume and was masked. He even wore a wig so that his identity was completely hidden. He introduced the court one at a time. Each of the debutantes was escorted by her father. They all wore magnificent white dresses with elaborate stand up collars and their fathers were in specially made formal evening suits with sequins and beading on the lapels.

Once the court had been introduced, the orchestra struck up the grand march from *Aida*. The king and queen of the evening were presented and everyone stood and bowed to them as they promenaded around the arena, waving to the crowd with their scepters in hand. They took their place on the thrones at the center of the stage. Then last year's court processed around and paid respects to the new court.

Then it was time to entertain royalty, and the krewe members came out in rollicking frivolity dressed as all manner of flowers. There were daffodils and tulips, irises and daisies, violets and marigolds to name a few. It was hard to imagine that these clowns were the pillars of society! No wonder they wore masks. They did little dances, acted out short skits, pretended to fight battles, and behaved much as young boys might. Then the captain indicated that it was time for the call-outs to begin. Each member went to a section of the audience and gave a name to the usher and the usher called for the lady to join her partner. Mary Rose felt sure her first dance would be with Jeff. He had as much told her so. But she was very surprised when her first call out went to a gentleman dressed as a columbine who was over six feet tall. Jeff was much shorter than that. Who could this be?

The gentlemen mumbled a few grunts as they danced, but would not be included in any conversation. As he returned her to her seat, he thanked her for the dance, and presented her with a small box.

"Thank you, strange gentleman. I wish I knew your identity," responded Mary Rose.

The second call-out was even stranger. This person appeared to be a crocus, and had difficulty walking, much less dancing. Again, Mary Rose felt sure this was not Jeff. As he handed her a gift after the dance she responded, "May all your dances be slow ones! That is quite a costume you are carrying around with you."

The call-outs continued, and still Mary Rose could not figure out who any of her dance partners were. Each gave her a gift as they brought her back to her seat. She conferred with Hannah, but she thought Hannah was holding out on her.

Her last call-out was with an anemone. His petals slapped away as they did a polka. He grabbed her close to him so his costume would not accidentally hit her as they danced. This was Jeff. She could feel it in her heart. Oh, how good it felt to be held so closely. She probably was blushing as red as the rose that Hannah was dancing with. He gave her the smallest of the gifts she had received.

Another grand march followed with the king and queen leading the way and all of the court following. The masked krewe members followed the entourage. Hannah turned to Mary Rose and asked her how she had enjoyed the evening so far.

"Was Dr. Bloom the anemone? He had told me he would be my first dance, but I am certain that columbine was not him. Which one was Mr. Stern?"

"I think Maurice was the rose. I will have to get it out of him later. He loves to make me guess. Have you opened any of your call-out gifts?"

"This all seems so unreal. What a fairy tale! I have not dared to open any yet. Is this the proper time to open them?"

"I have a hard time waiting this long! Please join me and let us see what we have been given."

Mary Rose opened the last and smallest one first. It was a tiny gold heart on a chain. She gasped when she saw what it was. The other gifts were much less personal—a book mark, a rhinestone bracelet, a box for holding treasures, a barrette, decorated hat pins, a broach of the Mardi Gras masks, a golden thimble, a small vase, a set of four napkin rings, a silver whistle, and a lace handkerchief. As she opened the last, Jeff returned to claim her.

"May I have this dance?" he asked.

"Of course," smiled Mary Rose. What did he mean by that heart? She certainly hoped he would explain exactly where he planned this relationship to go. Right now she just wanted him to hold her in his arms as they waltzed around the room.

"It is much easier to dance without all the petals, isn't it?" Mary Rose smiled.

"Oh no, you figured me out. How did you know?"

"Your call-out gift gave you away. It is beautiful."

"I wanted to give you something special, so I gave you my heart. I think I actually gave it to you the first time we met, although you quite thoroughly rejected it. I should have put some little dents in it for all the times you injured it!" he smiled.

"I am glad you did not mar it. I never meant to hurt your feelings. It just took me awhile to find out what a wonderful man you truly are."

"Patience is a virtue, as they say, and I have been very patient. Have you gotten to know Hannah during the tableau?"

"Oh, yes. She explained everything that was going on to me. She is a lovely lady and very proud of her older brother. She said she has invited one hundred people for breakfast! I do not think I know one hundred people that I could invite to a party."

"A lot of the guests will be business acquaintances of Maurice's. You will meet my brothers Louis and Arthur and their wives. Hannah will have a good many of her friends there as well. She is involved in many volunteer organizations. I do not know that you will know anyone there besides me. I doubt if she has invited any of the doctors."

"Well, obviously I will meet a lot of new people. May I wear my new heart?"

"That is why I gave it to you, hoping that you would keep it near yours forever."

"Oh, Dr. Bloom, you do make me blush. I never thought of you as a romantic."

"I have never been a romantic. Somehow you just bring out this side of me. But please call me Jeff when we are away from the hospital. By the way, Mardi Gras itself is in two weeks. Have you ever been to the parades?"

"I have volunteered at the hospital every year since I have been here. They are always so shorthanded, and no one else seems to want to work on that day."

"Well, this year you will not be free either. Do you think Miss Faircloth would be willing to join us?"

"She would love it. Although she would not say anything, I think she was very upset that I came tonight without her, so many of our adventures have been together. I will see to it that we are both cleared for the day. What can we look forward to?"

"I will make reservations for us at the Pickwick club. It is on Canal Street and that is where Rex stops to toast his queen. The queen and her maids are the most prestigious debutantes of the season. You can see all the throngs of merrymakers without actually having to be in the midst of them. I like it much better that way."

Several gentlemen came to Jeff to ask Jeff to introduce Mary Rose to them. She was asked to dance every dance that evening, and only got to dance with Jeff three other times. After the last dance, they gathered their treasures and headed to the Stern home.

As they entered the home, liveried waiters offered glasses of champagne on silver trays. Other servers brought around trays of delectables, from fried shrimp to stuffed mushrooms. Jeff proudly introduced Mary Rose to everyone he knew. There was a constant flow of champagne and hors d'oeuvres. At one-thirty, breakfast was announced and they all took their seats in a huge dining area. Waiters brought trays of Eggs Benedict, garlic cheese grits, strawberry stuffed crepes, beignets, fresh fruit, smoked trout, ham, and, of course, more champagne.

"This dress will not allow me to eat another thing," laughed Mary Rose.

"Hannah has certainly put on a spread. She loves giving parties. I have even asked her to host the soiree for the American Medical Association when it meets next June. It will not be a sit down dinner, just hors d'oeuvres and the like, but there will be hundreds invited. Her new home is ideal for large crowds. She was really excited when I asked her if she would be willing to offer her home. Hopefully, it will not be too warm. The conventioneers can ride the St. Charles trolley here, and get to see part of the city they would otherwise miss.

"It is a shame you did not meet her beautiful children. I am sure she has them locked upstairs and out of the way. They are delightful. I will have to arrange a dinner at Pa's soon where all the family can meet you."

"Dr. Bloom, are you sure they are ready for that?"

"Remember, it is Jeff, not Dr. Bloom, and I know I am ready for that."

After the breakfast, the crowd slowly dissipated. Mary Rose thanked her host and hostess for the lovely party, and said that she hoped they could get together again soon. To which Hannah replied something about she thought it would probably be very soon. Jeff helped Mary Rose into the carriage, and on the ride back to the hospital, he kept a tight grip on her hand.

"Miss Wenban, thank you so much for coming with me to the ball this evening. I have never enjoyed one more, and I am sure it is because of my lovely companion."

"Well, if I am to call you Jeff, you must return the compliment and call me by my Christian name as well, Mary Rose."

"I would love to do just that, but I think it will be just Rose! I have been doing that in my dreams already."

"There you go again, making me blush! You have quite a knack for that. But it is you who needs to be thanked. The ball was exquisite and what fun it is to not know with whom you are dancing. And the call-out favors are lovely, especially my little heart drop. Hannah's breakfast was the perfect final touch."

"How did you know I was the anemone?"

Mary Rose blushed again. "I could tell as soon as you took me in your arms," she said looking down.

Jeff reached over and kissed her cheek. "You are different from any woman I have ever met, and I love all of your differences. I do not know how I am going to let you go at the Nurses' Home. Will you ride with me out to the lakefront and we can watch the sunrise? It will only be a few more hours."

"And both of our reputations would be ruined! It is already past three in the morning. I would wager to guess that Mary Ellen is sitting up waiting for my return. How could I explain not returning before breakfast time?"

"Just tell her that I stole you away and refused to bring you home."

"The nurses would love that, once that word got out. They would chuckle every time they saw you. And if Sister Agnes got wind of it she probably would never speak to you again."

"I could care less about the other nurses or Sister Agnes; I just do not want this night to end. You are so beautiful."

"There you go again, making me blush. I must refuse your offer to view the sunrise, although I am sure it would be magnificent. Please do tell the driver to take me home," Mary Rose said curtly.

"Oh, no, it is the old Nurse Wenban returned. I hope I did not offend you, but I am so enamored with you, I sometimes lose my sense of propriety. I would hate to besmudge your stellar reputation, at least not until I get to know you a lot better," he said smiling. He kissed her quickly, but this time on the lips.

"Dr. Bloom, that is very impulsive of you. How dare you take such liberties!"

"It is Jeff, remember, and I just had an uncontrollable desire to kiss those lovely lips. Again, I apologize for my poor manners, but I think I am falling in love with you. I have never done this before, and I am not sure how to act. I just knew I had to taste those lips before the night was over."

At that, the carriage arrived at the Nurses' Home, and Jeff helped Mary Rose descend. He walked her to the door and said, "Thank you for such a perfect evening."

Mary Rose smiled and gave him a quick kiss on the cheek before disappearing behind the door.

Chapter Twenty-seven

The Morning After

As predicted, Mary Ellen was sitting on the edge of her bed when Mary Rose came in.

"Tell me all about it! How was the ball? Was it elegant? Did you have a good time? It is so very late. What have you been doing?"

"Give me a chance to catch my breath, Mary Ellen, and help me out of this dress. We had so much wonderful food at the breakfast after the dance; I thought I would pop my corset! It was all wonderful."

She went on to give Mary Ellen all the details of the evening, including the dancing with the unknown krewe members. She did not relay the feelings she felt in Jeff's arms. She showed her all the favors she received, however, did not mention the heart.

"Mary Rose, what is that necklace you are wearing. I have never seen it before. Is it a heart?"

Mary Rose blushed brightly.

"Did Dr. Bloom give you that as his call-out favor? Oh, my goodness. He is in love with you! Did he tell you so?"

"Mary Ellen, I am not one to kiss and tell."

"YOU KISSED HIM!!!!"

"Shhhh, you will wake everyone!" The blushing became more intense. "Oh, Mary Ellen, it was so romantic. I did not think I would experience anything so wonderful in all my life. Jeff is the sweetest, gentlest, most loving man I have ever met. But I cannot fall in love with him! He is not even a Christian, much less a Catholic. He was a complete gentleman, of course, although he did ask me to go out to the lake to watch the sunrise with him. I explained that would destroy both of our reputations. I am quite sure you are not the only one waiting to see when I got in this morning.

"His sister, Hannah, sat next to me at the ball. All of the men go backstage and put on costumes. Jeff was an anemone! They come out and do silly dances and skits, before the call-out dances begin. They are fully masked so you cannot tell who anyone is. Hannah explained to me what was going on and what to expect. When you are called-out, a krewe member comes to your area and gives your name to an usher, who calls for you. That is why they call it a 'call-out dance.' You dance with that person, not having any idea who they are! They will not talk to you or give themselves away. As they bring you back to your seat they give you a wrapped gift. I knew Jeff was the anemone as soon as he took me in his arms to dance. It was magical.

"After the dance, we went to Hannah's home for breakfast along with one hundred close friends. It was wonderful. She has a huge three story mansion on St. Charles Avenue. The servants greeted you with flutes of champagne, and every imaginable hors d'oeuvre. After an hour or so we were called in for a breakfast you could never imagine in your wildest dreams. Hannah was very friendly, and her husband Maurice is an elegant host. I met Jeff's brothers also. But the carriage ride home is what dreams are made of . . ."

"Tell me what he said when he gave you the heart!"

"He said that I had stolen his the moment we met and that he almost banged the little charm up to show how I had damaged his. He was so sweet."

"I think you will dream well tonight, but not for very long. Mass is in three and a half hours, so let us see if we can get some sleep."

*　　*　　*

After Mass, Sister Mariana stopped Mary Rose and inquired about her evening. Mary Rose blushed as she told her about the elegant ball and the wonderful breakfast afterwards.

"I noticed how early it was when you returned this morning. I am not used to my girls being out that late!" remarked Sister Mariana.

"Oh, Sister, I have never stayed out that late in my life. I know why they call it a ball. It was quite a unique experience, and Dr. Bloom is such a gentleman. His sister Hannah sat next to me at the ball and explained what was happening. After the ball, we went to her home for a breakfast."

"Was it just a small breakfast?"

"It was a huge breakfast. Everything wonderful you can possibly imagine. That is why I could not receive communion this morning, because we were eating at two a.m.! They served biscuits and beignets, eggs benedict, crepes, and so much more. The servants greeted you with flutes of champagne. There were about one hundred people there. I have never been to a breakfast like that. So many things I am experiencing for the first time now that I have moved to New Orleans. I do not imagine they have anything like that in Boston. And you should see the lovely call-out favors I was given. It was a fairy tale night I shall always remember."

"Mary Ellen, you had better watch over your friend more carefully. I think I may see some stars in her eyes. We certainly do not want her whisked away by a certain gentleman, do we?"

"Oh, Sister Mariana, you are as bad as Mary Ellen. There is no way that could happen. Dr. Bloom is Jewish. I am a devout Catholic. Mixed marriages like that do not work. It would be a nightmare. But I do enjoy his company, and he has been showing me a wonderful time."

"Just be careful, my dear. You have done wonders here at Hotel Dieu. Our infection rate has been reduced to the bare minimum since you girls have taken over and reformed our techniques."

"Sister Agnes is always teasing Dr. Bloom about converting him. I would not be surprised if one red headed nurse was the inspiration to make him find the Lord," smiled Mary Ellen teasingly.

"I will be remembering you in my prayers this evening, Mary Rose. It is hard to know what direction the good Lord has intended for you to take. He does work in mysterious ways."

*   *   *

A personal card was delivered to Mary Rose that afternoon. With it was a note from Jeff: "Thank you so much for such a wonderful evening. Please talk to Nurse Faircloth about joining me for Mardi Gras day. I have already made the reservations for us."

Mary Rose blushed again.

"Mary Ellen, Dr. Bloom has invited us to join him at the Pickwick Club for Mardi Gras Day! He has already made the reservations for both of us. What fun that will be! We have never seen the parades on Mardi Gras Day. I hear they are something to behold."

"Are you sure he wants me to join you?" asked Mary Ellen. "Is Dr. Danna coming as well?"

"He did not mention anything about Dr. Danna, but he had made the original invitation after the ball last night. He especially mentioned my asking you to join us, and today I received a formal invitation for both of us. Please say you will go. Remember all these adventures were to be done together. This is one you should not miss."

"Mary Rose, I will be delighted to go. I shall send Dr. Bloom my own response letting him know that I am thrilled to be included. Do we need to wear costumes? I hear most of the parade goers are dressed up as clowns or amusing disguises."

"We need to get advice from one of the locals and find out. Perhaps we could go as nurses? That is the only costume I have."

"I thought the reason for the costumes was to disguise yourself so that people would not recognize you. That way you can 'let your hair down' and as they say '*Lessez le bon temps rouler*.'"

"Oh my, I do not know if I can do that. I am going to talk with Jane Calhoun. She seems to know a lot about the local culture, and what would be appropriate for us to wear. We may have to go shopping again!"

"That is a great idea! You might also ask Dr. Bloom. That would be a great excuse for you to see him again. I know you would just dread that," teased Mary Ellen with a twinkle in her eye.

"I will do just that. When I send my response it will be with the question of appropriate attire for the event. But I am still going to ask Jane. I am not sure that Dr. Bloom is very aware of women's couture. He is always dapperly dressed, but I think he depends on his tailor to see to that."

*   *   *

"Jane, may I join you for supper this evening?" asked Mary Rose.

"Please do. We have not had enough chances to visit lately. I hear you have someone else showing you around our Crescent City."

"Oh indeed, Dr. Bloom has been taking me on several adventures. It has been great fun, but that is one of the reasons I need some advice. He has asked Mary Ellen and me to attend the Mardi Gras with him. We will have seats at the Pickwick Club. What is the appropriate attire for such an event? Should we wear costumes?"

"Wear a costume to the Pickwick Club, no indeed! That is where the queen and her court will be. That is where Rex comes to toast his queen. I have never been there for Mardi Gras, but I hear it is the best spot on the parade route. I would think a nice suit would be the best choice. No one at the Pickwick Club will be in costume."

"I am so glad I asked your opinion. Thank you. What else should I expect?"

"You will have the best possible view of all the magnificent floats and the beautiful costumes the maskers wear, and you will be mingling with the high society of New Orleans."

"Should I bring a picnic lunch?"

"There will be a lovely buffet provided for you at the club. That would be very uncouth to bring food with you. Be sure to wear a hat with a veil, and your gloves, of course.

"But, tell me, where else has the good doctor taken you?"

"We have been to the yacht club, but that was after we have been out on his boat, *The Miss Lillian*. He took me for a sightseeing tour through the St. Louis cemetery—that was spooky. And the best was to the Proteus Ball and breakfast afterwards at his sister's home. The ball was magnificent. I have never seen anything like it before."

"Well, wait until you see the Mardi Gras. It is unmatched in its magnificence. I think you will enjoy it very much. Perhaps I should take you to the Cathedral for Mass this Sunday. Mary Ellen should go too. Jackson Square is just outside the door and there are always street vendors and performers in the square. With Mardi Gras just two days away, I am sure there will be plenty to see. We can go to Café du Monde for breakfast afterwards—*beignets* and *café au lait*. It is a tradition. I feel I have neglected my duties as mentor for you as I promised when you arrived here."

"Things have been so hectic for all of us. Mass at the Cathedral sounds wonderful. I will ask Mary Ellen to join us, and I can assure you she will be as excited as I am. I can hardly wait. What time is Mass?"

"There are Masses at 6 and 8, but I would prefer the one at 8 a.m. if that is agreeable?"

"That sounds wonderful. We will be ready to go with you at 7:30. That should give us sufficient time."

"Perfect! Let us enjoy this delightful supper and look forward to next Sunday."

CHAPTER TWENTY-EIGHT·

Jackson Square

"Jane, tell me more about the cathedral. How old is it? Why is Andrew Jackson astride his horse out there in the square? What are the strange buildings on either side of the square? And is that a brewery across the street?" asked Mary Ellen.

"I can only answer one question at a time, please! The first cathedral was built here in 1727. It was dedicated to Louis XIV, the sainted king of France. At that time Louisiana was under French rule. Unfortunately, it burned to the ground in 1788. The new building was completed about a century ago, but it had to be greatly enlarged because the population of New Orleans had grown so much. There are several important people who were buried beneath the cathedral. That practice continues today, but you probably have to be a bishop to be buried here now. Most of the people whose funerals are held here are buried in the cemetery on St. Peter Street.

"Andrew Jackson was the hero of New Orleans and saved us from the British during the battle of 1812. He returned to New Orleans in 1840, and a huge oration was held in the cathedral. A party celebrating lasted for a week, ending with the planting of the cornerstone in the center of the square, which at that time was the *Place d' Armes*, where the soldiers drilled. It was renamed Jackson Square.

"Zachary Taylor visited the cathedral in 1847. He was a hero of the Mexican War. After a ceremony in the cathedral, he rode his battle horse Old Whitey through the city to the St. Charles Hotel. He was elected president just three years later. He lived in Baton Rouge and had a plantation in Mississippi. He was probably the last president who actually owned slaves. They called him 'Rough and Ready' because he always looked tousled. He was a man of the people, and the people loved him.

"The building to the left of the Cathedral is called the Pontalba Apartments. The Baroness Pontalba built those in 1852 with its fancy iron grillwork balconies and arches. She was the one who arranged to have the military grounds transformed into a lovely park with benches and radiating landscaping. It is a lovely place to sit and relax.

"To the right of the Cathedral is what is called The Cabildo. That is where the Louisiana Purchase was signed. Today the city council meets there and a lot of the government offices are located there. When the Baroness was building her apartments she insisted on having the Cabildo redone as well, so that it completed the square in a pleasing manner. They all went along with her. She must have been a remarkable lady!

"Across the street you noticed the Jackson Brewery. It was built about ten years ago and is said to be the largest independent brewery in the south. The German who built it is Dietrich Einsiedel. Its beer is very popular here in

New Orleans. Its main product is known simply as Jax Beer. The brewery is owned today by the Fabacher family.

"The French Market is just down the street to the right. Farmers come from miles around to sell their produce here every morning, except Sunday. The only place you will see open today is the Café Du Monde. Let us walk that way and see if we can get a table."

"I feel like I am in a foreign country. Look, over there, is that a juggler?" asked Mary Ellen.

"Indeed you will find a variety of artists and beggars in the square, and sometimes they are one and the same. They will have their hats strategically placed so that if you like their repertoire, you are expected to make a donation. Look, over there are some mimes putting on a show. The tables set up on the outside of the square are for the artists who will gladly draw your picture, for a price, of course."

"Mary Ellen, look at that juggler! He must have six plates spinning around at once. That is unbelievable," exclaimed Mary Rose.

"And look at the artwork on display. That looks like a picture around Lake Ponchartrain," asked Mary Ellen.

"Indeed, it does. The artist even captured many of the birds we saw. There is an alligator sunning himself on the shore. And look—three turtles!"

"There is so much to see," remarked Jane, "but I am starved. We can peruse the talent after we get some breakfast. Let us head to the Café."

They headed to the Café and found a cute metal table just large enough for the three of them. A waiter came and Jane ordered for them: *Café au Lait* and an order of *Beignets* for each.

"Part of the fun coming here is watching all of the people try to eat the beignets without getting powdered sugar all over their chests. It is quite an art."

There was a wide variety of people enjoying *beignets*. That seemed to be the only thing they served. The customers were of every age and shape, but they all had the telltale white powder on their chests.

"Luckily, it usually brushes right off, so do not stress if you do not master it on your first try. Very few people do. As we go through Jackson Square you can see who enjoyed their beignets the most," Jane chuckled.

"They are delicious! I have never had anything like this before. Who cares about the dusting of sugar if you can enjoy this treat," Mary Ellen squeezed out between bites.

"I agree. These are so good. Do they serve anything else here?" asked Mary Rose.

"I believe you can order tea or cocoa instead of coffee, but that is all. They do a booming business with their coffee and sugar coated puffs. For some families, it is a tradition to come after Mass every Sunday. Many businessmen stop here on their way to work during the week. The hotels tell visitors to the city that this is one place to make certain they visit."

After finishing their delightful breakfast, they did the best they could to brush the sugar off their fronts, and then walked back over to Jackson Square to admire the talent on display. An artist grabbed Mary Rose and begged her to please sit for him—he had to capture her beauty on canvas. Jane pulled her away and told her this was a regular ploy they used. Once he finished the portrait it would be almost impossible not to buy it from him. Mary Rose declined, saying, "You are so kind, but perhaps another day." And as an aside, she told Jane that no matter how good he made her look in the portrait, she would not be tempted to buy it, because she had already spent all of her spare money on the dress she wore to the ball.

They walked quickly to the other side of the square where there were children doing acrobatics. They had formed a tower of three, and the top child jumped, did a flip, and landed on his feet right in front of the bottom child. The second level repeated the action, landing right in front of him. The crowd applauded wildly.

"Oh, my, what kind of parent would allow their children to do such a thing?" asked Mary Ellen. She then noticed a man passing a hat among the bystanders, taking up collections for the young acrobats. "Do you think that is their father?"

"Probably, this may be the way the family earns money," said Jane. "A lot of parents use their children to perform for the crowds. You will probably see some dancing as well."

"Well, I will not contribute to this misuse of children. My heart stopped when I saw that youngster do a flip. I thought for sure we were going to be patching his head back together," sighed Mary Rose. "And this is our day off!"

"Indeed, we do not want to patch any heads or anything else," agreed Mary Ellen.

"One of my favorite things to do is to watch the people and try to guess their stories. Let us sit on the bench over there and see what we can come up with. I will go first.

"Do you see that gentleman over there in his formal tuxedo? My guess is that he went to a ball last night and is just trying to find his way home. Perhaps he took refuge with some harlot down in Roseville. Do you see how rumpled his clothes are?"

"No, I think he was one of the band members who had to play all night long, and then had to help clean up the premises, and is just winding his way home to his wife and children. Can we ask him?" asked Mary Ellen.

"No, indeed, that would spoil all the fun actually finding out the true story. Mary Rose, look at that sweet little family over there. What do you think the father does for a living?"

"Obviously, he is a tailor. He makes fine clothing. Look at how well dressed his wife and children are. He takes very good care of them. I saw them in Mass with us this morning. This is part of their regular Sunday morning routine. If we get up close we can probably see a few sprinkles of sugar on his lapel!" Mary Rose laughed.

"Good guess! Who shall be our next victim?"

"I know. Look at that little old lady sitting on the park bench opposite us," chimed in Mary Ellen. "She is a very wealthy spinster lady. Her father was very rich, but refused to let her marry the man she fell madly in love with when she was nineteen. He told her that the young man was just after her money. She never married and her only joy is watching other people strolling through the park. She now lives alone in one of the Pontalba apartments over yonder. She is hoping her true love will come looking for her again."

"Your turn, Jane," Mary Rose quipped.

"Oh, my, let me see. The artist who wanted to paint your picture comes from New York City. He moved to New Orleans to be near a young lady he met while she was traveling through the North. He catches glimpses of her every now and then, but she will not have anything to do with him. That is why he looks so sad."

The girls continued making up stories. There was an ample supply of story material with the square filled with tourists. Two young black boys were on the corner attracting a crowd. One was playing a harmonica while the other was tap dancing. They put on quite a show.

A steamboat's calliope could be heard in the distance. Everyone moved toward the river, waiting for it to land. As soon as it did, the showboat's touring company came onto the dock and began a sample show. There were singers and dancers and actors putting on a brief skit. They wore magnificent costumes. They urged all the onlookers to come on board the showboat to see the complete performance. "For just 5 cents you can see a show that has played all up and down the Mississippi River to rave reviews," announced the barker.

"Would you like to go see it?" asked Mary Ellen. "This will be another first. Have you even been on a showboat, Jane?"

"No, I have not. My father would not allow it. But I am a grown woman now, and can make my own choices. That sounds like a great idea. It will be a first for me, too. Come on, Mary Rose. Let us go aboard and see this wonderful show."

All three purchased their tickets and made their way up the gangplank.

"This is the first time I have been on a riverboat," sighed Mary Ellen. "Shall we take a look around before we find our seats? That is a huge paddlewheel on the side of the boat. How do they get it to turn?"

"Mary Ellen, you would think it would have a steam engine to turn it, but that huge paddlewheel is just for show. The boat itself has no means of movement, but is pushed up or downstream by a tug boat. Showboats are basically very elaborate barges. Having a steam engine on board would take away much of the room for the auditorium. Steam engines have been known to explode, which would definitely be hazardous with so many patrons on board. Our boat will not be going anywhere while the show is in progress. The patrons have to be able to leave if the show is really bad. I understand they can be very corny, or even vulgar. I hope this one is not either of those," remarked Jane. "That is probably why my father would never let me see a show. Since this is an early Sunday matinee, I would think it would be very appropriate. Look at all the children coming on board."

"This must be the casino where all of the gambling goes on. I have heard about all that wickedness and we surely do not want to go in there," said Mary Ellen.

"That reminds me of the club car on the train we took from Boston. It is time to find the auditorium and get good seats for the show," urged Mary Rose.

The auditorium was huge and beautifully decorated. The stage was draped in red velvet, and all the seats were covered in a matching fabric. Gilt carvings decorated the walls. There must have been over 200 seats for the patrons, with box seats on either side of the balcony. The girls found three seats available on the fourth row center and decided that would be the perfect spot. The auditorium was filling quickly. The calliope was still piping its song, inviting everyone to come aboard. Apparently its music was like that of the pied piper, enchanting the crowds and dragging them on to see the show.

"This is another great opportunity to people watch. I expect we will see a wide variety of people on board. Do you see any who look like riverboat gamblers?" asked Mary Ellen with a twinkle in her eye. "Perhaps they have struck it rich and are seeking someone with whom to share all that wealth."

"Do not get that into your head! The only place they would go to share their wealth would be to Roseville, and you certainly would not want to be considered to be one of those ladies of ill repute," warned Mary Rose.

"Choose which outfit someone is wearing that you would most like to have. I see that maroon suit coming in the door that is stunning. The skirt drapes beautifully over her bustle, and the jacket is fastened with silk frogs. The lapels appear to be made of the same silk fabric as the frogs, but the rest of the jacket and skirt appear to be wool. I would love to be able to touch the fabric and see what it is."

"Mary Ellen, you have excellent taste. That is an exquisite outfit. I think I would choose the navy dress with the white trim. See the lady standing near the stage? The white lace edging all along the tucks on the bodice really make it a stand out, and then the lace repeats on the cuffs of the sleeves. I think it is truly elegant," sighed Jane. "Mary Rose, have you picked your favorite?"

"I love that dark green suit with the silk bow blouse. That is truly my style, and the color would be perfect for me. Do you think we could ask those ladies to donate their outfits to some poor nurses?"

At this all the girls chuckled. And then the music began. The lights dimmed and the audience became very quiet. The barker introduced himself and then pointed to a sign showing the program for the day. It began with a song by their "Little Meadowlark" as he called her. Next, was a juggling act performed by two brothers. The highlight was the melodrama which had much of the audience near tears as the brokenhearted "Meadowlark" bid adieu to her family and boarded a train for the big city. Luckily it ended on a happy note, as she returns realizing that true happiness can only be found where you have people you love. The finale was a song and dance number by all the actors in the melodrama.

As the curtain closed the audience applauded eagerly.

The girls gathered themselves and followed the crowd down the gangplank. The lady in the maroon suit happened to be in front of them, and Mary Ellen took the liberty of touching the skirt of the suit, supposedly by accident. Her friends had a difficult time controlling their laughter, but Mary

Rose brought up one of the jokes that had been told in the program and pretended that is what they were laughing about.

"And how can we complete this lovely Sunday?" asked Mary Ellen.

"I am getting hungry. Shall we splurge on a really nice dinner? I am sure it is past mealtime at the hospital," suggested Jane. "The Court of Two Sisters over on Royal Street has a delightful brunch all day Sunday that is reasonably priced. I believe they even have musicians strolling through the restaurant playing for all to enjoy. This restaurant has a remarkable history as well as wonderful food."

"That sounds grand," said Mary Rose. "I have heard a lot about The Court of Two Sisters, and will be glad to have a chance to experience it personally. Will we be able to meet the sisters?"

"I hope so. Perhaps they will tell us the history of their place."

They walked the four blocks over to the restaurant, but had to wait to be seated. It seemed many others had made the same plans. When they were escorted to their table, they were given a menu with the food selections available for the brunch.

"Jane, do you have some suggestions?"

"I think you should try some things you have probably never eaten before. Start with the turtle soup—it is out of this world."

Mary Ellen's and Mary Rose's eyes opened wide as they both said: "Turtle soup!"

"Indeed, it is a delicacy. You will love it. Next would you prefer Eggs Benedict or grits and grillades? Both are specialties of the house."

"We have grits almost every day, and I had Eggs Benedict at the breakfast after the ball. They were wonderful. I want to have that again." said Mary Rose. Mary Ellen nodded approval.

"And for dessert I would recommend the bread pudding, pecan pie, or the Bananas Foster. The Bananas Foster is set on fire and comes to the table flaming! The bread pudding may sound plain, but it is divine. And you will not find a better pecan pie."

"We should order one of each and then we can try one another's," suggested Mary Ellen. "I would hate to miss out on anything."

"Great idea!" exclaimed Jane. "I was having a hard time deciding which one I wanted."

The girls enjoyed a delightful lunch, and almost skipped all the way back to the Nurses' Home.

CHAPTER TWENTY-NINE

The Mardi Gras

"How nice it is to have such lovely ladies accompany me to the Mardi Gras," said Jeff as he helped Mary Rose and Mary Ellen into his carriage. "Is this both your first parades?"

"Yes, it is. We have heard so much about the parades, but never had the proper invitation," responded Mary Ellen. "It just did not seem right for us to go out on the streets unescorted and mix with the rabble."

"Are you calling the good citizens of New Orleans rabble, although they do look like that on Mardi Gras. You learn all about the parades as a child and never outgrow it. I am delighted to be able to introduce you to the greatest free show on earth. I think that is how P.T. Barnum described it. After you have been once, it is hard to miss them in the future.

"We will have a definite advantage over the rabble, though, because we have reservations on Pickwick's viewing stand. You will get a great view of all the floats and the bands."

As they arrived at the club, a young boy met the carriage, and Jeff helped the ladies disembark. They made their way through the club to the grandstand. Once they were seated, Jeff offered to get the ladies something to drink. He explained that the buffet would be open after the parade, but perhaps they would care for a cup of tea or coffee. They both refused his offer saying they were too anxious to see all of the revelry.

"Would you like to meet the queen?" asked Jeff.

"Indeed!" both girls replied in unison.

"Follow me," he said, leading them to the front row of the viewing stand. "Miss Charbonnet, you could not be more beautiful! May I take a moment from your revelry to introduce two young ladies who are very enamored of your position this morning? This is Miss Mary Ellen Faircloth and Miss Mary Rose Wenban. They are both nurses at Hotel Dieu who have been brought to New Orleans from Boston to instruct the doctors and nurses here. This is their first parade. Miss Charbonnet's older sister, Alice, used to go sailing with me. Mr. and Mrs. Charbonnet, it is a pleasure to see you again. Little Susan has blossomed into a real beauty," said Jeff smiling as he bowed to the queen's mother, and shook Mr. Charbonnet's hand. I am sorry that Alice is not here with you. I have not seen her in quite some time."

"Alice has just given birth to her third baby, another boy. She is still abed, and was very disappointed that she could not join us today. It would bring back many memories of when she was a maid in the Krewe of Rex," replied Mrs. Charbonnet.

"Do you still have that lovely boat?" asked Mr. Charbonnet.

"Yes, it is still my weakness. I try to take her out at least every other weekend," said Jeff with a sharing smile to the nurses. "I do hope Alice and her baby are doing well."

"Oh, Alice is quite the little mother. She seems to really revel in that role. Luckily she has excellent help taking care of all the little ones," smiled Mr. Charbonnet.

After sharing small talk for a short while, Jeff and the girls returned to their seats in the grand stand.

"To tell you a little about the history of Rex, it was organized in 1872, and was intended to raise the spirits of the city after Reconstruction. A Russian prince was visiting the city, and the town leaders wanted to put on a fantastic show for him. Mardi Gras has been celebrated since the city was born, but it was very wild and unruly. For a while it had been totally outlawed. There were motley groups of men who would ride their horses through the city celebrating the "carnival," which means the end of meat. The city fathers wanted something that would show the city in a better light, so a group of city leaders got together and the Krewe of Rex was born. The motto for Rex is 'Pro Bono Public,' which means for the good of the people. It definitely raised the spirits, in more ways than one.

"Mardi Gras means Fat Tuesday in French. It is a traditional festival that celebrates the last day before the Christian Lent begins, when Catholics give up meat for most of their meals, as I am sure you know.

"But here comes the beginning of the parade. The person leading it on the white horse and dressed in white velvet is the Captain of the Krewe, known only as Bathurst. Clap for him! He is the man responsible for putting all of this together. Behind him you will see three of his lieutenants. They will always be riding three abreast, one purple, one gold and one green—the official Mardi Gras colors. Supposedly the purple symbolizes royalty, the gold symbolizes wealth, and the green symbolizes fertility. As with the Krewe of Proteus, all the krewe members are kept secret with the exception of Rex himself, his consort, and the maids and their escorts. Their pictures will be in the paper, and every year after this they will hang a Mardi Gras flag from their homes as a symbol of their former royalty.

"Here is King Rex himself. Rumor has it that the first king had to borrow a crown and scepter from an actor. As you might guess, these were specially made for today's Rex. He will stop and toast his queen. We will all raise our hands as though we are joining in the toast as well. The music you hear is from the king's calliope playing his theme song, "If Ever I Cease to Love." This was in a play that was in town during the first parade and just seemed appropriate and so has become part of the tradition. The calliope follows on the next float."

"Is that real ermine edging his train?" asked Mary Ellen.

"Yes, the costumes have come a long way since the first parade. Seamstresses spend most of the year designing and embellishing these costumes. You will notice all the beading? And do you love his wig?

"Next is the *Boeuf Gras*, or fatted cow. All of the riders on this float are dressed as chefs, supposedly preparing the meat for the feast. What are your first impressions?"

"It is truly magnificent. I thought the ball was the ultimate in elegance, however these floats are overwhelmingly beautiful," sighed Mary Rose.

"The costumes are so elaborate," said Mary Ellen. "Each one must have taken weeks to make with all the beading and decorations. Who makes these floats? It must take months to put all of this together. And they seem to go on forever. How many floats are there?"

"There are probably about twenty floats," agreed Jeff. "That is why the captain has such a huge job. Oh, here comes the title float. It will tell us the theme for this year's parade: "Quotations from Literature." What a delightful topic! I can think of many I would choose to have in the parade. Perhaps some of our favorites are included."

Mary Rose and Mary Ellen became more enamored as the floats passed, with bands playing between the floats. The crowds on the street erupted in applause with each passing float. There were also troupes of clowns mixed in amongst the marching bands entertaining the crowd with their foolishness.

As the last float passed, Mary Rose turned to Jeff and said: "Thank you so much for arranging this for us. It is truly an amazing sight to see. I never imagined it to be quite like this. I had heard all the excitement about the Mardi Gras, but this far outdid anything I anticipated."

"Dr. Bloom, this was a real treat," remarked Mary Ellen. "Thank you so much for including me. This has given me a new perspective on what Mardi Gras really is."

"Now ladies, it is not over yet. Once the court has made its way into the clubhouse, we will join them for a delightful buffet. You may notice the crowds setting up their picnics on the grounds outside. Mardi Gras is a whole day affair, not just a parade."

CHAPTER THIRTY

Facing Pa

"It is so nice dat you could join us for dinner dis Sunday, Jeff. It seems dat you have been too busy for us lately," said Pa as Jeff came in.

"Oh, Pa, the hospital has kept me very busy," replied Jeff.

"Your sister, Hannah, says dere is someting else keeping you busy—a young redhead!"

"Hannah must be referring to one of the nurses, Miss Wenban, who came from Boston to train the nurses and doctors at Hotel Dieu on sanitary procedures. She and her friend, Miss Faircloth, have been doing a wonderful job on lowering the number of deaths from infection at their hospital. They have even come to Charity to make some recommendations for us. She is quite knowledgeable, and I really enjoy her company. Hannah must be referring to my bringing her to the Proteus Ball. We both had a delightful time that evening."

"Hannah said you ver almost drooling at der breakfast afterwards, and it was not over der food."

"Oh, Hannah is such a silly one. She has a vivid imagination."

"Vy do not you bring her to dinner next Sunday. I tink I vould like to get to meet dis young lady dat has der good doctor drooling."

"Well, Pa, next weekend I plan to do a little sailing upriver, if you know what I mean. I will not be back until late Sunday."

"Can I assume dat you are bringing a nurse vit you to help?"

"Not this time, Pa. I did bring both of the ladies for a consultation visit a few months ago, but it is hard enough for me to sneak out of town without raising eyebrows. I can imagine what would happen if I brought them also. They were a great aid, and pointed out some corrections in procedure that have helped a lot. It would be nice to have trained nurses with me when I take my little cruises."

"Tell me more about dis vonderful young lady."

"Well, she was born in Philadelphia, but orphaned when she was very young. Both of her parents died from diphtheria. She was sent to Boston to live with her sister who was a member of the Daughters of Charity. They also had an orphanage there, so the family decided that was the best place for her. She came to New Orleans about five years ago."

"She vas raised by dose sail wearing nuns? She must be Catlic!"

"Indeed she is, Pa."

"I knew dose nuns vould cast a spell on you. Dat is how dey finally did it. Dey brought an enchantress in to seduce you to dere vays."

"Really, Pa, I am still in my right mind, and I have had no spells put on me. Being so new to the city and so sheltered by the nuns, it is delightful to expose her to the traditions of New Orleans. She had not been to a parade until I took her to Rex. She and Miss Faircloth loved it."

"So not only did you take her to der ball, you took her to der Mardi Gras, too? Jeff, you know dis can come to no good. You need to stop seeing dis young lady immediately. I will not stand for der idea dat you are becoming entangled vit a Catlic. Dat is not acceptable."

"I am not planning to marry her. She feels the same way you do, in fact, it took years for me to get her to speak to me in a civil tone. She felt that not being a Christian made me some sort of monster. I think I may be the first Jewish person she has ever known."

"Vell, you are giving me heartburn just tinking about it. Oh, good, here comes Hannah and her brood. Louis and his family should be here soon as well as Arthur. It vill be good to have der whole family together. It happens so rarely."

"Please, Pa, do not let this upset you. My friendship with Miss Wenban is just that and will go no farther."

"You understand dat your sister vill keep me in der know! She loves to tattle on her brothers. Here she is now."

"My dear sweet sister, Hannah, it is so good to see you and your wonderful children. Maurice, nice to see you too," smiled Jeff.

"Uncle Jeff, Uncle Jeff!" the children clamored as they jumped in his arms.

"My goodness, how big you are all growing," said Jeff as he hugged them all.

"Like veeds, dey grow," said Pa. "And can dey eat. Just vait until you see dem in action. Dulcie has trouble putting enough food on der table."

"Oh, Pa, you exaggerate so," said Hannah, giving Jeff a kiss as she pried the children off of him. "They do have healthy appetites, but I think it is because Dulcie is such a great cook. One day, I am going to steal her away from you!"

"Over my dead body," replied Pa. "She has been busy all morning trying to get dinner ready for dis crowd. I do not tink she vould be villing to do dis on a daily basis."

"Pa, I am just teasing with you. I do not know how you would find someone to put up with you the way she does. But, Dulcie, you just let me know if he is not treating you right. We can straighten that out."

"Me and Mr. Bloom has had a great understandin'. We gets along great. He knows to stay out of my kitchen, an' I stay out his business! We kinda takes care of each udder."

"Well, Dulcie, he is lucky to have you, and we all know that," smiled Jeff.

"If ya'll would come on in the dining room, I can start serving the gumbo. Mr. Bloom said he needed some good seafood gumbo to start the meal off today, and that's what has had me in thar cookin' all morning. Don't you lissen to him about my not bein' able to cook for a whole gang of folks. I loves doin' it."

"You do not have to ask me twice. Come on folks. We do not want that gumbo to get cold. I think we are the only Jewish family that serves gumbo at the Passover feast. I think the okra counts for the bitter herbs," teased Jeff. "Pa will you begin the traditional prayers."

Chapter Thirty-one

Pa

"Dr. Bloom, Dr. Bloom," shouted the young lad as he rang Jeff's doorbell and banged on his door. Jeff looked at his clock and saw it was 3 a.m. 'What in heaven's name can this be?' thought Jeff. The hospital had never summoned him in this way. Jeff quickly threw on his robe and stumbled down the stairs. It was Dulcie's fourteen year old grandson, Leon, standing there banging on the door in a panic.

"What is this ruckus about?" asked Jeff, rubbing his eyes.

"It is your father, Dr. Bloom. He bees real sick and Mizzuz Bloom and Ma sent me to get you. She knew he would want you to take care of him. He always said you bees the best doc in Nawlins."

"Let me throw some clothes on and grab my bag and I will be right with you," cried Jeff as he hurried upstairs to his bedroom. With lightning speed he returned, throwing on his jacket, tie still untied. As they climbed into the carriage, Jeff asked "Tell me what you can about Pa."

"I doesn't know much. Ma just came and got me up and said to rush over to git you and bring you to take care of Mastuh Isaac. She said he didn't look too good. He is such a good man. I sure hope he bees okay."

Jeff grabbed the reins from Leon and flicked them wildly trying to get the horse to move faster. "Dr. Bloom, Ol' Buck just can't goes too fast anymo," said Leon. "He's a good old horse, but he's gettin' tireder and tireder. Whipping on him jus' tends to slow him down."

"I am sure you are right, Leon. I just am very anxious to get to my father. Has anyone else been called?" Jeff asked as he relaxed the reins.

"No, suh. Ma said jus' to get you thar as quick as I could. I can rig up Ol' Buck in a flash and knew that would be the fastes' way to git you back thar."

"That was quick thinking, Leon. Thank you for hurrying so."

"Mastuh Isaac has taken good cares of us for as long as I can remember, and this is one of the firstest times I could do somethin' fo' him. I wanted to does as best as I could."

"Your Ma has been with us for as long as I can remember. I think she was probably working for Pa before the war!"

"Yessuh, I knows she was. She tole me all about how your Pa gave her freedom long befo' he had to. And he tole her she and her family would always have a place to live and wouldn't have a care in de world if she just stayed wit the family, and that bees the truth." Dulcie had raised her children and was now raising her grandchildren in the servants' quarters behind the big house.

As they pulled in front of the house, Jeff threw the reins back to Leon and jumped out of the carriage almost before it stopped. He ran up the stairs to his father's bedroom and was taken aback when he saw how pale and still his father was as he lay in his bed. His stepmother was sitting on the side of his bed, holding his hand. Dulcie stood guard by the door.

"Oh, Jeff, I am so glad you are here. Isaac was complaining that his chest hurt him last night right after supper. He took some bicarbonate of soda hoping that would settle his heartburn. When I woke up in the middle of the night I could hear him moaning and came in to check on him. I knew I had to get you here as soon as I could, that is when I sent for Dulcie and had her send Leon over to your place. His breathing is very shallow and he looks so pale."

Jeff checked for a pulse, and propped an extra pillow under his head. He asked Dulcie to get a basin of water and a wash cloth. He rubbed his father's hand and tried to get him to talk to him.

"Pa, it is me, Jeff. I am here to take care of you. Can you open your eyes for me?" There was no response. Jeff gently placed his palm on his father's forehead. "You do not seem to have a fever. Ma was telling me that you were complaining of chest pains last night. Are you in pain now?" There was still no response, but there seemed to be some improvement in his breathing. He dampened a cloth, carefully folded it, and put it over his forehead.

"Dulcie, would you mind putting a pot of coffee on for me? I am going to stay with Pa, and see if I cannot help him get through whatever his problem is. Thank you so much for sending for me."

"Yessuh. I be right back wit dat coffee for you. I knows how you like it—strong and black," she smiled.

"Indeed, Dulcie, you remember everything," Jeff responded as she hurried out of the room. He gave his Ma a hug and suggested she go lie down. "I promise to come and get you if anything develops." Tears streamed down Jeff's face as he realized there was little he could do for his father. Apparently his heart was giving out, and there was nothing known to medicine to keep it going.

When Dulcie returned with the coffee, he told her to go back to bed and try to get some sleep. He knew she would not heed his advice, but hoped she would at least get some rest. The days ahead would be a strain on all of them. Jeff spent the rest of the night talking to his father, telling him about all his hopes and dreams, and also reliving many good memories of family times.

As soon as the sun rose, Dulcie returned with a fresh pot of coffee and some biscuits. "Master Jeff, can I get anythin' for Mr. Bloom? Some fresh milk or juice?"

"Thank you, Dulcie. Pa is not doing much better. I do not think he is up to eating anything now. But please send for Louis, Arthur and Hannah. They need to be at Pa's side too."

She rushed off, sobbing quietly into her bandana. He could hear her downstairs sending three of her grandchildren in three different directions.

Within the hour the three siblings had arrived. Isaac opened his eyes and smiled to see his wife and all of his children surrounding his bed. "Vhat are all dese long faces about?" he asked. They all immediately broke into smiles.

"Oh, Pa, we are so glad to see you still have your sense of humor," teased Louis. "We were just a little grumpy because Jeff got us out of bed so early this morning. We are going to have to suffer through one of Dulcie's breakfasts now."

"That is really going to be tough on all of us, eating her delicious biscuits. I heard all the chickens squawking as I came in, which means she must have been collecting eggs as well," joked Arthur.

"Jeff has been up vit me half the night talking his head off. The only ting he didn't mention was dat redhead. He probably thought that vould send me to the hereafter if he did," whispered Pa. He then coughed several times.

"Pa, you need to save your strength for now and not talk. As I told you last week, Miss Wenban is just a friend and you need not be concerned about her. I am so glad to see some color come back into your cheeks. Pa, would you like a sip of water? Hannah, please get Dulcie to bring Pa some orange juice."

"Whatever the doctor orders," responded Hannah flippantly, as she left the room.

"You really gave me a scare last night, Pa. Luckily Ma came to check on you, and then sent Leon after me as soon as she realized something was not right. You may have just had too much excitement lately, but we will see. After you have had a few days' rest, you may be back to your old self again."

"I am glad you ver here," Pa whispered. He then closed his eyes again.

"Jeff, you should take a break. Go clean yourself up and get some rest. I will stay with Pa," volunteered Louis.

"I am fine," retorted Jeff, "unless you are suggesting I really need cleaning up. I would rather stay with him for the next few hours and see how he is doing. I do need to send word to the hospital to cancel all my appointments for the day. I do not plan to leave Pa for a while."

Hannah returned with a pitcher of orange juice. She placed it on the bedside table along with a tray of glasses. "I will get Dulcie to send one of her young ones for you, Jeff," she added as she left the room again.

"I know how hard this is for Hannah. She cannot sit still for ten minutes, and would rather run up and down the stairs than sit quietly," whispered Arthur.

"That is what makes her such a good mother. She is so devoted to her little ones, and they do keep her running. I have lots of practice sitting by bedsides watching patients, looking for good signs. Pa just talking to us was a very good one," added Jeff, defending his little sister. "I think she is having difficulty seeing Pa like this. She was always his favorite."

"And he readily admits it," smiled Arthur.

Jeff put his stethoscope to his father's chest and listened carefully. "His heart is making its own tune today. The normal rhythm is being disrupted. His pulse is weak which is why he is so pale. He is not running a fever, and does not seem to be in any pain," Jeff reported to his siblings.

"Would you mind stepping in the hallway with us for a minute, Jeff?" asked Louis.

"Sure, but only for a minute."

The three men exited the room just as Hannah was coming up the stairs.

"Jeff, what do you think is happening?" asked Louis. "Is the end near?"

"It could well be. His heart is struggling just to keep going. I wish we had a medicine to rejuvenate it, but we have not found one yet. I could give him something for pain, but he does not seem to be in pain, and that could only compromise his heart. He is really in the hands of the good Lord. That is why I had all of you summoned so early this morning. I could not even get him to open his eyes or respond before you came, but apparently he could hear me. That is why we need to make sure all of our conversations in the room are positive. Hannah, would you sit next to him for a while and tell him about all your children's antics. Even if he does not seem to notice, I know it will warm his heart. He is always talking about your wonderful children."

"Only if you go down and get some breakfast. Dulcie has prepared a feast. I think she has been cooking for hours."

"A stretch would do me good, but let me know if you see any change, Hannah. Keep talking to him and let him know how much you need and love him," conceded Jeff.

The three men headed down to the dining room which Dulcie had spread with biscuits, pancakes and cinnamon rolls. Bowls of fresh strawberries were at each place. As they entered the room, Dulcie ran up to Jeff and asked: "Bees he any better?"

"He opened his eyes and greeted us, but it was a strain for him to even get a sentence out. He seems to be resting fairly peacefully now. His breathing is a little better."

"Can I send a tray up for him?"

"Oh, no, Dulcie, he is a long way from needing food. You might start up a pot of your magic chicken soup. I know it has cured me many times, perhaps later in the day that would be the perfect medicine for him."

"Yessuh, I'll do that right aftuh I brings you your eggs. I knows how each of you likes them and I will have them out to you in a flash," said Dulcie as she scurried off.

"Jeff, please tell us your evaluation of Pa's condition," begged Louis.

"Well, Louis, he does not look good. I am afraid his heart is giving out, and we really do not have much to do to help him other than make him comfortable. I cannot predict how long it will take. If we can get him to eat and drink some, that will prolong his life, but he is not able to do either right now. It is a major challenge just to get him to sip water. Maybe Hannah is using her charms on him and getting him to cooperate. His heartbeat is very erratic, and his blood pressure is really low."

"Well, Dr. Bloom, we need you to work some of your magic. It is a shame that you have yet to come up with some way to keep a person's heart beating. I hear you can keep people breathing, even when they do not want to," remarked Arthur.

"Dr. Matas developed a machine that keeps the lungs going. We also have learned how to add fluids to a person's bloodstream when they are dehydrating. But as of yet the heart is totally out of our league. Maybe one day we will be able to repair or reinvigorate hearts, but that will probably be many years off, I am sorry to say."

"Jeff, you did a lot for him just coming and being with him last night. Ma thought he was a goner when she called for you, but you must be exhausted. Go grab a nap after breakfast while the rest of us are watching over him. I promise we will get you if there is any change," Louis suggested. "I am sure your old room is ready for you."

"Would Pa be better off in the hospital?" asked Arthur.

"He will be much more comfortable in his own bed with people who love him caring for him. There is little we can do for him in the hospital. I can give him morphine if he starts showing signs of pain, but, other than that, bed rest is the only possible cure. If the trip to the hospital did not kill him, exposure to all the diseases that are there probably would.

"I think I will go rest for an hour or so. Louis, I am going to hold you to your promise to call me if anything changes. Try to keep things down in Pa's room. He does not need any excitement."

"I will be in charge, Doctor, until we need your services again," teased Louis.

As they left the dining room, Jeff went up to his old room and lay on his bed. Just being there brought back so many memories. He still had the collection of medical books he had hidden on the top shelf of his closet, way in the back. He remembered how upset his Pa would get whenever he would catch him reading them. Jeff removed his jacket and his shoes and climbed into his old bed. He was asleep as soon as his head hit the pillow.

CHAPTER THIRTY-TWO

The Funeral

"Jeff, come quickly. Pa is having trouble breathing. It just started a minute ago," shouted Louis as he shook Jeff into consciousness.

Jeff slipped on his shoes without even tying them and rushed to his father's side.

"Pa, let me slip another pillow under your head. It may make it easier for you to breathe," whispered Jeff.

"Jeff, promise me you will leave dat redhead alone," Pa struggled to say.

"Pa, I may need to work with her, but you should not worry yourself about her. Like I said, we are just friends and she is a very talented nurse. She has taught me some of the things I needed to know. But I promise it will go no farther. Right now you need to concentrate on getting better. Try to breathe a little deeper." Jeff took out his stethoscope and checked his chest sounds. He shook his head.

"You are hearing my broken heart, eh Jeff?"

"No, Pa, but I am hearing you struggling to breathe. Save your breath with the talking for now. Try and take a deep breath for me."

"Louis, Arthur, Hannah!"

"Yes, Pa," they all responded in synchrony.

"Find Jeff a good Jewish girl. Ve have to get him out of der clutches of dis redhead."

"Pa, we will try, but you know how hardheaded he is. I can remember you fighting with him about studying medicine and you see where it got you," teased Arthur trying to lighten the conversation.

"Sure, Pa, I will set him up with a stream of young Jewish ladies until we find him the right one," promised Hannah. "I have a lot of friends who would love to marry a doctor."

Just then Pa rose up and gasped for air. There seemed to be an obstruction in his throat as you could hear a rattling noise. The three siblings looked at Jeff. Pa breathed again and settled back on his pillows, but the rattling noise continued.

"What is that noise?" asked Hannah, in tears.

"That is just fluid in his throat, Hannah. It is very common," responded Jeff. "Hold his hand and talk to him. Let him know how much you love and need him." Hannah immediately grabbed his right hand.

Arthur grabbed his other hand, and squeezed it tightly. "Pa, we need you here. Louis and I both need your advice to keep this business going. You have done such a great job getting it started for us, but you know how many times we have flubbed up. Thank goodness you were always there to straighten out whatever errors we made."

"Pa, my children need their Papa. You know how much they love you. Their favorite days are when we come over to see you. I know how they wear you out, because they wear me out too. They are so full of energy and fun. Maybe I have been bringing them over too much. That is what Maurice has been telling me, that I should not be such a burden on you. I always tell him that you love having us here."

Pa nodded his head in agreement. "Take good care of those babies, Hannah," he whispered. "They are our future."

With that his eyes drooped and he stopped breathing. Jeff swooped in with his stethoscope to see if his heart was still functioning at all. He then gently wiped his hand over his Pa's face to close his eyes completely. He straightened the bed linens and placed his Pa's hands together over his chest.

"Pa is at peace," said Jeff.

The foursome locked arms and recited in unison: *Baruch dayan emet*, or Blessed is the one true Judge. Ma sat in the corner and sobbed. After a brief pause, Jeff sent Hannah to arrange with the rabbi for the funeral on the next morning. Arthur went to inform Dulcie and oversee the preparation of the front parlor for the visitation that would begin as soon as the body was prepared. Jeff and Louis began the ritual of washing their father's body. They found the perfect white burial gown, or *tachrichim*, in his armoire, apparently purchased recently in anticipation of its need. His prayer shawl was wrapped around his shoulders and one end of the fringe was cut off, as tradition prescribed. Arthur returned to let them know that the room had been prepared to receive their father, and the three sons carefully carried the body down to the front parlor, and gently laid him in state.

Dulcie's grandchildren had been sent to all the neighboring homes to spread the word of their grief. Hannah returned with the rabbi in tow. Everything had been arranged. The plain pine casket would be delivered that afternoon. The cemetery had been directed to prepare the family plot in the Hebrew Rest cemetery. He had purchased a prime plot in the new Hebrew Rest II. It was wide enough for four or five coffins. Instead of having the buildings, the Jewish cemetery had plots elevated two feet off the ground. Jewish law required that the body be buried in the earth. The funeral itself was scheduled for nine the following morning. It was considered humiliation of the dead to prolong a funeral more than a day, and Jewish law forbade cremation or embalming. The rabbi did his best to console them, also making sure they were aware of the rituals to be followed.

A black funeral wreath was placed on the door. Within minutes, the neighbors began to pour in to pay their respects. Louis had insisted on being the first *shemira*, or guard, over the body. He sat quietly at his father's head reciting the psalms. The sons would take turns with this duty. Jeff excused himself from the group, going to his residence to clean up and change. He also planned to stop at the hospital and arrange to be absent for the next week. Hannah acted as hostess, receiving the visitors and accepting gifts of food. Maurice had joined her as soon as he heard of her father's passing. Arthur sat disconsolately in a corner. His job was to write the obituary for the newspapers. Dulcie wept quietly, trying hard to muffle her sobs in her bandana.

Word had already spread to the hospital when Jeff arrived. Condolences came from everyone he met. Sister Agnes gave him a big hug, something she had never done before. He removed himself as quickly as possible and returned to the family home. He went into the kitchen and found Dulcie sobbing uncontrollably.

"Dulcie, Dulcie. Please do not be so sad. Pa was a good man and I know he is now reaping his heavenly reward. Are you worried about him having to face our Ma?" asked Jeff jokingly, trying to lighten the mood.

"Oh no, Mister Jeff," answered Dulcie with a smile. "I knows how good your Pa was, and I knows both of the Mrs. Blooms treasured him. That's not what's got me so sad. I beez thinkin' bout me. Who is gonna take care of me now? Miss Hannah has already asked me to come work for her, but I am gettin' ole and I doesn't knows if I can handle that big house and all those little chilluns. Master Bloom and I was a perfect match. It's gonna be hard to find someone willin' to put up with old me and all my grandchilluns."

"Dulcie, you do not need to worry about a thing. Ma still needs you here. There is going to be plenty to do taking care of this house for now. I will talk with Hannah and my brothers and see what we can decide. Perhaps you would prefer to work for one of us."

"Thank you, Mister Jeff. I knowed you could make me feel better."

"Now you can make me feel better by fixing me something to eat. I am starved."

"Yes, Mister Jeff. Thar is so much food heah, you can pick what you want. What you feel like?"

"You chose for me. You know what I like better than I do. I would be happy with breakfast leftovers right now."

Dulcie scurried about fixing Jeff a plate, and sat it in front of him. He devoured it, thanked her profusely, gave her a hug, and went back into the front parlor.

"I think it is my turn to relieve you," he said to Louis. Louis rose from his chair, put his prayer shawl around Jeff, and left the room. Jeff turned the chair around to face the wall while still at his father's head, he started reciting his favorite psalms from heart. Jeff knew that in this position he would not have to speak to the many neighbors and friends who were stopping by to pay their respects. He could have quiet time in his own mind to deal with his grief. They would leave him alone.

The boys alternated guard duty throughout the night, never leaving the body unattended. By eight the next morning the house was filled with mourners. Dulcie had prepared an indulgent spread in the dining room for all of the guests. At exactly nine, the rabbi began singing the ritual Hebrew hymns to ask God's blessing on the dearly departed. Each of the siblings ripped their clothing as a sign of their loss. The rabbi proclaimed the traditional: "*Baruch atah Hashem Elokeinu melech haolam, dayan ha'emet,*" Blessed are you, Lord our God, Ruler of the universe, the true Judge. A shorter version of the same blessing was recited by the rest of the congregation: "*Baruch dayan emet,*" Blessed is the one true Judge.

Because Hebrew Rest Cemetery was almost six miles away, carriages had been lined up behind the funeral hearse. The body was carefully placed in the pine box, and nailed shut and as it was carried out all recited the *Twenty-Third Psalm*: The Lord is my Shepherd . . . The coffin was placed in an ornate hearse which was drawn by four magnificent black horses. A carriage carrying the pall bearers followed. Louis and his family rode in the next carriage. Jeff and Arthur joined Hannah and Maurice in their carriage. Hannah had chosen not to bring the children. A long line of carriages paraded slowly through the city. Bystanders on the streets stopped and bowed their heads as the procession made its way. Gentlemen removed their hats, and women grabbed their children and made them stand silently in respect.

As they passed through the magnificent double cast iron gates, which had been made for the World's Industrial and Cotton Centennial Exposition in 1884, Arthur commented on how proud his Pa had been to have had a hand in obtaining these for Temple Sinai. The hearse stopped just ahead of the family plot. All of the mourners got out first and formed two columns which the family passed through. Then the pall bearers brought the casket forward followed by the rabbi, stopping seven times as all recited the *Ninety-First Psalm*: "He that dwelleth in the secret place of the most High . . ."

The congregation closed around the burial site. Once all the prayers had been said and the casket had been lowered, each of the children picked up a handful of dirt and dropped it on the coffin. The other mourners followed suit. They then formed the double column again and as the siblings passed they uttered the traditional condolences: "*Hamakom y'nachem etchem b'toch sh'ar availai tziyon ee yerushalayim,*" May God comfort you among all the mourners of Zion and Jerusalem. A basin was provided for all to wash their hands as a sign of cleansing before they left the cemetery.

The following week was spent in mourning, or sitting *Shiva*. All the mirrors were covered and benches were brought into the front parlor. The siblings sat and shared memories of their father. Close friends joined them and added to the stories. It was a time of closeness and healing.

CHAPTER THIRTY-THREE

Rejection

"Oh, Mary Ellen, why have I not heard from Jeff? I did not attend his father's funeral, because I knew I would be an outsider and did not want to attend a Jewish service. But I did send him a note of condolence letting him know how sorry I was that his father died. He has not spoken to me since the Mardi Gras. Did I do something wrong?"

"Mary Rose, he was totally enamored with you when he brought us home that evening. I definitely felt like a chaperone, and was glad that you had one. I am sure he is just in mourning, and is not seeing anyone yet. Perhaps Jane knows what the traditions for mourning are like. All the traditions here are so strange. Or perhaps he knows that it is Lent and that, being the good Catholic that you are, you probably were abstaining from any social occasions. Jane would know."

"Mary Ellen, it has been almost four weeks. That should have been enough time for him to mourn. He knows we do not hibernate during the six long weeks of Lent. Perhaps I should break the ice and invite him somewhere. To what can I invite him?"

"Mary Rose, you know as well as I do that there are no social engagements until Easter. We could perhaps make a professional call and see if there is some way we can assist the Charity Hospital, but I am unsure how we could arrange it."

"Let us go talk to Jane and see what she can tell us. I would love to run into Sister Agnes. I wonder how we could arrange that. Perhaps we could ask her if she would like us to talk to the students in the nursing school. That, at least, would give us a reason to be at his hospital."

"That sounds like the best idea so far. You are really taken with Dr. Bloom! I have never seen you this interested in a man. I thought you said you could never be serious about a non-Catholic. Do you plan to conspire with Sister Agnes and convert him?"

"What a glorious idea! I had not even thought of that. Let us go see if Jane is in her room and can give us some ideas."

When they went to Jane's room she eagerly invited them in. "We really need to have another Sunday in the Quarter. That was so much fun," she said.

"It was indeed. I loved every part of it, and the food was delicious—all of it. But we have come to find out more about some New Orleans traditions. How long do people here usually mourn the loss of a parent—I mean someone who is fully grown and their parent was old?" asked Mary Rose.

"Do you know how old his father was, Mary Rose?"

"Yes I do. The obituary notice gave his age as 62. That is definitely old."

"There is no specific time period for mourning here, but are you talking about Dr. Bloom? The Jewish people have very specific rules about death and burials. I am not familiar with them, but I have heard of some of them mourning for a year. Tradition requires them to not attend any social functions, or wear new clothes, and things like that. For the first week after a death they cannot even bathe or shave! But you would need to check with someone who is Jewish to find out for certain. You have been here long enough to know that there are no social functions in New Orleans during Lent, mourning or not. New Orleans is such a Catholic city, that everyone respects the solemnity of the season. The biggest celebration would probably be the Saint Joseph's altars prepared by the Italian communities. March 19, Saint Joseph's feast day, always comes during Lent, and I know you have seen all the food that is prepared for those festivities."

"The only way Dr. Bloom visited a Saint Joseph's altar was if he was dragged there by Sister Agnes," whispered Mary Ellen.

"A year! Oh my! I hope that is not the case," sighed Mary Rose.

"We went to the Saint Joseph's altar at Our Lady of the Assumption Parish last year. The altar was twelve feet high and fifteen feet wide and was loaded with every kind of treat. I understand the parishioners spent weeks preparing all the delicacies," remarked Mary Ellen. "It makes me hungry just to think of all that good food. We tried a lot of them, too. They had the best breads baked in all kinds of shapes. Some of them had boiled eggs baked in them."

"Were you there when the Holy Family came in? The parish always chooses three young people to represent Mary, Joseph and Jesus. They go from door to door in the parish begging for food which they bring to the altar. The center of the altar always has a picture or statue of Saint Joseph. After the Holy Family eats, everyone else does too. Leftovers and donations are always given to the poor."

"I do not remember seeing the Holy Family, I just remember all of that delicious food," drooled Mary Ellen. "Oh, those cookies were scrumptious."

"Mary Ellen, we are getting way off the subject at hand. So you think mourning could last a whole year?"

"It is possible. You might ask Sister Mariana. She might know more about the traditions," answered Jane.

"I am afraid to bring the subject up to her. She already lectured me about becoming too friendly with a Jewish person. I have always hated being lectured to!"

"Well, we will have to put our heads together and see what we can come up with," offered Mary Ellen. "I am sure we can find a way to get our lovebirds back together."

"Mary Ellen, we are not lovebirds, just friends, and I am very concerned about how he is taking his father's death.

"Tsk, tsk. You are such dear friends. If that is the case, then you would have no problem asking Sister Mariana."

"Fine, I will do it," stomped off Mary Rose, "but later."

*   *   *

"Jeff, I have never seen you so gloomy. I did not know that it would upset you so much to ask you to come with me to pick out the marker for Pa's grave. I did not want to do it by myself, and you have such exquisite taste."

"Oh, Hannah, it is not the tombstone that has me so down. It just reminds me of my promise to Pa."

"You had not realized how smitten you were with Mary Rose, had you? He made you promise to keep your distance from her. You cannot break a death bed promise, Jeff."

"I know, but I can tell you how miserable I have been thinking about never seeing her again. I am beginning to think she was the one for me and I am just realizing it."

"Well, I promised Pa that I would introduce you to lots of young Jewish ladies, and as soon as our mourning period is over, I shall do just that. Apparently you like redheads?"

"Not just any redhead. She is different from any woman I have ever met."

"Well, I will just have to find a way to get your mind off of her. She is history. You promised Pa."

"You are not cheering me up, dear sister."

"Oh, here we are at the stone masons. Let us see what we can find or design that we both think would fit Pa. It may end up being ours too, so let us choose carefully."

"Dr. Bloom and Mrs. Stern, it is a pleasure to have you come and view my craft. Did you have something special in mind?" asked Mr. Joliet.

"The plot is rather large, and we wanted something that would stand out. You know, different from all the others. Somehow angels definitely would not suit Pa," responded Hannah.

"I was thinking—is there a way you could show a drawn curtain. Pa always referred to a curtain closing on one part of man's life when he dies. I know he spoke of that often when Ma died. You were just a baby then, and I know you would not remember that. I am not even sure where Ma's grave is. It is a shame they cannot be together."

"Ma Hannah would never hear of that. She does not want to hear anything about how wonderful Sarah Schwartz was. She feels she is always being compared to her. Besides, Ma is over in the Schwartz plot at Beth Israel Cemetery. There is no room for Pa there, and he would not be comfortable if we put him there. They did not even put her married name on the grave. But the curtain idea is a good one. Mr. Joliet, can you design that?"

"I have never seen one quite like that, but it could be done. Let me see," said Mr. Joliet as he picked up a paper and pencil and began sketching. "What if we put a drape to one side, and hung a laurel wreath on the corner to show victory. Something like this." He paused so they could study the sketch. "I will get the measurements of your plot and make sure to build a headstone that would be proportionate."

"I love it. It is so much like Pa—boldly understated. He would love it too. What do you think Jeff?"

"I agree. I have never seen any tombstones like it, and I think it would be something Pa would like as his memorial. I cannot believe it was so easy for us to agree on something so quickly, Hannah. Mr. Joliet, it has been a pleasure working with you, but I hope I never have to visit your establishment again. I am sure you understand."

"Of course, Dr. Bloom, I am glad we could agree on a suitable headstone so quickly. I will go to Hebrew Rest tomorrow and get the measurements, and then we can get started on it. I would recommend using granite, because it holds up much longer than limestone or marble."

"Again, we agree. How long do you think it will take to make the headstone and install it?" asked Hannah.

"We should be able to have it in place within two months, perhaps earlier. I will get started on it right away. The size and availability of the granite will help determine the timeline."

"Thank you again, Mr. Joliet. Come, Hannah, our work is complete. I think Louis and Arthur will love it too.

"Now that this is done, what is next on your agenda, my dear sister?"

"Several months ago when you first saw my new home you mentioned that it was large enough to host the reception for the American Medical Association. Is that convention in June? Were you serious, because I would love to show off my home to all those doctors and their wives?"

"Hannah, that would be wonderful, but it is not until next June. I am scheduled to meet with the planning committee next week, and I feel sure they will jump at your offer. It is so convenient that the conventioneers could just ride the trolley to your home. They would see all the mansions along the avenue that they would miss otherwise. Are you sure Maurice will agree to this?"

"Maurice would like nothing better. We will have our names all over the paper and pictures of our beautiful home. My only requirement is that my staff is allowed to prepare all the refreshments. I would want to be certain that our guests had a true New Orleans reception. I know some of the hotel caterers are from up north and have their own ideas about food. My staff knows how to prepare the very best."

"I think that will be totally agreeable as well. Of course, the Association will reimburse you for the cost. That will be much less expensive than hiring a hotel to manage the event. Check with Maurice and do get his approval before we move ahead on this. I do not want to incur his wrath."

"Maurice is the most gentle soul you have ever met."

"Unless you are in a business deal with him. You forget that I know the professional side of Maurice as well. He is a cunning and capable competitor."

"Well this is not business, except that it will be wonderful publicity for him. I cannot imagine his objecting, but I will do as I am told and be a dutiful wife and get his permission. I will ring you as soon as I speak to him. I am so glad you have invested in one of those remarkable devices."

"In my position at the hospital, it was essential that they are able to contact me quickly, so a telephone is a necessity rather than a convenience."

"Well it is a necessity for me as well. It would have been so much better had Pa had one. Then Ma Hannah could have called you to come to his aid more quickly, but he would not contend with any of the new—fangled devices."

"Hannah, it would not have made a difference. Leon rushed over as quickly as he could. In fact, I think Old Buck almost had a seizure himself between the way Leon and I were pushing him to go faster. That old horse just is not what he used to be."

"Maurice is talking about buying one of those horseless carriages. It kind of scares me. They go so fast."

"I am looking into one myself. It would be so much easier than having to harness the horse and then have to have someone care for it while you are doing business. Just crank it up and off you go. No one has to muck stalls or bring hay. But I may wait a while until they get a little safer. Considering how few automobiles are in New Orleans we are getting a  disproportionate number of injuries from people riding in them. I took a ride in one of Wood's Electric Phaeton, and it was a thrill. I have been in a couple of the steam powered autos as well. What is Maurice looking at?"

"He brought home a Phaeton the other evening to try it out. It costs almost $3000! Of course, Maurice would not settle for one without all the bells and whistles. We all went for a ride in it and it was a thrill, but I still prefer my Nellie."

"Maurice has always been a forward looking man, and I think the horseless carriages will become more and more popular. Pa was teasing me about it just a while ago, saying he was expecting me to drive up in one any day. He was not one to jump on the bandwagon of anything new. He would get on me about having a steam engine in my sailboat, but he sure did not mind when the wind was not blowing if I employed its use."

"Pa was from the old school, may he rest in peace. I miss him so much."

"I used to go to him for advice all the time. He had a very good head for business which is why he was so successful."

"Oh, here we are back at my home. Will you stay for supper and play with the children? They love when Uncle Jeff is here."

"I would love to. I think I enjoy their company as much as they enjoy mine. It takes my mind off of all the other things going on in the world."

"Well then it is decided, and you can talk with Maurice firsthand about the reception."

CHAPTER THIRTY-FOUR

Easter Sunday

"I am so glad we decided to have an adventure this Easter," sighed Mary Ellen. "It is time we got out and had some fun again."

"Big Fred should be waiting for us outside church to take us to Canal Street to the Easter Parade. We both have our sassy new bonnets to show off, and I am sure we will be a sensation."

"Oh, Mary Rose, I had such a hard time concentrating on Mass with all these posies on my head."

"I think it was more of a problem for the people sitting behind us. Your posies look lovely. You were meant to wear posies, and it is a perfect match for your new violet dress. Of course, I had to have roses."

"Indeed they are the loveliest pink roses I have ever seen. I am sure they attracted attention as well. Oh look, there is Big Fred. Do you remember how frightened we were of him when we first saw him? How much we have adapted to our new city and its citizenry! He has been our driver so many times since then, and always shows us a little extra."

"Ladies, youz looks lovelier dan evuh. I hopes I didn't keep you waitin'."

"Happy Easter, Big Fred! We just walked out of church, but perhaps you can give us some suggestions. We are looking for an adventure and I had heard that the biggest Easter parade is on Canal Street. What would you recommend?"

"Thar's a big parade on Canal Street, but its not yo kind of people. I tink you would fit in much better up on de Avenue. Thas where de high class peoples shows off. What if I takes you up to St. Charles and Melpomene and drops you off? You can promenade down the avenue and stop at Delmonico's for dinner. It is just a few blocks. After dinner, walk on down to Lee Circle and I will meet you thar."

"And what will you be doing all that while?"

"I'll be doin my favrit pastime, people watchin'. I've packed me a poboy and will find me a good spot jus to sit back and enjoy all the fancy outfits."

"Would you do us the pleasure of joining us at Delmonico's?" asked Mary Ellen.

"Dey doesn't let the likes ah me in Delmonico's. I knows my place: sittin' in my carriage waitin' for my ladies to return. I'll be happy as can be."

"If you are sure? That does sound like a delightful excursion—another first. Please do take us to the Avenue. I have never eaten at Delmonico's, but I have heard so much about it," said Mary Rose.

Big Fred drove them to Melpomene and helped them out of the carriage. They chatted casually as they strolled down the avenue, nodding to the passersby. There were many families strolling with their prams, showing off their offspring. It was a beautiful spring day, and the girls were admiring the dresses of all the other paraders.

"I wish I could just sit on the sidelines and watch, like Big Fred. I love to people watch," said Mary Ellen.

"Well, if we did so we would not get to experience Delmonico's, and I am getting hungry. I think I see the sign just ahead on the right."

"I see it too, Mary Rose. I hope we do not have too long a wait to be served for I too am starving. I have been thinking about this lovely brunch since Big Fred mentioned it. It is just one block farther. Who is that waving at us? Is that Jane?"

"I believe it is. She seems to be very excited about something. Let us go see what it is."

"Mary Rose and Mary Ellen, what do you think you are doing parading yourselves up and down the avenue like a painted lady. You must know better!" cried Jane.

"Why, Jane, we just wanted to be a part of the Easter Parade. What is wrong with that?" asked Mary Rose.

"Have you noticed that there are only families out here—no unattached ladies? It is totally inappropriate for nice young ladies. Who told you this would be okay?"

"Why Big Fred dropped us off on Melpomene so we could walk to Delmonico's for brunch and enjoy all the others who are dressed up so elegantly. He thought we would really enjoy it," answered Mary Ellen.

"Since when do you ask Big Fred for advice on social issues? I thought you knew to consult me. I am embarrassed to introduce you to my parents."

"Jane Ann, who are these lovely young ladies?" inquired an older gentleman.

"Daddy, these are the two nurses I have told you so much about: Miss Mary Rose Wenban and Miss Mary Ellen Faircloth. They were just walking over to Delmonico's for brunch. Girls this is my father, Mr. John Calhoun."

"For a minute, I thought you were scolding them, Jane Ann."

"Well, Daddy, they have been relying on my advice for many of the customs of our city, and I was advising them that it did not look quite right for young, unescorted ladies to be prancing down the avenue on Easter Sunday."

"Oh, Jane Ann, you are such an old prude. Ladies, I think you look quite lovely, but to ease my dear daughters mind, perhaps I could escort you to Delmonico's. We were headed there for brunch as well. Would you like to join my family? This is Mrs. Calhoun and our younger daughter, Frances."

"I am so sorry, Jane, we should have asked you first. We knew you were going to be with your family for the holiday and did not want to bother you again. Mr. Calhoun, we would love to join you, and Mrs. Calhoun, it is a delight to meet you. Your daughter has come to our rescue so many times on helping us learn the ways of your delightful city. Frances, I did not know that Jane had a younger sister. She has been keeping you a secret," teased Mary Rose.

"It is my parents who have kept me far from the hospital," replied Frances. "They fear I will decide that I want to be a nurse like my big sister. We so rarely see Jane Ann anymore."

"Indeed. We have lost one daughter to the medical profession and would hate to lose both of them. Jane Ann has wanted to be a nurse since she read that book about Florence Nightingale. I really thought that once she got into the chores involved in nursing she would change her mind, but apparently she is not going to do so anytime soon. She keeps telling us how much she loves it, and how she knows she is doing what God meant her to do. I know I cannot argue with God," sighed Mr. Calhoun.

"We thought by now we would be walking our grandchildren down the avenue on Easter, but Jane has no indication that will happen any time soon."

"Daddy, will you stop all that talk of grandchildren. The time will come, I am sure, and if not, I am very fulfilled in what I am doing. Ask Mary Rose and Mary Ellen! They both traveled from Boston to help us learn how to treat patients properly. They are the pride of our profession, and I have learned much from them."

"Enough of all that. Here we are at Delmonico's. Yes, sir, a table for six, if you please."

"Right this way," led the maître d'. They were taken to a room on the second floor with a nice round table. "Today we have the special Easter brunch starting with Spicy Citrus Bloody Marys, Crawfish Quiche, Peach Glazed Ham Steak, Pecan Waffles with Roasted Pecan and Banana Syrup.

May I start you each with a delightful Bloody Mary?"

"That sounds wonderful to me. Mrs. Calhoun, is that to your liking as well? And ladies? But do tell the bartender not to make the Bloody Marys too spicy."

They all concurred and carefully placed their napkins in their laps. The conversation immediately went to Boston, and the Calhouns asked the girls a myriad of questions about it.

Had they seen the spot where the tea had been dumped into the harbor? What about Paul Revere's copper shop? Was it still there? And then the questions began on the train ride to New Orleans. How long did it take? Were the accommodations sufficient? What was it like to come to a city so far away? Mary Rose related the story of their arrival on All Saints Day and how different that tradition was from anything they knew. Jane pushed Mary Rose to tell about the Proteus Ball and how elegant it was. The time flew as they enjoyed the wonderful cuisine and conversation. When they were ready to leave, Mr. Calhoun insisted on paying for their brunch, and they all walked down to Lee Circle to meet Big Fred.

The girls chose not to reprimand Big Fred for his inappropriate advice. After all, this was another lesson learned. Big Fred was not an etiquette expert, but Jane was. They sat back and enjoyed the carriage ride back to the nurses' home. It had been a delightful day.

CHAPTER THIRTY-FIVE

The Nurses' Home

One of the highlights of early December was the graduation from the School of Nursing, which managed to coincide with the opening of Charity's new Home for Nurses. This structure was something the nurses had been clamoring for since the school opened several years earlier. Funds for the home were donated by A. C. Hutchinson. Unfortunately, Mr. Hutchinson died the week before the opening of the home which caused a lot of consternation.

"Dr. Bloom, the nurses and I feel torn about this celebration." whispered Sister Agnes. "Our graduates are so upset. They have looked forward to this day with such anticipation, but feel they are being disrespectful since poor Mr. Hutchinson is barely cold in his grave. We have tried to demonstrate our mourning by placing the proper bunting on the Home itself. I do not know what else we can do."

"Perhaps in this way we can give him full honor. Before his death, we were required to keep silent about the contributor whose donations made this home possible. Now I think it only appropriate that we name the building the A.C. Hutchinson Memorial Nurses' Home. Sister Agnes, Mr. Hutchinson would love to have been here to see the culmination of his desires, but I feel sure he is watching from above and smiling. He was suffering so much before his death. I will indeed make mention of our sadness in my address. Our students deserve to be happy about their accomplishments."

"My heart is heavy. Everything is prepared for the tour of the facility to follow the graduation. Dr. Miles' Amphitheater looks lovely. The volunteers have done a remarkable job. There seems to be shrubbery and potted plants in every corner. Governor Heard should be arriving shortly."

"Do you remember how Mr. Hutchinson smiled when we had the cornerstone ceremony in June? He was so proud of what he had contributed. Keep thinking of that smile. The plans were in order and he was delighted that it was under way. Unfortunately his health took a downturn shortly after that, and he has been bedridden for months now. This home for the nurses was to be his proudest accomplishment. Being president of Morgan's Louisiana and Texas Railroad and Steamship Company allowed him to accumulate enough wealth that he wanted to contribute something meaningful to his adopted home. After his wife died, he had no one to leave his money. It is good we have so many caring citizens."

"We still have a few minutes before we should go onstage. I am going to check on my girls and make sure they are ready. I hope Miss Waters, the salutatorian, can stop shaking long enough to deliver her speech. It is quite good, but she is very nervous."

"I will go corral our other speakers. I see the Honorable Mr. Merrick coming in, and there is Dr. Lewis. The orchestra is warming up. It should not be much longer. Smile, Sister Agnes, the good Lord would be proud of what you have accomplished."

*   *   *

"Would you stop fidgeting, Mary Rose? You are worse than a four year old today. You look wonderful, as usual. What has you in such a stir?"

"Oh, Mary Ellen, I am not sure we should be going to this graduation. What do I do if I run into Dr. Bloom there? I have not seen or heard from him since Mardi Gras last year. I have done my very best to avoid him, and now I feel like Daniel walking into the lions' den. Tell me again, why are we going?"

"We are going because Sister Agnes extended a personal invitation to both of us. She is very grateful for our help with the nursing school, advising on their sanitation curriculum. It would hurt her feelings if we did not attend. I thought you were over Dr. Bloom. You told me that many times."

"I know we were just friends. He did not owe me anything, but I just felt I guess you could say jilted when he disappeared from my life. It was right after his father died. I do not understand it."

"Well, you have had a lot of other gentleman friends since that time. None has had the effect on you that Dr. Bloom did. Perhaps it is because you knew all along he was the forbidden fruit."

"Perhaps you are correct. He was a very interesting escort, however, I must go back to my original unfavorable impression of his gentlemanliness. There are so many others I have met with much better manners. I feel sure he will not even give us the time of day if he sees us."

"Mary Rose, I find that hard to imagine. I can remember the look in his eyes every time he looked at you. I doubt he can ignore you, and I will make sure he does not ignore me!" joked Mary Ellen teasingly.

"You had better not do anything to embarrass me, Mary Ellen. You are my best friend, and best friends do not embarrass each other."

"Have no fear, my dear. I will behave myself, although I feel a little devilment creeping up on me."

"Control it, please. No devils here. Everyone seems to be going into the amphitheater. Let us go and find a discreet place to watch the ceremonies. I do not want to be on the front row."

"We can go and hide in the back if you choose." As Mary Ellen turned to enter the amphitheater she bumped into someone coming out.

"Oops!"

"Oh, do excuse me, Miss Faircloth. It is a pleasure to see you here, and Miss Wenban, charmed indeed. Please come and find a good spot in the amphitheater. Sister Agnes sent me to gather the speakers and help them find their way to the front. Perhaps we will see each other later at the reception. I do look forward to it."

"Well, we cannot stay long," blushed Mary Rose. "We are quite busy these days, and only came because Sister Agnes had personally invited us."

"In that case, you must come to see our new Nurses' Home. Sister Agnes would like to take you through it personally. Did you give her some advice on it?"

"She asked our opinion on the facilities in the early planning stages, which we shared with her. But do run on and tend to your duties."

"I do hope we can visit later, ladies." Jeff turned and shook hands with the governor as he entered the building.

"Well, he obviously has more important guests to tend do," sniffed Mary Rose.

"Would you stop being so silly? I can see the magic is not gone yet. We will see what develops as the day progresses. Let us go find our seat. Do you still wish to hide, or would you rather try to destroy his confidence? I will bet he has a hard time concentrating on his speech if he has to look at you," giggled Mary Ellen.

"You are such a scalawag! I wonder how we have been such good friends for so long. Let us do find a good seat down front. I will bet he has no problem at all," mused Mary Rose.

The girls were able to find a nice place on the third row, right in the center, making them at eye level with the speaker at the podium. "Great spot to put our theory to the test," smirked Mary Ellen. "We will see who is right."

At that time, the stage filled with Governor W.W.Heard, Chief Justice E.T. Merrick, the Honorable T.J. Kernan, Dr. E.S. Lewis, Sister Agnes, and

Jeff. They all took their seats. The orchestra struck up the Grand March from *Aida* and the thirteen graduates paraded on the stage. Sister Agnes came to the podium and asked everyone to rise and bow their heads as she asked for the blessing of the Almighty on the events of the day. She dedicated the proceedings to the late A.C. Hutchinson. She then introduced the Salutatorian, Miss May E. Waters of Alexandria, Louisiana.

After the salutatory address, strains of the *Ave Maria* filled the room. Sister Agnes wiped tears from her eyes as she began her report of the School of Nursing. She looked straight at Mary Rose and Mary Ellen as she thanked all of the volunteers who had helped the school become so exceptional. She then turned the podium over to Jeff.

Jeff went on to proclaim that the nurses graduating from Charity's nursing school will be a blessing not only to the city, but to the entire south. They will go out to dispel misinformation and inappropriate procedures, because they have been trained in the very best techniques. He proudly called out the names of each of the graduates, and recommended they be approved for graduation. His eyes did not leave his papers as he read his address, but Mary Ellen had noticed that during the other speeches his eyes did not leave Mary Rose.

Next, the Honorable Merrick dedicated the new Nurses' Home as the A. C. Hutchinson Memorial. He spoke very kindly of Mr. Hutchinson and how deeply he felt the loss of that great man.

Then the Honorable Mr. Kernan presided over the awarding of medals and diplomas with Jeff and Sister Agnes assisting. Miss May Campbell of Stonewall, Georgia gave the Valedictory address. Dr. E.S. Lewis, vice president of the Board of administrators gave a brief proclamation, and then invited all the guests to proceed to the new Nurses' Home. There he officially turned the residence over to the state, which the governor accepted. A delightful reception had been prepared there.

As Mary Rose entered the Nurses' Home, Jeff grabbed her elbow, escorting her into the building. "Hello again, Dr. Bloom, this is a lovely building. I am sure your nursing staff is delighted to have such luxurious surroundings."

"Compared to their old facility, it is indeed luxurious. Yes, the nurses are ecstatic. I am sure you can verify that by talking to any of them. But, to change the subject, how have you been?"

"Quite well, sir, and yourself?"

"Busy, as you might imagine. Since Pa's death I have thrown myself into the hospital and have tried to assure that it is operating as effectively and efficiently as possible. I have even given up my regular sails upriver, if you know what I mean. The colony is running very efficiently as well, and no longer needs my constant intercession. We have a fulltime physician at the facility, who is quite capable, and is making great strides in helping the residents. What has been keeping you occupied?"

"Well, Mary Ellen and I have been enjoying quite a social life of late. I had wondered why you were missing from so many of the events around the city. I assumed you had just climbed into a hole of some sort."

"Indeed, I had—a dark and dismal hole that suddenly brightened when I saw your smiling face in the audience today. I realized how much I missed your friendship."

"Oh, do go on, Dr. Bloom! If you will excuse me, I must go pay my respects to Sister Agnes."

"I know she will not mind if I take you off to the side for a few minutes. I have something I would like to say before we join that crowd. I promise to bring you in her direction shortly, but first hear me out. She has been asking me about you for months now, worrying why I had not seen you."

"She is such a sweet thing, asking about me, but actually I had been consulting with her on the nurses' home, so I do not know why she would ask you about me?"

"I think she had hoped our relationship would bud into something more promising."

"Well, imagine that. We both knew from the beginning that it was just to be a professional affiliation, nothing more. It is a shame you did not tell her that."

He pulled her to the side of the room and said, "Oh, I did. I told her that. In fact, I told her that my father made me promise on his death bed that I would no longer see you."

Mary Rose turned ashen. She stared at him dumbfounded.

"I see that has affected you. I know it must have been hard to understand why I disappeared from your life. It has been one of the most stressful things I have ever had to do. I even asked Sister Agnes for advice, especially since she kept pestering me about why I had not seen you."

"And what advice did she give you?"

"She said 'You must follow your heart. I know you loved your father, but he is no longer here. You need to do what you think is best for you.' What a wise lady she is!"

"And what have you decided?"

"Until I saw you again today, I decided I had to honor my promise to Pa. But my heart leaped at the sight of you and I heard Sister Agnes' words. I did not know how I would make it through my little speech today with you watching me. Did I fumble my words much?"

"I would not have known you were in distress, if that is what you might call it."

"Distress would be too mild a term. My heart was racing. I could not wait to leave the stage so that I could speak with you and try to explain my absence to you. That is why I grabbed you away before you could even enter the reception. I hope I am not being too forward again. I know how you disliked that when we first met."

"Please give me a few minutes to digest what you have told me, Jeff. It has come as quite a surprise."

"While you digest, let us go and make our pleasantries. I see your friend, Mary Ellen, is staring over this way wide-eyed. She is concerned for your well-being."

"We do look after each other. Yes, let us join the others and we can talk at a later point."

Mary Rose made her way to Sister Agnes and commended her on the new building. Sister Agnes smiled and said, "Oh, I see you were consulting with Dr. Bloom. He has been an angel in helping us get this built."

Mary Ellen gave her a look as if she would burst if she could not find out what was happening. "Girls, please enjoy some refreshments. Our residents have worked hard preparing a nice assortment of confections. I hope you will be able to take the tour of the facility as well."

"Yes, sister, we would love to see your new home for the nurses," responded Mary Ellen.

"Have some refreshments and I will have one of the nurses take you on a tour."

Mary Rose and Mary Ellen made their way to the buffet table. Mary Ellen whispered, "What is going on? Why did Dr. Bloom pull you aside that way? Are you all right? You have not said a word since he spoke to you."

"Mary Ellen, I cannot speak about it right now. You will have to wait until we return to our quarters. In fact, I may have to go talk with Jeff again after our tour. Would you mind if I deserted you for a short while?"

"I see that look in your eyes again. How can you let him smooth talk you after months of not even giving you the time of day?"

"I will explain it all later. These little petit fours are delightful. I think I will get a cup of punch," said Mary Rose, avoiding her friend.

After enjoying the refreshments, one of the resident nurses offered to take them on a tour. They went through the facility, Mary Rose checking out all the details, as though she was trying to make the tour last as long as possible. When they returned to the reception area, Jeff was standing there smiling.

Sister Agnes grabbed their hands and said "Now are you ladies ready to come to Charity?"

Both girls laughed and thanked her for the offer, but said they were committed to Hotel Dieu. They then turned to walk out of the door. Jeff ran to open the door and asked, "May I give you ladies a ride to your home. My carriage is just outside."

Mary Rose responded quickly, "Yes, that would be delightful." Mary Ellen's mouth dropped, but she followed along obediently. As they neared the carriage, Mary Ellen said: "It is such a beautiful day; I think I would like to walk home."

"It is a lovely day, and if that is what you would like to do, I will see you later," replied Mary Rose.

Jeff bid Mary Ellen adieu and helped Mary Rose into the carriage. Then he suggested "Mary Ellen is right about the beauty of the day. Would you like to take a stroll along the river? It is one of my favorite spots."

"In December, we would have ice floes on the Charles river in Boston. Any chance we will see anything like that?"

"Winter has not arrived here yet, has it? Even so, the ice usually melts by the time it gets to St. Louis. I do not think I have ever seen ice floes on the Mississippi. I am sure that you would agree that today is spring like. No chance of ice."

"A walk along the river sounds lovely."

"I have missed you so much. I had not realized it until we started talking and it seems like we never stopped. I am so sorry I ignored you for so many months. It was not easy."

"Jeff, why would your father do such a hateful thing? I do not understand it."

"Pa had seen a different side of the world than I have. He had a great distrust of anyone who was not like him. He chose his friends and business relations to have a similar background. Pa never talked much about Alsace and why he and his brother ran away from there. He especially had a great fear of Catholics. The French who took over his country were Catholic. I wish I would have had the chance to talk to him more about it, but he was very German in many ways. He knew what he thought was right and was not willing to discuss it with anyone, especially someone so much younger who had never known suffering and sacrifice. He never returned to the old country. Once he left, he never saw his family again. We suggested he go back for a visit many times, but he would not entertain the idea for a minute. He had no desire to go back. It must have been dreadful for him. I am scheduled to go to a conference in Philadelphia later this year. I may well go seek out his brother who lives there and see if he will share any information with me."

"How can you go against a promise you made to your father on his death bed?"

"Mary Rose, until today I could not. My heart has been torn to shreds since he made me promise. I realize now that it was a promise made under duress. Had he been healthier I would have argued with him, but I could not cause him any stress in his condition. I do not know where our friendship is going, but I do want to renew our friendship. Today is the first day I think I have smiled since Pa died. I like how I feel when I am with you. If you can be so kind, please forgive me for my negligence."

"Jeff, I too have missed our friendship. I could not understand what I had done that had cut off that friendship so abruptly. Of course, I forgive you. I was very young when both my parents died so that my grief was quite different from yours. The only promises my parents made me make was that I would be a very good girl. If you would talk to the aunts and uncles who cared for me shortly afterwards they would tell you I ignored those promises as well. I must have been a very difficult child to have been sent to the orphanage in Boston."

"So we both have dishonored our parents," smiled Jeff. "Another thing we have in common. We must look for our similarities rather than our differences."

"Jeff, I do believe you planned this walk so we could be here on the river as the sun sets. Let us throw all our cares into the burning orb as you told me the Indians did, and enjoy the beautiful view."

"It is a beautiful sight, almost as beautiful as you. Are you getting chilly?" asked Jeff as he put his arm around Mary Rose.

"The temperature seems to have dropped a bit," smiled Mary Rose as she snuggled into his side. They walked along the river, discussing all the things that had been going on in their lives.

"Would you care to join me for supper tonight?" asked Jeff. "I may have kept you out past your supper time. We could go over to that new German restaurant, Kolb's. Have you ever eaten schnitzel? I hear theirs is exceptional."

"I have never had German food. You will need to educate me on it. Schnitzel it is."

They walked back to the carriage arm in arm.

CHAPTER THIRTY-SIX

The Christmas Tree

The third floor playroom of the Milliken Children's Hospital had been transformed. A magnificent tree stood in the center with its star touching the ceiling. Its branches were adorned with stars and tinsel of every color. Stacks of toys and dolls could be seen beneath the tree. Streamers, holly and mistletoe decorated the walls and ceiling. Guests of honor were seated around the edges of the room; many were the donors who had contributed gifts. Tables were filled with bonbons, cakes and cookies. And then the procession began.

Leading the parade was Dr. Bloom carrying a very small bundle wrapped in a blanket. He was followed by a procession of the Sisters of Charity each carrying her own swaddled child. Nurses followed with additional patients. Impromptu pallets were placed around the tree. The room was soon filled with children, each wide eyed and awestruck. Many had never seen a Christmas tree. When the last patient was carried in, the distribution of gifts began. Each child was asked what it was he or she most wanted, and soon it was theirs. Little girls cuddled their new dolls, and the boys played with their locomotives or horses. Even the sickliest of the children brightened immensely; undoubtedly the best medicine had arrived.

After the gifts were dispensed, refreshments followed with punch and cookies for all. As they filled their tiny bellies, another surprise arrived, for there was jolly old Saint Nicholas in all his glory with a huge sack on his back. He visited with each child and gave gifts from his bag. The children were ecstatic. Most had only heard tales about Santa Claus and had never actually seen him.

Miss Lily Mae Scooler's gift of a phonograph was set to playing carols. This was a marvel most of the children had never seen or heard played. They were totally transfixed. The guests of honor milled through the room visiting with the children.

"Sister Agnes, I am so glad you invited my sisters and nurses to come assist in this celebration. What a wonderful way to celebrate Christmas with these poor little ones," sighed Sister Mariana.

"It is I who needs to thank you. I do not know how we could have transported all of them to the playroom at one time without your help. We wanted all who could join in the merriment to come. Those who are too ill are getting a special visit from Santa himself, but I think just being in this room is enough to raise anyone's spirits."

"I find it hard to imagine Dr. Bloom leading such a procession."

"Dr. Bloom is wonderful with the children. I think they are his first love. He spends a great deal of his time here at the Milliken Hospital looking after the little ones and making sure they are well cared for. It was his idea to have this huge party, in fact he solicited gifts from many of the donors. He told them Santa this year was a Jewish gentleman," smirked Sister Agnes.

"I know this has uplifted the sisters and nurses almost as much as the children. Looking at the faces of your donors, I would expect this could easily become an annual event."

"The Christmas spirit is quite contagious, and it is one of the few things we would like everyone to catch!" teased Jeff as he walked up on the two nuns.

"Dr. Bloom, this has been stupendous. I am sure all of these little darlings will sleep with a smile on their faces tonight."

"I just hope we can get them all back into their proper bed. This has been quite an undertaking. Thank you so much for your assistance. Your sisters and nurses have been wonderful," said Jeff as he looked around the room.

"They jumped at the opportunity! They were eager to make Christmas a happy occasion for these poor sick children. What a horrible fate, to be stuck in a hospital at Christmas time."

"Well, I think they are not minding it so much now," smiled Sister Agnes. "Let me get the recessional underway. I know many are totally exhausted after all this excitement."

Each of the sisters and nurses gathered up her assigned ward along with their treasures and headed back to the patient rooms. The donors milled around and visited with Sister Agnes and Jeff. Many of the nurses returned to the playroom to assist with the cleanup. All had smiles on their faces.

"Dr. Bloom is just beaming!" remarked Sister Mariana.

"I think one of your nurses is responsible for his wonderful moods of late. For months he has just been moping around. I invited some of your nurses to the opening of the new nurses' home trying to entice them to come to

Charity, but I think an old spark was rekindled," smiled Sister Agnes. "There she is now, trying to pretend to pay him absolutely no attention. It is probably driving him crazy."

"Do you mean Nurse Wenban? I have noticed a definite improvement in her spirits as well. I was assuming it was just the Christmas spirit having its influence on her, but now I see it may well be more than that. Oh, there he is going over to talk to her. I guess she will have to pay him some attention," snickered Sister Mariana.

"Well, let us not stare. That would be impolite. You know, I think my prayers may be answered, but not at all as I had expected."

"What are you talking about?"

"I have been praying for the conversion of Dr. Bloom since I met him many years ago, but I could not make an inch of headway. I think our Miss Wenban may be the answer to my prayers."

Chapter Thirty-Seven

The Fire

When Jeff arrived at the hospital on the morning of April 14, all were talking about the fire that was sweeping the west end of the city where the Southern Yacht Club is located. Apparently all of the fire trucks from the city had gone out to battle the blaze. Jeff immediately got back in his carriage to make his way to the inferno. From a distance he could smell the fumes and before long he could see the blaze. The *Miss Lillian* had a prize berth very near the club itself. She was one of the most valuable boats in that harbor. Someone surely would have taken her out of harm's way.

As Jeff neared the location, all he could see was smoldering embers. The flames had been extinguished, but the carcasses of burned yachts lined the harbor, including the *Lillian*. The fire had started in the saloon of Morris Hayman, around three o'clock in the morning. The barking of dogs awakened tourists who were staying in the resorts there, and soon they were embattling the blaze as well. There was a heavy wind from the west which made the flames travel rapidly along the shoreline, catching everything in its reach on fire. Some amateur fire fighters used hoses attached to a cistern to try to calm the flames, but with little success. Some of the nearby residents evacuated boats that were on the farthest docks from the fire, but more than twenty yachts were totally destroyed, including the *Lillian*.

The local paper reported: "Several of the employees of the West End Hotel had been busy trying to save the company's property. They had secured ladders and gotten on top of the one-story frame structure formerly known as the Mirror Maze. They fought the flames there as long as they could, and succeeded in getting enough water to drive the flames away before the cistern gave way. While they were on the building the wind blew their ladders down.

There was no escape for them but to jump. The heat from the burning Capitol and Oliviera Hotels was intense. The fighters pulled off their coats and wrapped them around their heads. They dashed water on each other to save themselves from being suffocated. They gave up hope of saving the buildings when they saw the cistern fall."

The estimated damage was over $70,000. Jeff stood solemnly by his former boat house when Harry Miller and his son came up to him. "Jeff, I am so sorry we could not save the *Lillian*. My son and I jumped on board the *Seminole* and put out a fire on its deck while moving it out of the basin. My poor boy burned his bare feet stomping on the flames, but we did rescue her. At that time, the *Lillian* was already aflame."

"Harry, you and your son did an admirable job in rescuing the *Seminole*. You can be very proud of your heroism. Did most of these buildings go up quickly?"

"Like tinder. The blaze was unreal and the wind spread it rapidly. I have never seen anything quite like it. I hate to bother you at a time like this, but could you look at my son's feet and recommend some treatment?"

"I will gladly treat a hero's feet! Come sit over here and let me get a look at them," directed Jeff. "You have some second degree burns here. Much of the epidermis has been removed, and there is redness, swelling and tenderness. You can expect to have some redness for a month or more, but probably will not have any permanent scarring. Let me wrap your feet right now in a dressing soaked in salt water. When you can get home, change the dressing to one soaked in a mixture of linseed oil and lime water. Thoroughly saturate the gauze with it, so that it does not become attached to the skin. Keep that on his burns for the next twenty-four hours, changing the poultice every four hours. Then prepare an ointment composed of one dram of boric acid to an ounce of petroleum jelly. The ointment should be sterilized by placing the jar in a pan of water and boiling it for five minutes. Use a butter knife to spread it over the wounded area and then wrap it in a loose gauze bandage. You should be able to walk on your feet in a couple of days. There does not seem to be much I can do for poor *Lillian* now. Perhaps I can use my skills to help some other heroes today."

After seeing that the young Miller boy was bandaged and in his carriage so they could go home, Jeff spent the rest of the day treating others with injuries. It seemed to help alleviate some of the pain he felt in losing the *Lillian*. Over forty boats were destroyed as well as the two hotels and numerous houses nearby. There were many burn victims Jeff bandaged and instructed on how to care for the burns. As night fell, he sat on the dock with tears in his eyes. The charred remains of the *Lillian* had finally stopped smoldering. There was nothing to salvage. Luckily insurance would pay for some of the damage, but she was irreplaceable.

'Another chapter of my life closes. Last year I lost Pa, and now this. As they say, never two without three. I wonder what is next for me,' thought Jeff.

Jeff made his way back to his carriage. He had not realized how exhausted he was. He slowly drove home letting his trusty horse do most of the directing. Luckily his stable boy was on hand to take care of the horse and carriage when he got home. He climbed into bed without washing or eating, and collapsed until the bright sunlight wakened him the following morning.

CHAPTER THIRTY-EIGHT

The Confederate Veterans Parade

"How can they have such a huge celebration? They do know they lost the war?" asked Mary Rose as they watched the parade of former Confederate soldiers pass.

"Oh, we know we lost the war. We paid for it dearly," remarked Jeff. "You should have been here when all those scalawags and carpetbaggers moved in. Thank goodness they are gone. Pa struggled to keep his business going. But these men you see marching through the city streets are very proud of their heritage. They are proud that they stood up for what they believed in, and the throngs lining the street support them. There was no dishonor for our Confederate veterans, in fact, they were highly honored and, as you can see, they still are."

"But how can men be proud that they owned other men? I do not understand how anyone can say that slavery was not the worst affliction our country ever had."

"Pa owned slaves; in fact, Dulcie was one of his slaves. Many of the darkies who work for him now were his former slaves. You have to understand that these poor souls were brought over from Africa with absolutely no skills. Had they just been turned loose they would have starved to death. Someone had to take care of them and train them to do the jobs that were available. Admittedly there were some very cruel slave masters who abused their subjects, but as Pa used to say "Dey costs so much der is no vay I vould hurt dem so dey could not vork." He took very good care of his slaves which is why most of them stayed with him even after they were given their freedom."

"That is not the story we heard in Boston. We heard that they were all whipped constantly and starved and lived in abhorrent conditions."

"Compared to the conditions they lived in in Africa, living conditions here were very nice. Many of the slave traders felt they were rescuing them from the jungles. Food and housing were provided for them. Those who showed extra abilities and talents quickly moved up the ranks. There were all levels in their society, just like there is in any society. They did not have the freedom to quit their jobs and move on to another place, that is true, but if they were extremely unhappy they usually acted up and the slave master would sell them to someone else. Sometimes families were separated, which was bad. I worked with a lot of Pa's former slaves when I helped with the logging operations, and they greatly respected Pa. They never said an unkind word about him and they were very loyal to him. I understand right after the Emancipation Proclamation some of the slaves took off for other parts, but a good number came right back looking for honest work. They had learned a trade, and knew that Pa was a fair boss. He hired them back and told them to spread the word to others looking for work. It took a lot of strong backs to run his lumber operation."

The United Confederate Veterans were having a huge reunion in New Orleans. It was mid-May and the weather was ideal. There were parties and dinners, meetings and speeches, and this huge parade. It wound through the streets of New Orleans, stretching six miles from Canal Street down Saint Charles Avenue. The crowds were three and four deep all waving Confederate flags.

Mary Rose stood in amazement. "Have you read *Uncle Tom's Cabin*?"

"No, I have avoided it. I have heard enough about it that I do not want to read it. I lived here and saw a lot of what was happening. The people who were at fault were the ones who went to Africa and stole those people away from their homeland. I wonder what they promised them."

"Why did your Pa come to America? He was from Germany?"

"Actually he was from Alsace which changes from German to French hands regularly. We are German and at the time he was a teenager, Alsace belonged to the French. The French were at war with Germany, and Pa and his brother, Jacob, were going to be drafted into the French army to kill Germans. They just could not do it. So they hopped a freighter coming to the Americas with what clothes they had on their backs. From the tales Pa told, conditions on his boat were very rough. They nearly starved to death by the time they docked. They arrived in New Orleans in 1851. Luckily Pa got a job on the north shore cutting lumber. Through a lot of hard work and ingenuity, he turned that job into a very successful business. His lumber yard provided much of the cypress used to build New Orleans homes. Jacob took off for the east coast. He lives in Philadelphia now, and has done very well. Strangely enough, his son, Jacob, just moved to New Orleans because he was appointed the head of the commissary. Captain Jacob Bloom graduated from West Point and has a reputation as a great Indian fighter. I have met with him several times, and he is quite a character. Uncle Jacob is doing fairly well, but not well enough to come to Pa's funeral. I did meet him once on my travels to visit hospitals in Pennsylvania. He looks just like Pa. They could have been twins. And his accent is just as strong as Pa's was."

"I wonder if I will ever go back to Philadelphia. Did you know that is where I am originally from?" sighed Mary Rose.

"I heard you were from Boston! When did you leave Philadelphia?"

"Both Ma and Pa died from diphtheria when I was very young. Several relatives offered to take me in until they learned about the disposition that came with my red hair. Being the baby of the family, I had been somewhat spoiled. Eventually it was decided that I would go with my older sister who was a Daughter of Charity and lived in the orphanage where she served. I saw a lot of Elizabeth, or Sister John, but have not seen any of my other sisters or brothers since I was five. I get letters from some of them, and one day I hope to see them too.

"I guess watching Ma and Pa die is what made me want to become a nurse. Working with the Sisters, it was easy to get into nursing school, and I just loved it from the very start. My only regret was not being able to travel. When the opportunity arose to come to New Orleans, I convinced Mary Ellen that this was the chance of a lifetime. I think she is glad we came too. It is a very different world here, but I never thought I would see this!"

"Would you like to go to one of the speeches?" smiled Jeff. "You could hear how wonderful the confederacy was, and what a shame it was that we lost."

"I do not want to hear that. I would have a hard time keeping my mouth closed. I can remember when we arrived in New Orleans and Big Fred had been sent to pick us up. Mary Ellen and I were scared to death. We had never seen a black man, and he is very black."

"Oh, Big Fred is one of the nicest Negroes in town."

"Indeed, we call on him to take us whenever we need a carriage. I think he works almost exclusively for the sisters and the hospital."

"I will bet he could tell you some stories about being a slave. Next time you are in his carriage, ask him. He loves to talk."

"Indeed, I will."

"Look, they are handing out Confederate flags. Let me get you one," smirked Jeff.

"No, thank you. I am a citizen of the United States of America and do not support anyone who thinks they can own other people," retorted Mary Rose indignantly.

"I thought you might like a souvenir to show your grandchildren one day."

"Dr. Bloom, you are so irreverent some times. I do not know what to do with you."

"Let me make some suggestions. As you probably have heard, the American Medical Association is having its convention here next month. New Orleans is becoming a very popular spot for visitors. Over a year ago I persuaded my sister Hannah to volunteer her home for one of the socials, which she did. Now, my question is: would you do the honor of accompanying me to the social?"

"I wonder if you have a hidden agenda here. I noticed that you never invited me to join you for occasions when we might run into any of your family. Now, suddenly, you want me to go to a social at your sister's home? Hmmm," wondered Mary Rose.

"It is high time that my family knows that I am seeing you again. I would rather expose them to you in a setting where they will be required to be civil. I do not want them to embarrass either of us. I figured this was the perfect occasion. Only Hannah will be there and she will keep her cool—she is the ultimate hostess. Then she will tell the others in private and they can blow their steam, if that be the case, in private."

"And you do expect explosions?"

"They were all there when Pa made me promise him. They will let me know that I am dishonoring my promise to him."

"If you feel so strongly about it, why are you doing it? Why are you seeing me?"

"Mary Rose, I went for months with this huge hole in my heart. At first I thought it was for the loss of Pa, but when I saw you at the opening of the Nurses Home, I knew what I needed to feel whole again. I missed you and our friendship. I do not know where this is leading. I just do not want to feel so empty again. We have so many strikes against us, I know, but I am drawn to you in a way I have never experienced before. This Confederate parade is a great example of that. I am proud to be a Confederate with the name of our honorable president. You are horrified that we still celebrate that era of our history."

"Mary Ellen will tell you how upset I was when I no longer heard from you. Luckily I had her to take my wrath out on, and she handled it well. She is such a dear friend and she knew how hurt I was. Our relationship has been like a roller coaster, but I do not want to get off. I will gladly accept your kind invitation to the social for the AMA. It promises to be a very interesting afternoon."

CHAPTER THIRTY-NINE

The Convention

Doctors were arriving from all over the world. The American Medical Association was descending on New Orleans. Over 4000 were expected. Never had they had such a large assembly of physicians. A lot of excitement surrounded the arrival of Dr. Adolph Lorenz from Vienna whose treatment and cure of cripples, especially children, was of great interest. Dr. George Brown, secretary of the American Tuberculosis Congress had also arrived. The oldest member, Dr. Alonzo Garcelona would celebrate his 90th birthday, and 50th year as a member.

Meetings would be held all over the city for the next week. The general meetings would be held at the Tulane Theatre. Thirteen different breakout sessions for various specialties would be held at the YMCA, Touro Synagogue, the College of Pharmacy, The Washington Artillery Hall, and the Carondelet Street Methodist Episcopal Church. Famous physicians from all over the world delivered papers on the wide spectrum of medicine.

Jeff was glad to be so busy with arrangements. He had worked with several committees to make sure New Orleans put on an exceptional show. Entertainment had also been provided. Jeff was very involved with the opening reception at Hannah's home. Streetcar fare for conventioneers was free. Champagne and food had been donated by numerous vendors. Everything was in order. Hannah was ecstatic that she was going to show off her beautiful home to so many doctors and their wives. It was the premiere event of the convention and she was going to be center stage. Jeff made certain not to mention whom he was escorting.

"Well, Mary Rose, are you ready to make your grand entrance. I am sure we will get at least Hannah's attention when we arrive," smiled Jeff, as he helped Mary Rose from the carriage.

"Indeed. I see several of the doctors from the hospital. I imagine all of New Orleans medical society will be here," commented Mary Rose.

"The premier physicians from all over the world will be here! We have had a phenomenal turnout. I think a lot of people just wanted to visit New Orleans. It has such a great reputation for its good food and good times."

"I know I had heard a lot about it in Boston," remarked Mary Rose. "It seemed there was always a party going on in New Orleans. It seemed like such a mysterious city, so full of glamour and fun. That is why I talked Mary Ellen into coming."

"Well, were you disappointed?"

"No indeed! There have been times when all I have seen is the inside of the hospital, but there have been so many adventures I never would have had in Boston. It is an enchanting city."

"Well I am very glad you chose to come to my fair city. Were you here for the last yellow fever epidemic when Sister Agnes had to rescue me from the mob?"

"I read all about it in the newspaper. She was quite your hero," smiled Mary Rose as they entered the party.

"Good afternoon, Dr. Boudreaux. You remember Miss Wenban, I am sure."

"Of course, Dr. Bloom, how could I forget such a gifted sailor?" smiled Dr. Boudreaux. "That was quite an adventure we had!"

"One I will never forget, that is for certain. It is good to see you again. Have you returned to your bayous of southwest Louisiana, Dr. Boudreaux?" asked Mary Rose.

"Yes, and I love being home. Luckily I can return to the city for special events such as this. Have you ever seen so many doctors? I am looking forward to learning so much in the seminars. Dr. Bloom, your sister's home is magnificent."

As they entered the residence, the mill of people began with Jeff proudly introducing Mary Rose to everyone he met. And then they came face to face with Hannah.

"Hannah, everything looks wonderful. It was so good of you to volunteer your home. I know our visiting doctors and their wives are impressed." As he reached to give Hannah a hug, she shrugged away from him.

"Well, Miss Wenban, I am surprised to see you here," replied Hannah icily.

"Your home is more beautiful than I remembered. Thank you for having us for the reception."

"I did not realize the surprises that would be in store for me," answered Hannah as she turned away and greeted other guests.

"Well, that went well," smiled Jeff.

"Oh my, I do think my presence has upset her! I hate to come between the two of you. Perhaps I should not have come. At least she did not make a scene, as you predicted, but the afternoon is still young."

They wandered through the parlors meeting many other doctors, chatting with acquaintances and making new associations. As they walked through the gardens, Maurice suddenly came up behind Jeff.

"I cannot believe you. How could you do this to your sister? Do you know how upset she is?" he shouted.

"Please calm down, Maurice," cautioned Jeff. "Let us keep this civil, if we can."

"I do not know that I can," he responded in a lower tone. "Hannah has worked so hard to prepare this lovely reception for you, and you turn around and slap her in the face with your betrayal of your own oath to your father. How could you be so mean?"

"I had hoped she would not take this the way she has. The reception is indeed lovely, and I know how much Hannah loves showing off her beautiful mansion. I asked her to do this because I thought she would enjoy hosting these festivities. Word of her beautiful home and hospitality will be spread throughout the world."

"Do not be so glib, Jeff. You know you decided to demonstrate your lack of honor at a time when she could not respond. She was almost in tears when she pulled me aside to tell of your treachery."

"This is a very inappropriate time to discuss this matter. Perhaps we can sit down tomorrow and confer on the situation. People are already looking this way. Let us not ruin the setting. I would hate to make the newspaper because of a brawl at the Medical Convention reception at your home," smiled Jeff coyly. "I had hoped we would get more positive coverage."

"It is a shame that dueling has gone out of style, because I would love to challenge you on the field of honor, but then you have none," smirked Maurice as he turned and went back inside the mansion.

"Perhaps we should leave, Jeff," Mary Rose said as she pulled him aside. "Neither of us would want this public display of animosity."

"I am proud to have you on my arm, and no one is going to tell me whom I can see. Look, there is Dr. Liberman. You must have met him before, Rose."

They continued to stroll among the guests avoiding contact with either Hannah or Maurice. Hannah looked as though she was having a grand time, showing off her home, smiling and chatting with all of the guests.

As they were leaving, Jeff stopped to thank Hannah for hosting the lovely soiree. She simply smiled a fake smile but did not say a word. Maurice chimed in "I will see you tomorrow, Jeff."

CHAPTER FORTY

The Confrontation

Jeff received a note from Maurice to meet with him at his office at 2 p.m. When Jeff arrived he was surprised to find all of his brothers there as well.

"I did not realize we were having a family meeting," smiled Jeff as he entered the office.

"Close the door behind you, Jeff. I do not want everyone in the building to hear what is about to happen."

Maurice was seated behind his mammoth desk and the brothers had chairs facing one solo chair on the other side of the desk.

"Please, take your seat. Your brothers were as surprised as I was to hear of your betrayal. We all thought you were more honorable than you obviously are," snapped Maurice. "We all thought you were a man of your word. Apparently, you are not."

"How could you do that to Hannah after all she did to host the reception for you?" asked Louis. "You promised Pa that you would never see that young lady again, and yet you show up at Hannah's home with her on your arm. Did you not mean what you said?"

"When Pa was on his death bed I would have promised him anything in the world to try to calm him down and make him better. You know how much I loved Pa and how distressed I was that I could not fix him. When he made me promise not to see Mary Rose, I took it to heart, and I did not see her for over a year, but then I happened upon her at the opening of the Nurses' Home. Sister Agnes had invited her to come. As soon as I saw her I realized how much I had missed her company. Mary Rose is like no other woman I have ever met. I do not know where our relationship is going. I know we have insurmountable differences; the main one being religion. But she makes me happy like no one else has ever made me happy. I am not going to give up her friendship, and I want all of you to get to know her as well. I had hoped Hannah would accept her in a more positive way, and I certainly did not mean to offend her. Louis, perhaps we could go out to dinner this weekend, so you can get to know her as well."

"You have lost all of your marbles, Jeff. It is bad enough that you are stomping on Pa's grave. Do not expect your brothers to join in. I do not want any part of this woman, and I wish you would come to your senses as well," responded Louis.

"What about you, Arthur? Will you go out on the lake this weekend? I am looking at a new boat, and wanted to take her out for a trial run. That would be a perfect time for you to get to know her," chimed Jeff.

"I stand with Louis and Hannah. One of us insulting Pa is enough. I do not wish to ever meet this paramour of yours. I agree that you need to remember your oath," responded Arthur.

"I am very sorry to hear that. Pa had a lot of very old-fashioned ideas. Just because I am seeing Miss Wenban does not mean we have formed any permanent relationship. I enjoy her company very much and I thought you all would too. I am sorry you are so offended by my continuing my relationship with her. I am a very busy man and do not need to waste any more time on this sort of hostility. Good day, gentlemen," said Jeff as he walked out the door.

"Do not bother coming back," shouted Maurice. "We do not want to see any more of you."

Jeff's face flushed. He was stunned, but he did not give them the pleasure of even turning around to see the expression on his face. How could they be so cruel? They were his family. He needed to talk to someone he knew he could trust. Where could he go?

He headed towards the hospital and found himself wandering around aimlessly. He knew he could not concentrate on patients or problems now. His heart was heavy. As he walked through the corridors, Sister Agnes greeted him with a serious look on her face.

"Dr. Bloom, just who I was looking for. Could we go to your office to discuss something I have on my mind that is really bothering me? My, you look as though you just lost your best friend. I am sorry. Is this a bad time?"

"Actually, Sister, this would be a good time. I was looking for someone to talk to and you may be the perfect sounding board. Please come with me and perhaps we can resolve both our problems."

They walked briskly through the hospital, and as they entered Jeff's office, he offered Sister Agnes a cup of coffee.

"Dr. Bloom, you know we do not eat or drink in public, but please do help yourself," smiled Sister. "You look like you might need something stronger than coffee."

"Indeed, it has been a rough afternoon. Let us talk about your problem first, perhaps that will calm me down."

"Well, Dr. Bloom, I doubt that, but here it is. I overheard some of the physicians talking about one of the convention speakers pushing the idea that the house surgeon in any hospital should be replaced every four years. That it was good to get fresh ideas into any institution."

"Oh, is my job in jeopardy too?" smiled Jeff. "What else will befall me today?"

"Your job is in no danger. It would be very difficult to find someone to replace anyone as hard working and dedicated as you are. I just thought it would be wise to be aware of such talk. The board has been totally thrilled with your service. So much has been accomplished since you took over."

"Much of what I did was a continuation of Dr. Miles' plans, all with the help of you and so many more."

"The real challenge is to finish what you start. Dr. Miles had started the plans for the new wing, but you built it. He did have the plans for the Leper Colony, but you have taken it to a very successful reality. I believe you do have to take full credit for the Children's Hospital and the Nurses Home," she smiled.

"You are too kind, Sister. I had great shoes to fill when Dr. Miles died. I hope he is smiling down on what we have accomplished. I admired him greatly."

"Now I have given you something else to worry about and it looked like you already had a great deal on your mind when I ran into you. Can I help you resolve your problem?"

"I think you Catholics have a great advantage with your confessional. You get to go behind a curtain and talk to someone trained in counseling and tell about your most egregious sins. And then you are blessed and told that as long as you are sorry for your sins they are forgiven. What a blessing that must be!"

"It is indeed. You know I have been trying to tell you all the wonderful things you have been missing by not converting," she smiled. "But what has brought you to the point that you are looking for absolution. You are not guilty of malpractice, are you?"

"No, it has nothing to do with my professional life. My family has just ostracized me for what I have done. I have been told that they no longer want to have anything to do with me."

"And what horrible deed are you guilty of? I promise to keep this conversation between the two of us. It will go no farther."

"Before Pa died, his last request was that I break off my friendship with Miss Wenban. He deemed her an incredible threat to my salvation, even though he had never met her. To calm him down, I promised him I would. And for many months, I did. But I ran into her at the opening of the Nurses' Home, and I could not resist renewing the friendship. We have been seeing each other regularly since then. I escorted her to the convention reception that was at my sister Hannah's home yesterday. I was called to a family meeting this afternoon and told what a worthless individual I was."

"They think she has cast a spell on you, just like your Pa thought I had done?"

"I think she has too. I have never met a woman that I have enjoyed being with so much. We have so much in common. She really makes me happy. I do not want to break off our friendship. I enjoy it too much."

"Oh, and I remember what a rocky road that was to start with! She thought you were the devil himself. I am glad she has seen what a wonderful man you are. It sounds like love is in bloom, Dr. Bloom!"

Jeff blushed. "I do not know that it is love. We have not ventured into that area at all. It is truly just a friendship. What do you think I should do?"

"The best marriages are based on friendship. I think your family is being very cruel to you. I know how much you grieved your father's death, and I know you would not take your promise lightly.

"But to get to the matter of the promise to your father: A promise is a promise, but a deathbed is a horrible time to make such a promise. You only agreed to it to try to calm your father down, which it did. You did not rationally consider what you were promising. It was not a promise freely given; it was coerced, and, because he is no longer here, you cannot go back and renegotiate it. In my opinion, it is always ethical to violate promises to the dead if they were made under pressure and can harm those living. I would suggest that you go talk with your rabbi about this promise. Perhaps he can ease your conscience about not keeping it."

"That is wonderful advice, as usual, dear sister. You have lightened my load and made me feel much better. I will schedule an appointment with my rabbi soon and discuss the matter. There were many deathbed promises made in the *Torah*—some were kept and some were not. I feel sure he will have an answer for me."

"Go in the peace of the Lord, dear doctor. I will be praying for you," she said smiling.

"Please do let me know of any dissension you hear. I appreciate your warning me."

CHAPTER FORTY-ONE

Absolution

"Rabbi Levy, I am so glad that you could meet with me today," said Jeff shaking hands with the rabbi.

"How can I help you, my son? I so greatly miss your dear father. I know you must miss him also."

"Pa is the reason I am here to get guidance from you. I am hoping you can help settle something for me, and I was advised by a dear friend that you might be the perfect counselor."

"Jeff, I hope I can fill that role for you, but usually I only help people find the answers to their problems in their own hearts. Please tell me what is hanging so heavily on yours."

"Rabbi, what is your opinion of deathbed promises? I made one to my Pa that I cannot keep. How horrible of a son does that make me?"

"That is a formidable problem. Probably the most sensational of those promises can be found in Genesis regarding Joseph. You may remember that Joseph promised he would bring Isaac's bones back to the land of Israel, which he did. Because Joseph was very prominent in Egypt at that time he was able to bring Isaac back to his homeland and arrange an elaborate funeral procession. When Joseph was on his deathbed he made his descendants promise to bring his bones out of Egypt when the Israelites were finally released from slavery. However, according to rabbinic tradition, the Egyptians made a casket of metal for Joseph, and sank it in the Nile River. This was supposed to bless the waters of the Nile.

"In both Genesis and Exodus it tells that Moses took with him the bones of Joseph into the Promised Land. Now according to tradition, as Moses was preparing to leave Egypt he went to the Nile and called out to Joseph saying that the exodus from Egypt was being held up by him—to reveal himself so they could leave or else they would be released from their oath. Immediately the casket floated to the surface, and Moses was able to retrieve the bones.

"Pretty extraordinary event! Rabbinic tradition often uses miracles to show how our people survived. Whether they are true or just fables is yet to be decided.

"This story immediately comes to my mind when I am asked about deathbed promises. We do not all have the help of miracles to keep those promises. The problem with something pledged on a deathbed is you cannot go back and obtain release. My guess is that the only reason you made that promise was to comfort your father. Apparently now it is causing you tremendous grief. You made the promise unwillingly, under pressure. Your Pa was trying to control you even after he was no longer able to do so. Is that right?"

"I have tried very hard to keep that promise, but now I find it greatly affects my own happiness. I feel great guilt about failing to keep it. I cannot remember ever making Pa a promise I did not keep, until now."

"Jeff, I do not know what the promise was, but it does not matter. Your Pa was unfair in putting you in that position. He probably was trying to protect you from something he saw as a danger. Jeff, you are a grown man and able to make decisions for yourself. I hereby absolve you from whatever promise you made your Pa on his deathbed. As stressed as you are, I can tell it was not something that would improve your life, even though your father thought it would. He did not know everything. Do not be angry with him. Ask the Lord to help guide you. He is the One who knows what is best for us. Sit with me and we will pray together."

The two sat and prayed together. Jeff felt a tremendous sense of relief. Even if his siblings would not release him from his promise, he felt his father had, and that was what was important.

Later that day, he ran into Sister Agnes at the hospital. The smile on his face gave away his elation.

"Dr. Bloom, I like your new countenance. Apparently something has changed your attitude."

"Oh, dear sister, you gave me such wonderful advice. I took it and did not realize that I could get so much peace of mind from talking to my rabbi. We did not even get into the specifics of the promise. He just assured me if it would not improve my life here on earth and would be detrimental to my happiness, then it was a promise falsely given and I was absolved of it. I do not think my brothers will ever accept that explanation, but that is for them to fret over. I feel my father's absolution. That must be what you Catholics experience in confession. I am now at peace with myself."

"Yes, it is like bathing your soul and getting a fresh start with a clean spirit. I am glad to see you so relieved. You have enough pressures without having so much guilt with which to deal."

"I have also been thinking about the rumors you relayed to me, and have been wondering if perhaps I have overstayed my welcome as House Surgeon. The hospital has been my life since I started medical school. Perhaps it is time that I seek other outlets for joy and satisfaction."

"Now you listen here, Dr. Bloom, I in no way intended for you to start thinking that way. You have done wonders at Charity. Your dedication has been phenomenal, and I certainly did not want to start you thinking about stepping down. Get that out of your mind immediately."

"Well, I am looking at a new sailboat and I would love to take it on a long cruise—perhaps to Havana. I can think of a lot of enjoyable things I might do if I were not so tied down to the hospital. I would have great difficulty remaining at Charity under someone else's leadership, which is why I plan to pray over it for some time before I take any action. I just wanted to let you be the first to know that change may be in the air. I have not decided anything definite yet, and will continue to keep you informed. Please do keep this between us. I would hate for these rumors to expand."

"Well, Dr. Bloom, I will keep you in my prayers as always. Perhaps Miss Wenban has been a greater influence on you than even you know," she smiled as she turned to go on her way.

"God bless you, Sister Agnes."

"Indeed, He has."

CHAPTER FORTY-TWO

The *Miss Lillian II*

"Jacob, I am so glad you chose to join me to try out my new boat. I could not have had a better person to judge the quality of this vessel. I am even thinking of taking her on a cruise to Cuba later this year."

"Jeff, do you think the hospital could survive without you for such a long trip? Who would you take with you as first mate? That would be a difficult cruise by yourself, especially if you came across some stormy weather. You know I spent quite some time in Cuba during the war; perhaps when I can take leave I could join you on your adventure." Captain J.E. Bloom had been appointed in May as the Commissary for the U.S. Army in New Orleans. Jacob was the son of Issac's brother, Jacob, who had immigrated with him in 1846. Jacob had continued his travels up north and finally settled in Philadelphia. Young Jacob was a graduate of West Point and had most recently been serving as Commissary in Chicago.

"That is one of the many decisions I have on my mind right now. I have always found that getting out in the open water helps to clear my brain so that I can make decisions. They weigh very heavily right now."

"Well, tell me, Jeff. What is it that is stressing you so much, besides your banishment from the family? I would think that would be enough!" Jacob smiled.

"Indeed that is part of it. I hate that Hannah, Louis, and Arthur are so angry with me. I even went to the rabbi and consulted him about it."

"And what did Rabbi Levy have to tell you? I have only heard the other side of the story. According to them, you had promised dear Uncle Isaac that you would stop seeing some young lady of which he did not approve, and then you showed up at Hannah's home with this same young lady on your arm."

"The Rabbi explained that a promise made under extreme pressure is not one that must be held in conscience. Ideally one should renegotiate the promise with the person receiving the promise, but in the case of deathbed promises that is impossible. He said that he had seen many such promises. Apparently it is a very common practice among parents—when you cannot get your children to succumb to your wishes, you force them to promise you they will before they die—which is exactly what Pa did. Rabbi Levy absolved me of the promise and told me that I should not feel guilty about not complying with it. He did not even ask me the nature of the promise. He said that Pa simply thought that he knew what was best for me, and resorted to simply ordering me to comply. The Rabbi said that I am an adult, no longer under the tutelage of my father, and am quite capable of making my own decisions. No harm is done if I do not follow Pa's wishes—harm other than the admonition of my siblings."

"Are you in love with her, Jeff?"

"I don't know that yet. I have never met anyone like Rose. Intellectually she is my perfect match. I would like for you to meet her soon. She is a beautiful redhead from Boston. She came to New Orleans as a trained nurse to improve aseptic practices at Hotel Dieu. The problem is that she is Catholic. That set Pa off, as you can imagine. We debated about it many times. He has been trying to match me up with the perfect Jewish wife since I reached puberty. I would tell him that I want a wife with whom I can discuss the problems of my day, and someone who could give me worthy advice on some of the decisions I have to make. I am not just looking for someone with which to breed. He did not understand that. Pa kept telling me to marry someone who is not very intelligent, and I would have a much more peaceful life. He never let either of his wives know anything about his business. He would rather consult the family dog, than talk with Hannah. I was too young to remember his relationship with Ma, but I would assume it was similar. According to Pa, a wife's job was to keep the home as a veritable refuge from the outside world, and to produce offspring. I want more than that, which is probably why I am still single!"

"Well, I can help you make a decision about one of the ladies in your life. This yacht is magnificent. I love the way she responds. The sails went up in a flash. It is possible that one very skilled person might be able to handle her, despite how large she is. You have sleeping accommodations below, as well as a head and very limited galley. Is she bigger than the *Lillian* was?"

"She has a bit more room astern, and her hull is deeper and wider. She has a displacement hull which should make her go faster. I really do like her cabin. In looking for a boat, I was hoping to find one that was seaworthy, and that I could even live on for a number of days as I go from port to port. The

Miss Lillian was a dream boat, and she will be hard to replace, but I am ready. I miss being able to get out on the water, and I would like to go for longer voyages. She does have the steam engine like the *Miss Lillian* had which really comes in handy if I am sailing alone or if the wind is not cooperating. Let us turn her around and see how well she responds when we try to sail alee. Gently turn the wheel while I maneuver the sails. We do not want to capsize by turning too quickly."

"No, let us not spoil all this bright work with the murky Ponchartrain! I will be gentle with her, Jeff."

As they turned her, she responded beautifully. "She reminds me of a butterfly, hovering over the water. She is a beautiful boat," declared Jacob.

"Indeed she is. I just need to get her owner to come down some on her price."

"Jeff, you can afford her, whatever the price."

"I hope Pa did not hear you say that. He would be rolling over in his grave. As if, pay whatever the asking price is? I am sure you are a skilled bargainer as well. I think it is in our blood. Getting a seller to come down on his asking price is half the fun of buying something! I received $3500 from the insurance company for Miss Lillian, so that will give me a good start on paying for my new boat. The owner is asking $4500 for this one, but I plan to talk him down."

"That is more than I paid for my home! You cannot be serious. It must be nice to be a rich doctor," teased Jacob.

"Please remember that I am not practicing on my own, but work for the state at a charitable institution. The only reason I can afford such a luxury is that I do not have anyone else to take care of but me. That is my problem. I really want more in my life."

"Now that we have turned around and are heading back to the dock, tell me what else is on your mind. Jeff, you seem to be very troubled."

"I am very troubled. One of the speakers at the medical convention went on and on about how no man should have an unlimited tenure as the house surgeon of a hospital. Perhaps it is time that I seek a new direction for my life. I have been so involved at Charity that I have barely focused on anything else. Pa used to lecture me about it all the time. It is a very time consuming job if it is done right, and I have tried very hard to do it right. I am tempted to step down and start enjoying life more."

"Have you heard any of the doctors or administrators suggesting such a thing?"

"Sister Agnes mentioned that she overheard some doctors discussing it, but she assured me there was no way I could be replaced. She is one of my staunchest supporters, but when she mentioned it, it got me thinking. Here I am over forty years old and who knows how much longer I have on this earth. There must be more to life than the hospital, although I love what I do. Why should I be totally consumed by my profession?"

"I agree that your devotion to that hospital has been commendable. The army is now perfect for me. I am so glad that my family can travel with me on most of my assignments. It is so comforting to have them near. It was really hard when we were separated for long periods. But what are some of the things you are thinking of doing?"

"Well, I want to travel more. I would like to have more time to write journal articles. I want to have a more active social life and perhaps even start a family. I am not sure exactly what I would spend my time doing, but I am suddenly feeling the hospital is an onerous burden that I am ready to pass to my successor. Am I being selfish?"

"Who will look out for you if you do not look out for yourself? I do not think you are being selfish at all. Will you still practice medicine?"

"Without a doubt I will continue to practice! Maybe I will move to a smaller hospital, or open up an outside practice. I am sure many of my patients will continue to seek my expertise."

"Now does this Mary Rose have anything to do with this decision?"

"I do not know. That is yet to be decided, but I know I am not happy any more putting in 14 to 16 hour days and still feeling that I have not completed my job. It is a huge decision. Can I be happy working under another house surgeon? I have gotten used to giving orders, can I take them again?" Jeff smiled.

"You do have a lot on your mind. Let us sail over to Mandeville and enjoy this lovely boat. Did you have to return her by a certain hour?"

"I think her owner would be delighted if I decided to keep her indefinitely. There are two bunks below, we could even spend the night on board and get away from it all."

"My wife would be a fright if I did not return until tomorrow. That is one of the many people I have learned to take orders from," Jacob smiled.

"Well take the wheel and head her north. Let us go straight across the Ponchartrain and see how difficult she is to handle. We will see how hard it is to sail her solo."

"Cardinal idea, sit back and relax and I will take her across the lake, then I get to cruise while you bring her home. We are here to help each other if deemed necessary, but she seems to be a lady who wants to please. I think I have her under control."

CHAPTER FORTY-THREE

The Resignation

As the Board of Administrators gathered for their monthly meeting, Jeff gave his monthly report citing how many patients had been served and how many ambulance calls had been made and on and on with much detail. He then excused himself from the meeting. A few minutes later a messenger appeared with a note for the board. The board chairman, Dr. E.S. Lewis, read the note and sat down as all color drained from his face.

"Gentlemen, it seems our agenda has changed. In my hands is a note from Dr. Bloom dated today, July 6, 1903, and I shall read you his words:

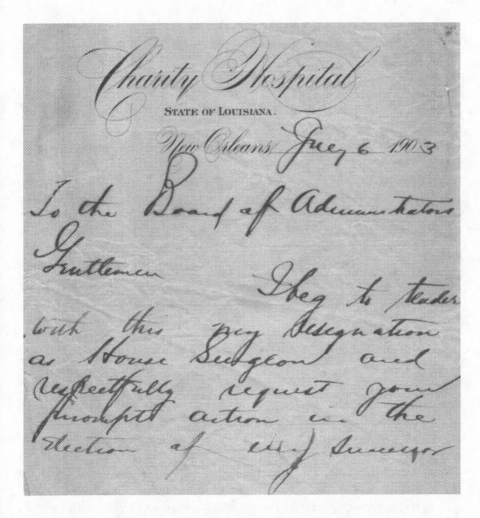

"Do any of you gentlemen have any knowledge of why this has happened? Did Dr. Bloom give any of you any indication that he was going to take such an action?"

The board immediately broke into an uproar which ensued for several minutes. All agreed that this was a total surprise and needed some explanation. A group decided that they would go to Dr. Bloom's office and try to reason with him. The meeting was put on hold for a time until the committee could confer with Dr. Bloom. They immediately left and went to his office in the hospital where he refused to give any details or reasons or reconsider his resignation. He told them he had been considering it for a time. They returned to the meeting thoroughly dejected.

In a release to a newspaper, Dr. Lewis said: "The purpose of the conference was to request Dr. Bloom to withhold his resignation, or express his reasons for resigning so that we might possibly induce him to withdraw it. But the Doctor has not seen fit to do so, and desires that his resignation be accepted. He said that he has contemplated this move for some time and had decided to make it at present. His resignation has been accepted with regret. Dr. Bloom said that he appreciated the Board's waiting upon him, but could not see any reason why he should change his intentions."

A reporter for the paper questioned the good doctor and his only comment was that he wanted to go into private life. He noted that Dr. Bloom had served Charity Hospital for seventeen years, with the last nine as House Surgeon. The reporter also mentioned how "many would regret this resignation, as he had won his way into the hearts of many people and is loved and remembered by those who have been the beneficiaries of his skill."

The Board departed from its original agenda to determine that future house surgeons would hold the position for only six years. They then went on to consider the sale of horses at the Crescent City Jockey Club.

*   *   *

"Dr. Bloom, what is this I am hearing? Are you really leaving us?" cried Sister Agnes. "Where are you going? Has someone made you a better offer? The board will do whatever it takes to keep you. One of the members asked me to talk to you and persuade you to change your mind."

"Sister Agnes, you are the reason for my resignation. When you mentioned the hubbub about limiting the term of house surgeons, I started thinking about it. I am forty-two years old and have devoted seventeen of those to this hospital. That is the summation of my life. I want to do more. I want to travel and meet new people. The ones I meet here are all sick! As far as where I am going, I am not sure. I am looking for a quieter place. I may just rent a little office and hang my shingle out and see what develops. I want a life outside of medicine. Is that too much to ask?"

"What will we do without you? You have made so many wonderful changes here at the hospital and you get along with all of the staff, even the surly ones. But I do understand. When I renew my vows each year, I think about the same thing, but I am perfectly happy serving the Lord and aiding the sick. Have you had any offers from other hospitals?"

"I decided to resign this afternoon, so word is just getting out that I am leaving. This weekend, I took a new boat out on the lake with my cousin, Jacob, and we talked about all kinds of things. I realized that I am burning out, and it is time for new energy to come to the hospital. I want to do something much more peaceful. Do you have some suggestions?" Jeff smiled.

"Well the peace of the Lord is always an option! I will gladly be your sponsor to teach you about the one true religion."

"I knew that was coming. No, I am not ready to convert, dear Sister. Do you have any other suggestions?"

"Sister Mariana was talking about adding an orthopedic surgeon to Hotel Dieu. You might inquire about a possible position."

"I feel sure you would put in a good word for me, would you?"

"Dr. Bloom, as if you needed someone to vouch for you. Your reputation has spread throughout the world. I know many of the doctors who were here for the convention told me how impressed they were with what you had accomplished at Charity. I, of course, agreed with them wholeheartedly. When do you actually plan to leave?"

"Well, I asked the board to take prompt action on finding my replacement. I want to clean up some loose ends and leave everything in good order. I was very fortunate to follow such a meticulous doctor as Dr. Miles. I hope to be able to help my successor as well."

"The board mentioned that they have called a special meeting for this Saturday to look for your replacement. I do not know if they plan to do a national search, or if they already have someone in mind. Time will tell, but you need to consider your future. Drop by and visit with Sister Mariana and see what she has in mind. It might be the perfect place for you." 'I can only imagine how my family will respond to that,' Jeff thought to himself. 'Leaving Charity to go work where Mary Rose is working. Perhaps that is the perfect spot—I will get to know her better and find out how well suited we are for each other.'

"Thank you so much for the idea, Sister Agnes. I may well pursue it, after all I have no other options at the moment."

*   *   *

Word spread rapidly. It felt strange to Jeff that there was no one he had to clear this with before taking the action he did. Pa was gone—he was the traditional clearing post, or at least he would tell him before he heard it elsewhere. There was no point in confiding in his brothers or sister—they were not on speaking terms.

Letters from his patients came wishing him well in his future endeavors. One patient remarked that she was delighted he was leaving Charity so that now he could make house visits! Another eloquently went on about how the blooms in the garden must eventually bear fruit, and hopefully he had a beautiful bowl of fruit to enjoy.

The following day a note arrived from Sister Mariana. It read:

Dear Dr. Bloom,

Sister Agnes advised me of your recent decision to leave Charity Hospital, and your desire to find a new location from which to practice medicine. We are seeking a physician skilled in general surgery with a specialty in orthopedics. If you are interested, please arrange an appointment with me at your earliest convenience. We would love to have you join our staff.

Sincerely,
Sister Mariana

Jeff got notes from other institutions. The head of Touro stopped by to confer with him. The New Orleans Polyclinic also called on him. He received letters from hospitals from near and far. He knew he did not want to leave New Orleans permanently. This was his home. He decided he was going to go for a long weekend cruise and mull over his possibilities. It was always easier to think out on the water. After his cruise with Jacob he had haggled the owner down to an even more reasonable price and had purchased the *Miss Lillian II*. Sailing it alone was not a problem. The new boat was even easier to handle than his original one. He sent his card to Sister Mariana requesting an appointment early Monday morning. He had intentionally decided to stay far away from Mary Rose until he had made his decision. He did not want anyone to think she was influencing him.

Saturday morning, Jeff loaded his new yacht with provisions for the weekend. As he sailed away from the yacht club he felt a heavy burden lift from his shoulders. He had nothing to do but enjoy the magnificent day. It had been a very long time since he had felt so free. The *Miss Lillian II* and the weather cooperated beautifully. He knew he had made the right decision to leave the hospital.

Monday morning, Jeff kept his appointment with Sister Mariana.

"Dr. Bloom, it is so good to see you. You appear to have gotten a little too much sun this weekend! Have you been enjoying our great outdoors?"

"Indeed, Sister, I spent the whole weekend on the lake pondering my future. I am hoping you may have some suggestions for me."

"We are looking for a surgeon to locate his office in the hospital. He could still have patients outside the hospital as well. We are especially in need of someone skilled in orthopedics. I understand that is one of your specialties."

"I will consider your offer, but only if you have an X-ray machine available. I understand that you have not added one to your facility yet."

"We are far behind on that, in part because we had no place to put it and had no doctor who wanted to take on the responsibility of training staff to use it. We have contemplated its purchase for some time now. If that would be a condition for you to come on staff here, we will be glad to arrange for one to be delivered as soon as possible. In fact, we would love for you to select which model would be most suitable for our use and where would be the best place to position it."

"Without a doubt, any good orthopedist needs one of these instruments. It is a modern marvel. I would gladly help you with the selection of the machine even if I am not selected to join your staff. Please tell me more about the position you have available."

"Come with me, Doctor, and I will show you where your office would be located. As you know, our hospital is much smaller than Charity and you would not be involved with all of the management decisions, although we might call on you for your recommendations. Your sole job would be practicing medicine. I am sure you have a large pool of patients who would want to continue to call on you. In fact, now that you are not at Charity, I would expect that pool to grow considerably," she said as she led him out the door and down the hallway.

"This is the office we have available. You will notice it is not one, but three rooms; one to serve as a waiting room, the second as your office and the third as an examining room. We will also provide you with someone to manage your appointments and waiting room. The hours you chose to work will be yours to decide. As far as salary, you will not receive any salary from us. Instead you will bill your patients depending on the services you render. We will bill them separately for any hospital services provided to them. Your receptionist will take care of that for you as well. Now, what do I need to do to convince you that this is exactly the spot where you want to begin your private practice?"

"Oh my, this is lovely. I have the perfect place for the X-ray machine as well—in the corner of the examination room in my office. The room is definitely large enough and that way it will be readily accessible and I can monitor its use by other staff members. They are very delicate machines and do have to be handled carefully. Do you have specific hours you would want me to be here?"

"Because we do not pay you for your time, your time is your own. Many of our doctors work part time, some take leave for months at a time, as long as you keep your patients informed, that is no problem. What else can I resolve for you?"

"Sister Mariana, you have made this decision very easy for me. If you will have me, I would love to join your staff. When would you like me to start?"

"Would today be too soon? Since I heard of your leaving Charity I have been asking the good Lord to please direct you over here. I think He has heard my prayers."

"I have agreed to stay on at Charity until my replacement is hired, but I do not think that will take very long. Would it be all right if I looked into purchasing the X-ray machine as soon as possible? And I would like to begin moving some of my books and other paraphernalia into the office also."

"Consider this office as yours. I would suggest that you send notices out to your former patients and friends letting them know where they can find you. If you will come back to my office I have several catalogs with X-ray machines in them, perhaps we can find one that is exactly what we need and order it today."

"I do believe the good Lord is looking out for both of us. I will gladly join you and see what we can find."

CHAPTER FORTY-FOUR

Relocating

The news about Jeff's resignation traveled rapidly. Letters were sent to Governor Heard and others asking them to use their powers of persuasion to convince Jeff to withdraw it, and return to duty. Articles in the paper listed the many accomplishments that had taken place during Jeff's tenure at the hospital. Saturday evening, the board came together. No one had applied for the position of House Surgeon, as many hoped Jeff would be persuaded to change his mind. Therefore the Board followed its most common order and chose the first assistant house surgeon, Dr. J.M. Batchelor, to succeed Jeff as House Surgeon. Dr. J.A. Danna, a very young 26 year old who had served at Hotel Dieu before coming to Charity, was named first assistant, and Dr. S.W. Stafford was named second assistant. Because Dr. Batchelor was vacationing in the Great Lakes, Dr. Danna would take over immediate responsibilities until he returned. This caused quite an uproar, with several members of the board questioning how someone so young and inexperienced could handle the job.

"Jeff, there has been much ado about you in the newspapers," quipped Sister Mariana. "I hear they are turning the governor and all of his friends loose on you to get you to change your mind. Can I still count on your remaining with us?"

"Indeed, Sister. I have never felt so free. It is as though a huge load has been lifted from my shoulders. No one can talk me into changing my mind. Dr. Danna had mentioned how wonderful you were in managing this hospital, but I thought he was exaggerating. I have been touring the facilities and trying to decide how I can be of more value to you. One of the things I wanted to talk to you about was taking a few weeks off to travel. While my patient load is small and you are not used to having me around here, I thought I would like to go up north to tour some of the facilities there and see how they are improving care for their inmates."

"Dr. Bloom, when you accepted this position, I thought I made it clear that your time is your own. How strange it is that you mention just that, because I came here with the purpose of asking you to help the hospital in a unique way. As you probably know, the Daughters of Charity have been planning to build a new facility here in New Orleans. We have spotted a suitable location and are currently negotiating for its purchase. When we build this hospital, we would like for it to have every modern convenience. The Sisters have recently built two new infirmaries one in Birmingham and one in Waco. I want ours to be even nicer than theirs. I would like for you to take an extended tour or the Northeast and Canada and get ideas for our new facility. You will have the liberty to purchase or order equipment you think we will need. I spoke at length with Sister Agnes about this, and she said you were the ideal person for the job. I would like to give you a list of hospitals we would like for you to visit. Perhaps you could work a little sightseeing in among your travels. This would be an ideal time for such a trip, as it is so warm here, and yet the snows in the north will not interfere for several months to come. I am glad we did not order your X-ray machine; because that is one of the things you might want to investigate in your travels. We can indeed call it a sabbatical as you go and travel to your heart's content. Since you will be doing the hospital's work on your sojourn, we would cover the cost of your travel as well as give you a generous stipend for your time."

"Sister Mariana, I do not know what to say. With the temperature as hot as it has been this July, the thought of going up north is very appealing. Traveling to Canada as well had not even entered my plans. I jump at this opportunity. A time away from New Orleans may be just what I need, and I would love to investigate all the changes taking place in other hospitals. What a grand adventure it will be! We are talking about months now instead of weeks!"

"And it always gets warmer in August, as you well know. Please do plan to take off as long as you deem necessary. We will gladly consider any improvements you can recommend. Have you noticed something already?"

"Actually, I have and was reluctant to bring it up. I was wondering if there were a way that the children might be isolated into a separate ward. I was appalled to see them interspersed with the adult patients. I guess I had been spoiled by our addition of the Milliken Home. I assumed similar conditions existed here as well."

"Our board will be meeting in two weeks and I will bring up that idea. In the meantime let us work together on figuring out how we could make this happen. You do not think Mrs. Milliken has some more money she would like to donate, do you?"

"I think Charity tapped Mrs. Milliken to her full extent. She was very generous. However, I have become very capable at asking for contributions for worthy causes. As I spend more time socializing these days, I will see if I cannot locate some other eager donors—especially when it comes to the children—they are very dear to my heart."

"You are such a good man, Dr. Bloom. I am delighted to have you here at Hotel Dieu. I feel this is the start of a wonderful future for all of us. Please do start planning for your sabbatical. You deserve it!"

As Jeff worked at unpacking his books and organizing his office, he heard a tap at his door. "Come in," he responded.

"I hope we are not bothering you too much, but we did want to welcome you to Hotel Dieu," smiled Mary Rose. Mary Ellen was standing next to her. "We were totally taken aback when we heard you were leaving Charity, and even more so when we heard you were moving here. Was this a sudden decision?"

"Well, I have been thinking about it for quite some time. One of the speakers at the AMA convention spoke about how important it was to have turnover at the House Surgeon's position, just to keep things fresher, and it got me to thinking. I was burning out at Charity and it was time for new blood to take the lead, so I quit! Luckily this position became available, and I think it will suit me quite nicely."

"You will love it here at Hotel Dieu. I know Mary Rose and I do," smiled Mary Ellen. "If there is anything we can help you with, please let us know."

"Actually, I probably will not be here for a while. I just spoke to Sister Mariana about taking a tour of hospitals up north. She has asked me to visit numerous hospitals in the northeast and Canada and get ideas for the new infirmary that is now in the planning stages. This is an ideal time, because I have no patients and no encumbrances tying me down at this time. I probably will be gone for several months."

"Oh, my!" responded Mary Rose, blushing. "We thought we would be enjoying your presence here, but I guess we will just have to wait our turn. Have a nice trip." She turned and walked out quickly, leaving Mary Ellen standing awkwardly with her mouth ajar.

"I am sorry, Dr. Bloom. We should not have imposed ourselves on you. I am glad you will be here, and do wish you well on your journey," curtsied Mary Ellen as she turned to leave.

"I have done it again!" said Jeff shaking his head. "I certainly did not want Mary Rose to think I was coming here on her behalf, but I also did not mean to offend her, and I think I did. Please try to explain my actions.

Under the circumstances, I think a few months of travel will help me decide the direction my life needs to take. Please give her my apologies."

"Of course, Dr. Bloom, I will try, but I think she would be more likely to accept it if it came from you. I hope we will see you again before your journey," said Mary Ellen as she closed the door behind her, smiling.

Jeff sat down at his desk and put his head in his hands. 'I really have a knack for saying the wrong thing to that lady. When am I going to learn not to offend her? It just seems to come naturally. I need to do something to make amends without giving the wrong impression. Flowers? No, that would imply something too intimate. Oh, I know exactly what might work.' Jeff jumped up and ran down the hall.

"Miss Faircloth, I am so glad I caught you. I have recently purchased a new boat. You know the *Lillian* was lost in the West End fire a few months ago. I was wondering if you and Miss Wenban would join me on a cruise this Saturday?"

"That sounds lovely, but I will need to check with Mary Rose before I give you a definite answer. Would it just be the three of us?"

"Unless you have someone else you would like to include. The *Miss Lillian II* is even easier to sail, and has more room on deck. I may ask Dr. Danna to join us. Please do let me know if we can arrange it. I know I will not be leaving until at least next week. As warm as it is in the city, it is delightful out on the water. I know you will enjoy it."

"I will let you know, Doctor. Thank you for the kind invitation."

As she caught up with Mary Rose, Mary Ellen said: "Dr. Bloom is so smitten with you he does not know what to do. He asked me to apologize to you if he offended you, but he did not want you to get the wrong idea—that he was coming here because you were here. To offer amends he invited us to go sailing with him this Saturday on his new boat. I told him I would let him know if we would join him. Dr. Danna may also be coming. Please say yes!"

"You have had a crush on Dr. Danna since he came here. No wonder you are so eager to accept, you silly goose! Well, you have done so many things for me, I can hardly refuse to help you out this time, besides a sail on the lake sounds wonderful. It is so hot already this summer. Please do accept for both of us. I do plan to keep my distance from the dear doctor here at the hospital," quipped Mary Rose.

Mary Ellen proceeded to write a note of acceptance and had one of the orderlies bring it to Jeff. He smiled broadly when he received it, and sent an immediate reply that he would pick them up at 10 on Saturday, please let him know if that would not be acceptable. He had renewed spirit as he unpacked and stored all of his office materials.

CHAPTER FORTY-FIVE

The Farewell Voyage

"Well, I am so glad you ladies could join us on our voyage today. I hope you will find my new *Miss Lillian* even more delightful than the old one. I know I am enjoying how easy she is to maneuver. Despite her size, she is easy to handle, even when I sail alone. Of course, it does make it easier to have a capable first mate like Dr. Hanna on board." They easily took the boat out onto the lake. There was a swift breeze which filled the sails. Pelicans flew alongside.

"Dr. Bloom, I would imagine you will have a lot more time to spend yachting now," smiled Mary Rose.

"Please call me Jeff. I had thought I would indeed have more time, but now I am off on a great adventure, and I have to leave poor *Miss Lillian* in dry dock. That is one reason why I wanted to have you join me for a farewell voyage today. As I mentioned, Sister Mariana is sending me on a fact finding mission up north. With the city as hot as it is these days, I do not think that I will suffer greatly, but there are some people that I will miss in my travels."

"Exactly where and when are you going?" asked Mary Ellen.

"My train leaves Monday morning. I have been as busy packing my steamer trunk as unpacking my office. My stops will include Toronto, Quebec, Niagara, Saratoga, New York and Boston. There may be other stops, as I hope my colleagues in the various institutions will guide me in my endeavors. I am eager to see the advancements they have made, and Sister Mariana wants me to include these in our new facility. She and Dr. Lewis are determined that Hotel Dieu will become the finest facility south of the Mason Dixon line. I am the lucky one who gets to travel to all the major institutions and see just what they have to offer."

"Well, Dr. Bloom, you can thank Mary Ellen and me for your grand tour. We had suggested it to Sister Mariana about two months ago. We had hoped she would send us! I am so disappointed," said Mary Rose stomping her foot.

"Oh my dear Rose, I had no idea! But I cannot imagine sending you two lovely ladies traipsing across the country, bouncing from hospital to hospital! That just would not be proper. Not only that, but it would not be safe."

"Do not tell me about proper or safe. Mary Ellen and I took it on ourselves to volunteer to come here almost nine years ago. They all told us how daring we were to venture into that "heathen land" so recently conquered. Well, we not only ventured out, but we made the trip in grand style and have contributed immensely to the backward civilization we found here."

"Please do not be angry with me. I had no idea you had wanted to take on such a venture."

"Mary Rose and I had suggested that we would like to go home for a visit this summer, and we could tour some of the hospitals while there. Sister Mariana insisted that she could not survive without us here and immediately dismissed the proposal," declared Mary Ellen.

Dr. Danna sat quietly and observed the tirade. "Perhaps we could suggest that you could escort the nurses as far as Boston to assure their safe travel," he interceded.

"Well, there is no way we could make the arrangements at this late a date. Only two days to prepare! That would hardly give us proper time."

"What if I postponed my trip for a week? Do you think that would be acceptable? I would love to serve as your escort," offered Jeff.

"I think Sister Mariana was afraid that if we went back home we would never come back," smiled Mary Ellen. "She knows we both have been a little homesick and was afraid that the temptation to stay up north would be too great to resist. I do not think she would approve of any such arrangement."

"Does she think she is holding us captive here, Mary Ellen? She has her new slaves!" snapped Mary Rose.

"Mary Rose, how absurd, you are not even homesick. You just wanted to travel. Isn't that the truth?" retorted Mary Ellen.

Mary Rose turned away from the trio, sniffling into her handkerchief. Jeff came up behind her and put an arm around her. "Please do not cry. I seem to always upset you, and all I want to do is make you happy. I wanted to spend time with you before I took off on my journey. I know how much I will miss you while I am gone. I do wish I could take you with me, and maybe one day I will be able to do just that. We have much to work on in the meantime."

Mary Rose looked up at him with a startled look. 'What is he saying?' she thought.

"The reason I was so upset when you first announced your plans to travel was knowing that our plans had been hijacked. I did not know how you had heard of our request, but felt you had undermined us. I apologize. Apparently it was Sister Mariana who undermined us. I am so disappointed."

"Please do not let this ruin our day on the lake. I will talk with Sister and see if there is some compromise that can be reached. Where exactly had you planned to go?"

"First, we would return to Boston. We could stay at the Nurses home there and visit the hospitals in that area. I have a sister in New York City whom I would love to see again, and we could stay with her. And then we would go on to Philadelphia, where most of my family still lives. There are several relatives that would host our stay there. I had explained that the main expense would be the train ride. But she would not hear of it!" Mary Rose seemed to get more and more irritated. Her cheeks became brilliant red. "I knew there had been great changes taking place in New England, and thought we could really benefit from learning the intimate details. So she takes my great idea and offers you the opportunity instead. I am sure she is even offering to pay all of your expenses!"

"That sounds like you had really thought this through. I am sorry that I am benefitting from your plans. You were brave to come here and help so much in reforming our medical practices. I would never question your courage. It is indeed a shame that your plans were thwarted," added Jeff.

"But I have an idea. Miss Mary Rose will you marry me and join me on an extended honeymoon touring hospitals of the Northeast and Canada?"

Mary Rose's mouth dropped open. "Dr. Bloom! As though I would even consider such a proposal! You must have been in the sun too long."

Dr. Danna laughed. "You know I understand that is exactly what Dr. Lister and his wife did on their honeymoon—traveled all over Europe visiting hospitals and studying their practices."

Mary Ellen was dumbstruck. She could not quite figure out whether Jeff had been serious or not. She knew he was smitten, but was he really considering marrying her best friend?

"Am I to take it that you are refusing my offer?" asked Jeff smiling. "In that case, let us change the subject quickly before it becomes any more painful. Shall we head over to Slidell and stop there for a picnic? I do not have the spread I used to provide. Unfortunately I can no longer call on Dulcie to supply my picnic basket, but I think you will all enjoy what is available."

No further mention was made of Jeff's upcoming adventure. The conversation was kept to pleasantries about the weather and such.

When the nurses got back to the nurses home, Mary Ellen almost popped. "What would he have done had you said yes?" she shrieked. "I have had the hardest time keeping my mouth shut. Mary Rose, you were so calm and composed! It must have affected you!"

"I thought my heart would come out of my chest," she smiled. "Can you imagine the sane, calm, controlled doctor doing something so out of character? I am so glad my quick wit saved me. How totally out of the blue was that proposal! You know he knew what my answer would be. Do you think he really meant it?"

"He would have been in a very compromising situation had he backed down. After all, you had two witnesses to his proposal. He has been madly in love with you since the first time you crushed him when you refused his offer to take you out for dinner. How do you really feel about him?"

"Mary Ellen, there is no way we can ever marry or even think about it. He is a devout Jew and I am a devout Catholic. No priest would ever marry us, and I could not imagine being married by a rabbi. I greatly admire Jeff and love being with him. He knew the idea of going with him to investigate hospitals up north would be a real incentive for me, and, in truth, it was very hard to turn down. But there is so much more to marriage than just traveling the world doing what you love to do. Oh, but how wonderful does that sound! I need to make a novena to get these ideas out of my head. I cannot even consider such a proposal. It is out of the question."

"But if you truly love him, there should be some way you could make this work. We will have to pray on this. Jesus wants us to be happy, and if Jeff will make you happy then maybe you were meant to bring him to Jesus. Think how proud Sister Agnes would be if you actually converted him."

"Well, I have several weeks or even months until I have to confront this predicament. Jeff will be gone for quite some time. Oh, how I do wish I could go too!"

CHAPTER FORTY-SIX

The Adventure Up North

"Sister Mariana and Dr. Lewis, I am so glad you could both meet with me so soon after my return to New Orleans. My trip was very rewarding, and I was disappointed that I had to cut it shorter than I had anticipated, but I have much to report to you."

"Yes, I understand that Governor Blanchard has asked you to serve as a delegate to the tuberculosis congress which is convening here soon. It is hard to get away for an extended time when your city and state have come to depend on your knowledge of medicine," smiled Dr. Lewis. "But tell us, how do we need to improve our facilities?"

"First, I am delighted to see that during my absence you were able to provide a children's ward to separate the youngsters from the other inmates. I think you will find this causes an immediate improvement in the little ones' health and well-being. Something we need to develop as well is a gymnasium. There was one at the Boston's Children's Hospital that was amazing. They demonstrated how it was greatly improving children with deformities—strengthening their muscles to counterbalance their infirmities. Also I observed a "bloodless" surgery—a way to repair deformed limbs by manipulating them. The original apparatus was designed by Dr. Lorenz, but an attorney who had a crippled child redesigned it into an amazing instrument that Dr. Lorenz probably would not recognize. It can be used to cure children up to 14 who have congenital deformities. The results are amazing. I have ordered one for the hospital; in fact, I purchased it and have it with me."

"That was your assignment, Dr. Bloom, but tell us of your other discoveries," added Sister Mariana.

"Another remarkable device I observed is called a 'thermophar.' It will replace every hot water bottle in the hospital. At room temperature it is a solid, but when you submerge it in hot water it assumes a temperature of 110 degrees. It will retain that temperature for seven hours and to reactivate it all you have to do is stir it with a stick. It can assume many different shapes so that it is easily applied to almost any location on the body in need of heat therapy. It is most remarkable. We need to order several of these. I have the name and address of the provider."

"I have read about these in the literature and am anxious to see it put into use," said Dr. Lewis. "It actually sounded too good to be true."

"It does work remarkably well, and I think you will be pleased. Some of the other new devices I observed included electric vibration machines, the newest in X-ray technology, galvanic current machines as well as ones that use static electricity and high frequency currents. We definitely need to work on our pathology department. It is the up and coming way to find the cause of diseases so that they can be treated properly. The Children's Hospital in Toronto has practically eliminated diphtheria. It has a branch hospital on an island and brings their small patients there for fresh air. It also inoculates them with antitoxin every three to four weeks. They have not had a case in the hospital in some time now. I am submitting to you a list of the devices we should certainly order for the new hospital, and possibly we could begin using them here while the building process is ongoing."

"You have come back to us with so much valuable information. I knew you were the man to send on this exploratory mission," smiled Sister Mariana.

"I did get the impression that someone else had requested this adventure before I was even hired by Hotel Dieu."

"Did those girls give you a hard time about that? How could I send two young ladies off exploring hospitals by themselves? They would have gotten nowhere. You have the credentials and the reputation that got you easily accepted into any institution. I admit, it was their idea and they were sorely disappointed when I refused to allow them leave to go. I was also afraid they would not come back. You may know they both are originally from up north and have family ties there. We would be at a great loss if they did not return. They both have been so important to our nursing staff."

"That is exactly what I told them," smiled Jeff. "What would we do without them here? But they thought I had gotten wind of their idea and had usurped it. They were quite angry before I left. I hope they have cooled their tempers by now. Miss Wenban's cheeks and ears were as red as her hair when she confronted me about it."

"Well, I will speak to her about that! I will make sure she does not bother you any more, Dr. Bloom."

"Oh, please, do not interfere. I love to have Miss Wenban's attention, even if it is not favorable. She is a very interesting young lady and I would not want to have her chastised in any way."

"As you say, Dr. Bloom, I just hate to have any of my nurses accusing one of our most prominent physicians of something so underhanded. I will not even mention it to her if that is your desire."

"Thank you, Sister. I am sure I will hear more from her about it, but I can handle her Irish temper! I have yet to run into her since my return, but hope to do so soon."

"Well, perhaps I can arrange that for you. If you do not mind, would you please go to the children's ward? We have a new patient with a malformation I would like for you to observe and see if the new procedure you mentioned would work for him. He was born with a twisted knee, and has been crippled since birth. Perhaps your amazing device is exactly what we need to 'fix' him."

"Certainly, Dr. Lewis, I will proceed there directly. May I give you this list of suggested equipment I feel would greatly add to our hospital? By the way I did stop by the Provincial Offices of the Daughters of Charity and met with the Mother Superior. I was very impressed with the plans they have for the new infirmary here, and also what they have recently opened in Waco and Birmingham. I was equally impressed with the Mother Superior. She is a charming lady who is determined to make a difference in this world."

"Apparently the feeling was quite mutual, Dr. Bloom," smiled Sister Mariana. "She wrote me of your meeting and told me how delightful the encounter had been. It seems she had already heard about you from Sister Agnes, and asked me to please continue working on your conversion. In fact, she was quite adamant about it."

"That is probably why she insisted that I go to Quebec," Jeff smiled. "What a delightful town that is! Not much in hospitals, but such a wonderful city. There is a magnificent shrine there to St. Anne-de-Beaupre, which seems to have a huge effect on the entire community. There was not a soul in the prison there. Criminal court was cancelled because there were no cases. This is a town of over 200,000 and yet I did not see a single display of drunkenness or foul language during my stay. Even the cabmen were very polite and courteous. There were no beggars to be seen. It is quite a remarkable place, and, of course, mostly Catholic. And it was timed so I was there for the celebration of Saint Ann's feast day on July 26. It was quite a beautiful ceremony."

"The Lord works in mysterious ways and apparently so does Mother Superior," chuckled Sister Mariana.

"Indeed," grinned Jeff.

As he entered the children's ward he was taken back, because seated at the charge desk was Mary Rose.

"Dr. Bloom, it is so good to see you again. I hope your trip was pleasant and not too exhausting," she greeted him icily.

"It was most remarkable, Nurse Wenban. I hope to share all of the details with you some time soon, but my mission here is to see a young lad with a deformed knee. I observed a procedure that could possibly help him considerably. Do you know which youngster to whom Dr. Lewis was referring?"

"Of course, that must be Rodney. He is eight years old and has never been able to walk. He was brought to us two weeks ago, although he was born with this defect. His parents are praying for a miracle."

"Perhaps I can provide that. Please lead me to him. I am so glad that they developed this children's ward. Are you seeing a difference in their well-being?" asked Jeff.

"It is much easier to provide the care the youngsters need with them all in one place, and they seem to take comfort from seeing others in the hospital of their own age. They are very sympathetic, and no matter how serious their circumstances; there always seems to be someone here in worse condition, so they take comfort from that. Here, let me introduce you to Rodney. Rodney, this is the famous Dr. Bloom, who may be able to help you. You are very lucky that he could take time from his travels to come and see patients," added Mary Rose.

"Well, Rodney, as Nurse Wenban said I did just return from an extensive visit to hospitals up north. While I was there I observed the most amazing piece of equipment, and I think it may just fix your knee. Let me take a look at it."

After Jeff examined the knee, he smiled and said "Yes, I think we can fix this. Rodney, are your brave enough to be the first of my patients that I try this out on? I practiced a little while in Boston, but you will be the first south of the Mason Dixon line to experience this treatment. Where might I find your parents?"

"Actually his parents have a farm in Thibodaux and had to leave Rodney and go back to take care of the animals and crops. They gave us permission to do whatever we can to help him," added Mary Rose.

"They will really be surprised when they come back and find you walking around!" smiled Jeff.

Rodney beamed. Tears came to his eyes. "Do you think I will be able to run one day?"

"I will bet you will be one of the fastest runners in Thibodaux, and then perhaps you will come back here one day and teach me how to do the Cajun two-step. I have seen it performed by folks, but have not ever tried it myself."

"Mere and Pere go dancing all the time, but I do not yet. But if you fix my knee, *mon ami*, I will go home and learn how to do all the Cajun dances and come back and teach you!"

"Well, Rodney, I am going to go back to my office to get the new equipment, but I will be back soon. It may hurt some, but I think it will be well worth a little pain."

"*Oui, Docteur, Je sais très brave*. I do not fear *un petit incommode*. Whatever you say, *c'est bon*."

"You are *très* brave, indeed my little one. We will be arranging for those dance lessons very soon."

Jeff returned in short order and found four other doctors had come to observe the procedure. Jeff brought along a copy of the written instructions he was given to go along with the device. He immediately went to Rodney and said "I am going to take you into another room to do the procedure. There is no need to be afraid. I will have one of the doctors make you breathe in some happy gas, so that you will not feel any pain. It will help you relax, and will make my job easier."

They placed Rodney on a stretcher and rolled him into one of the operating rooms. By this time, several more doctors had joined the entourage. One doctor placed a mask over his nose and mouth and told him to breathe deeply and count back from ten. They were surprised to hear the young man counting in French. "*Dix, neuf, huit, sept, six, cinq* . . ." He was fast asleep as the ether took effect. Jeff attached the device which stretched the tendons and ligaments and adjusted the bones. He then splinted the knee and wrapped it in plaster of Paris.

"We will have to keep the knee immobile for a few weeks, but he will be able to put some pressure on it, and we can begin to teach him how to walk. He should be fine."

They rolled him back to the children's ward, and a nurse was assigned to keep a close eye on him. The doctors all congratulated Jeff on the procedure and said they wanted to learn how to use the device as well.

Jeff went in to check on Rodney just as he was waking. "Well, my brave young *garçon* how was that?"

"I did not expect this big *blanc* thing on my leg, doctor!"

"That is to hold the bones in place so they regrow properly. We will take it off in just a few weeks and will have you walking in no time. Be patient. You have been suffering for long enough. You will be surprised how quickly this time will pass. The nurses have promised me they will give you extra special attention—especially that one with the red hair. She loves to sing and has a beautiful voice. If you ask her, she will sing to you."

"*Merci, docteur.* I will trust you, since I do not have a choice," the boy smiled.

"We will be dancing soon," Jeff said as he turned to go. On his way out he stopped by the desk to see if Mary Rose had warmed up any, but she kept her head buried in her paper work and would not even look up at him. He said quietly "I do have stories to tell that you will love. I hope you will let me share them with you."

CHAPTER FORTY-SEVEN

Consulting with the Rabbi Again

"Rabbi Levy, thank you for seeing me again."

"Jeff, I am always here for you. Never forget that. What can I help you with today?"

"I have another dilemma that I do not know how to deal with and thought you might have some suggestions. You will recall that I came to you about the promise I made to Pa that I so greatly regretted."

"I believe it was something you promised him as he was dying, and I assured you that your promise was made only to calm him. Has this new problem something to do with that?"

"My Pa was from the old country and was very set in his ways. I had been seeing a young lady from Boston who is Catholic, and Pa made me promise to stop seeing her. I tried very hard and succeeded for several months, but when I accidentally saw her at a reception my heart raced. She is beautiful inside and out. She is my true soul mate. She is delightful company. She is a nurse and loves medicine as much as I do and even understands me professionally. I want to marry her and be with her forever. She is a very devout Catholic. How would such a marriage ever work?"

"Oh, Jeff, you have gotten yourself into quite a pickle. You sound like a teenager in love."

"I am hardly a teenager, Rabbi, but I am in love."

"You know her Church will never approve such a wedding."

"I felt sure that would be the case. We have not made any commitments yet. I did propose to her once, but it was rather flippant, and she responded equally flippantly. I think she thought it was a joke. But since that day it is all

I can think of—how wonderful it would be to have her as my wife. How can I make that happen?"

"I am assuming she is also not a teenager."

"No, she is not."

"First, I would invest in a beautiful diamond ring. Does she have a father you would need to get approval from?"

"Her parents are both deceased. The only person I would need approval from is her best friend," smiled Jeff.

"Talk to the friend before you buy the diamond, and get her ideas. If she thinks you have a chance, then make plans. I would suggest that you arrange a lovely dinner, or picnic, or walk—you have a better idea of where your young lady would be most comfortable. Explain your feelings to her and get down on one knee and offer her the ring while begging her to make your dreams come true. If she accepts, then I would arrange for a wedding by one of the judges—that way you can have the marriage blessed by her Church at a later date. If the wedding were performed in the synagogue there would be great difficulty getting approval later."

"Rabbi, do you think such a marriage can be a happy one?"

"That all depends on how hard you both work at making it happy. Our religions have much in common, after all Catholicism was based on Judaism. Jesus Christ was a Jew. They respect and abide by the same Ten Commandments we have. Your father came from a world where the enemy was represented by Catholics. The Catholics are not your enemy here. You have worked closely with them for many years in the hospital. You know they wish you no harm."

"I have several who wish to convert me!"

"I have met Sister Agnes many times and I am sure that is one of her pet projects."

"Indeed, she mentions it regularly. I am not ready to convert. I love my faith as much as Mary Rose loves hers. Now my job is to convince Mary Rose to marry me! Pray for me, Rabbi, it will not be an easy undertaking," smiled Jeff.

As they shook hands to part, the rabbi said: "May God go with you."

*   *   *

"Miss Faircloth, may I speak with you in private?" asked Jeff coyly.

"Why Dr. Bloom, I have a few minutes. How may I help you?"

Jeff took her arm and escorted her into an empty examining room in the hospital.

"I am in severe distress and I need your help," pleaded Jeff.

"Oh, dear doctor, should I call a doctor?"

"A doctor cannot alleviate my pain. I am suffering from a broken heart. I have become acutely aware of how fond I am of your dear friend, Mary Rose, and I am serious about wanting to marry her. You heard me propose on the boat, I am sure, but everyone took that as being in jest. However, since that time I have longed to make a serious proposal. All the while I was traveling, I thought how much more I would have enjoyed my travels if Mary Rose were at my side. I could hardly wait to return and was glad to have an excuse to cut my travels short. Luckily, the governor provided that. Since she has no father to ask for her hand, I thought you would be the person most dear to her that I should ask permission. I also hoped you could give me a positive outlook on her response."

"Dr. Bloom, I am totally stunned. I do not know what to say! I know that Mary Rose feels very strongly about you, sometimes great admiration and other times great animosity. Unfortunately her feelings right now are the latter. You will have to do a lot of charming to get her to agree to marry you. Have you considered the problems you will face with religion? I am astonished that you are even considering such a possibility."

"Miss Faircloth, I consulted with my rabbi, and he said that sometimes mixed marriages can have very successful outcomes. It will take extra work on both parties, but he said that someone who is so in love can overcome major obstacles. The rabbi suggested we get married by a judge and have it blessed by a priest later. I asked him to please keep this news to himself as I had quite an ordeal ahead to convince her that I am worthy."

"Dr. Bloom, I do not think worthy is the problem. You are one of the finest doctors in the city and looked up to by everyone in high positions. I have never heard anyone demean you, other than Mary Rose, and that was only when you had done something that really exacerbated her. On the positive side, you have so much in common—medicine and healing, the most important of those. And she would love to travel, which is something I think you also enjoy. Improving our world is one of her greatest desires, and you work constantly to do that. But there is the huge chasm called religion which would be difficult to build a bridge across. Have you considered converting? That would do the trick!"

"Now you sound like Sister Agnes. I wish it would be that simple, but much as I love Mary Rose, I fear the Lord even more, and would hate to displease him by giving up my faith just to be with the one I love. That is out of the question. Would you encourage her to think about the possibility?"

"Oh, Dr. Bloom, you remind me of a heart sick puppy. How can I deny your request? I think you would be a very good husband to Mary Rose. I do not think you would interfere with her practice of her religion, and I know she would not interfere with yours. The children, if any, would have to be raised Catholic, of course. You might consider discussing this with Sister Marianna, but, then again, you probably should not until after Mary Rose is swayed. I promise to keep this news between us, although it will be very difficult not to confide in my very best friend. I will ask the Lord to help me seal my lips."

"You have been a great help, and you are a dear friend to Mary Rose. I know you want her to be happy, and I believe I can make her very happy. Just a good word from you every now and again may help me in my pursuits. Thank you so much, Miss Faircloth."

"May God bless you on your pursuit. I feel you have a very difficult task ahead, but I will do my best to encourage her."

Mary Ellen was stunned. How was she going to keep this news to herself? She had confided everything in Mary Rose, and had never kept any secrets from her. This would truly be a challenge, but she believed Jeff would make Mary Rose very happy.

*   *   *

When Mary Ellen returned to her room at the Nurses' Home, she found Mary Rose sitting staring out the window. She was fingering her rosary beads, but it was easy to see that she had been crying.

"Mary Ellen, whatever am I going to do? I am so perplexed. I watched Jeff perform a miracle today on a young boy. It is a technique he learned in his travels and shared it with many of the physicians in the hospital. He took the leg of a cripple, and straightened it. The leg was set in a cast, but Dr. Bloom indicated that he would be walking soon, even running and dancing. It was so amazing. The boy had been born with a deformed leg and had never been able to walk!"

"My friend, why has that brought you to tears and prayers?"

"I do not know what to do. I do not want to encourage Jeff, but he offered to tell me stories of all the things he saw and learned on his travels and I am dying to hear them. Sister Marianna made the right decision; you know the doctors up north would not have availed themselves to us as they did for him, but I will die before I admit that to him. I need guidance. I am so attracted to him, but I know I should not be. What do you think I should do? You have always been there to give me the very best advice."

"Mary Rose, you are a hopeless case. You have a wonderful man who is madly in love with you, and wants to share his life with you, and you keep turning away from him. Perhaps it is your mission in life to bring him to Jesus, and at the same time have a wonderful life. You have shut him out so many times, it is a wonder he keeps coming back. I am sure there are many women in New Orleans would jump at an opportunity to get any attention from the great doctor."

"But he is Jewish! I am Catholic! And he is as devout as I am. His family has already cast him out because he was seeing me. Imagine what will happen if we married. My parents are probably rolling in their graves at the very idea. They would have been horrified. You can probably visualize the reaction Sister John would have if she knew I was seeing him.

"When he so flippantly proposed on the boat, my heart skipped a beat! Thank goodness my mind kept functioning so that I could come up with an equally glib response. What would I do if I thought he were serious? I need to prepare my answer in advance so I am ready to respond. I cannot be caught off guard."

"What would be so horrible about marrying Dr. Bloom? Are you prejudiced against Jews?"

"Oh, Mary Ellen, you know better than that. How would we raise our children? Where would we be married? No priest would marry us, that is certain."

"There are ways to get around all of those problems if you are truly in love. Do you think you are?"

"That is why I am here praying and asking the Blessed Mother to guide my steps. I have never been in love, and am not sure what it feels like. I know that my heart beats faster whenever he is near. I blush whenever he speaks to me. I want so much for him to put his arm around me and draw me near, but I have to shut all of that out of my mind. This can never be."

"Mary Rose, you are closing your mind to the possibilities. I think you do love him. He is a wonderful man, and you have much in common. I know you admire him and what he has accomplished. Do not hold it against him that he is not Catholic."

"I do not know anyone but Catholics. I have been so sheltered all my life that I have seen very little of the outside world. I have always envisioned my little family going to church together on Sundays, and having the priest over for dinner. All that would never be."

"Who did you see as your spouse? Did you ever dream about Dr. Bloom?"

"Too many times, I am ashamed to say. Today in the ward, I had to keep my eyes buried in my papers. I could not even look up at him after he had worked on the boy. There will be too many times when we have to work together that I will have to face him. Perhaps I should leave and go to another hospital. I know Sister Agnes would take me in!"

"Not if she knew you were moving to get away from Dr. Bloom! She thinks he is wonderful and has been trying to set you two up for years now.

She thinks you are his salvation. You know how long she has been trying to convert him; I think she believes you may hold that special key that will make him change his mind."

"I know I cannot speak to Sister Marianna about this, and I do not dare ask Sister Agnes, I know what her response would be. Tomorrow morning, before Mass, I will go to confession and ask Father for advice. I think the Blessed Mother is putting the steps to take in my mind. She does work wonders!"

"Oh, Mary Rose, that is a wonderful idea. See what Father has to say about your predicament. He will not be able to go discuss it with anyone, so your secret remains one, and yet you can get some good advice."

"I feel so much better already, but I am starving. Let us go down to supper," Mary Rose cheerfully wiped her eyes and led her friend out.

CHAPTER FORTY-EIGHT

The Confession

"Bless me, Father, for I have sinned. It has been one month since my last confession," Mary Rose began. She went on to confess the minor infractions she had committed and then said, "Father, I come to ask advice from you. I asked the Blessed Mother to guide my steps and she sent me to you."

"She is a wonderful role model to follow, my child. How may I help you?" responded the priest.

"I think I have fallen in love with a wonderful man. I expect he is going to ask me to marry him soon, but I do not think I should."

"Do you love this wonderful man, my dear?"

"Yes, Father, I do. The problem is that he is a devout Jew. His family has already ostracized him because he was seeing me. I know the Church frowns on mixed marriages, and I am a fervent Catholic. What am I to do?"

"You do indeed have a problem. The Church would never approve of such a union. There would be serious disparities between the two of you. How would you raise your children? The Jews honor the Sabbath on Saturday, whereas Sunday is our Holy Day. Do you celebrate Christmas or Chanukah? Passover or Easter? There would be so many conflicts. Would you have to keep a kosher kitchen? Do you know how to do it? There are many foods the Jewish people are forbidden, and would he be willing to keep your abstinence from meat on Fridays? So many questions! I would never approve of such a marriage."

"Father, another devout Catholic advised me that perhaps my purpose on this earth was to convert this wonderful man to our Church. Under those circumstances would your opinion change?"

"Only if you converted him before you married and then the question would be moot, because you would both be Catholic. Do you think that is a possibility?"

"No, Father, I think that is highly improbable. What is your advice?"

"Avoid this man at all cost. Do not encourage him in any way. For your penance, I want you to say three rosaries and ask our Blessed Mother to give you the strength to remain faithful. This man will only lead you astray. I am sorry, my child, I know this is not what you wanted to hear, but this is the best advice I can give you. God bless you and keep you. Go in peace. Your sins are forgiven."

"Thank you, Father."

Mary Rose knelt in a pew by the statue of the Blessed Mother. She spent the next hour praying her rosaries and begging for guidance. When she finally felt she was calm enough to leave, she headed to the hospital. As she was opening the door to the hospital, Jeff was leaving and almost bumped into her. He could tell she had been crying and immediately pulled her aside.

"Why are you so sad on such a beautiful morning? It breaks my heart to see your beautiful face so tear stained. Please come for a walk."

"And lead me not into temptation," she said. "I am sorry, but I must get to my duties. I must look a fright. Forgive me." She darted quickly for the ladies room to wash her face. 'Blessed Mother is this how you lead me—straight into his arms. What am I to do? I need better guidance,' she thought. 'Three rosaries must not be enough.'

After calming herself again, she headed to her nurse's station and began immersing herself with her patients. She was working in the children's ward and it was easy to be totally consumed with their needs. She had a group of children surrounding her as she read them a book, when Jeff walked into the ward.

"Good morning, Nurse Wenban. I have come to check on my patient and get him out of that bed."

"But, Dr. Bloom, you just adjusted his leg yesterday. We usually do not get patients up that quickly."

"Well our procedures will be changing. One of the things I plan to install is a gymnasium for the children. By lingering in their beds they are slowing their recovery. We need to get them up and moving around and using the muscles that work. I want to show you how we are going to teach this young lad to walk—something he has never done. If you would not mind, please come be my assistant so that I can teach you this procedure."

She nodded assent and followed him over to the young man. He took two of the hospital beds and placed them a foot apart. He then helped the boy from his bed and told him to stand up, holding on the rails of each of the beds.

"Soon we will have a device for doing this that will be much better than two beds, but we must not wait to start Rodney's rehabilitation. That is what they call it up north. Rodney, I want you to put most of your weight on your arms and your good leg, and gently manipulate your legs in a walking motion. Nurse Wenban, would you please stand at the other end of the beds and help him turn around. Rodney, I want you to do this twice this time, four times this afternoon, and at least four times again tomorrow morning before I come to check on you. If you think you can go farther, do so! The more you push your muscles, the faster they will become strong. You had no broken bones, only misplaced ones. Had they been broken, we would not put any weight on them yet. Young man, you are doing wonderfully. Do you agree, Nurse Wenban," Jeff beamed.

"It is indeed miraculous, Dr. Bloom. Rodney, how do you feel about your new legs?"

"Mon Dieu, I feel as though Christ himself has come to my succor," Rodney smiled.

"Well, he was also Jewish, I believe," smiled Jeff. He then helped Rodney back into his bed and instructed him to sit on the side of the bed as much as he possibly could during the day.

"I will be back to check on you, Rodney, and you too Nurse Wenban." Jeff smiled as he rushed out of the ward and on to his other patients.

'Oh, Blessed Mother, this is not helping my situation. The more I see him working wonders, the more I realize I am falling deeper and deeper in love with him.'

Mary Rose chose to skip lunch and go to the hospital chapel where she said another rosary. 'Help me, Blessed Mother,' she prayed.

After lunch, she was helping Rodney do his walking routine again. Because she was doing it by herself, she ran to the other side to help him turn each time.

"Mademoiselle Wenban, tell me about this miracle worker. I want to know more about Dr. Bloom."

"Well, Rodney, I can tell you some things about him. He just came to Hotel Dieu this summer after serving as the House Surgeon at Charity for many years. The procedure he did on you is one he learned this past month when he went to study the hospitals up north. He is a very talented doctor."

"Indeed he is, and very much in love with you."

"Why, Rodney, why would you say such a thing," said Mary Rose blushing profusely.

"I can tell by the way he looked at you and spoke to you. It is very obvious. And I think you return his feelings, *oui*?"

"Are you trying to be a matchmaker, Rodney? You are much too young to be worried about such things."

"Being born a cripple I have had the opportunity to study people. Since I could not move around I had much more time to watch and observe and learn. I am *très bien* at picking up such things. People at home tease me about it all the time, they think I have some strange voodoo powers because I can interpret people's feelings. It is not hard, it just takes paying attention. I also can tell that you are very upset by something, but I cannot tell what it is. You seem to try to avoid Dr. Bloom, but he seeks you out. Are you trying to play hard to get?"

"That is enough of your foolishness! How old are you anyway—ninety-two?"

"*Mais non*, I turned huit last *Mai*, but they tell me I am very old for my years."

"And nosy," she teased, as she helped him back in his bed. "Now remember to sit on the side of the bed for a while this afternoon. If you want to, we may do this walking exercise again before my shift is over. Would you like to do that?"

"*Oui, nourrice*, did not the good doctor recommend additional practice?"

"Yes, *mon chere*, that is why I suggested it. I will be back to work with you again later."

Mary Ellen had come into the ward while Mary Rose was working with Rodney. "Can you take a short break, Mary Rose?" she asked.

"Not now, dear, but is there something I can help you with while I am here? I am the only nurse on duty and cannot leave these darlings unattended," she said as they walked back to the nurse's station.

"What is that you were doing with the boy with the cast on his leg?"

"That is a new procedure introduced by the remarkable Dr. Bloom. That is the lad I was telling you about last night. They are both determined he will be dancing out of here in just a few weeks. That is something he called 'rehabilitation.' Rodney is eager to do it as much as I will help him with it. He is quite a cutie and determined he will walk."

"I guess we will all be learning new things thanks to Dr. Bloom's journey. He came to see me this morning because he was very worried about you. He said he thought you had been crying. Are you all right?"

"I am fine. He just caught me at a bad time. I think all the pollen in the air was affecting me."

"You know you cannot get away with lying to me, Mary Rose Wenban. I know you too well. You can tell me about it later, if you wish, but you seem to be fine now. I did not see you at lunch today and I just wanted to check on you."

"Oh, I spent my lunchtime in the chapel. I have been adding some pounds lately and decided I could skip a meal or two."

"You will have to go back to confession for lying to me twice in one day, but I will get the truth out of you sooner or later," she smiled as she left the ward.

CHAPTER FORTY-NINE

The Lighthouse

Jeff was waiting for Mary Rose when her shift ended. "Would you honor me with your company at dinner this evening, Miss Wenban?" he smiled.

"Why, Dr. Bloom, you take me by surprise. I would love to hear the stories you promised to tell me about your adventures up north, but I would have to change from my nurse's uniform. Would you give me about an hour to prepare?"

"I will be pacing anxiously, my dear," he teased. "My carriage will await you at your residence."

Mary Rose rushed home and, of course, Mary Ellen was waiting for her. "Now I have you cornered. What is going on?" she asked.

"Dear me, I do not have much time. Dr. Bloom will be here to take me to dinner soon. I am more confused than ever, but I will give you a brief synopsis of what my day has been like."

The two friends chatted as Mary Rose changed and carefully coiffed her hair. "Mary Rose, I think the Blessed Mother is telling you something. It seems the more you pray, the more you see of Dr. Bloom, and the more enchanted you become. I think she is approving the match."

"Mary Ellen, I am getting the same message. The more I fight it, and the more I pray, the more attracted I am to him. He offered to tell me about all of his travels up north. How could I turn that down? You know how much I wanted to go on such an adventure."

Jeff arrived at the appointed time and helped Mary Rose into his buggy. "Where are we going for dinner this evening?" she asked.

"I have reserved a table for us at the Yacht Club. I thought the nice drive out to the lake would give us time to chat. It has been too long, and I have much to tell you."

"That will be lovely. Do tell me about all the things you saw and did up north. What cities did you visit? Did you get to Boston?" They chatted without stopping until they reached the shore. Jeff recanted all the tales he could remember, but saved the best until they stopped.

"You know, Rose, the one thing I kept thinking about in all my travels was how much more enjoyable they would have been had you been with me. I missed you."

Just then, the stable boy came to take the buggy, and Jeff escorted her into the main dining room. He had arranged a quiet table next to the huge window so they could look out over the lake. "What a beautiful setting for a beautiful evening!" Mary Rose remarked.

The waiter brought a stand with a magnum of champagne. "As you ordered, sir." He proceeded to remove the cork with great flair and poured two glasses, and then quietly receded.

"I took the liberty of preordering for us. I hope you do not mind."

"Champagne! What are we celebrating?"

"Being together—here is to us," and he lifted his glass in a toast. "To a stellar friendship; may it continue to flourish!"

She joined him in the toast, despite being somewhat shocked by it. At that time the waiter appeared with shrimp cocktails.

"This is indeed a treat," she smiled. "I should let you order for me all the time."

After the shrimp cocktail, a small salad with crabmeat topping was served. The waiter continually refreshed their champagne glasses. The salad was followed by trout amandine. The waiter insisted that the fish had been caught in the lake that very day.

While eating they had admired the yachts coming into harbor and Jeff named each boat and who owned it. As the moon rose over the water, it gave a mystical beauty to the gentle whitecaps stirring the coastline.

The finale for the dinner was a bread pudding smothered in hard sauce, a specialty of the house. Because the champagne had been depleted, Jeff ordered two Brandies.

"I believe you are trying to get me tipsy, Dr. Bloom," Mary Rose smiled.

"Just relax, my dear. You seemed so stressed earlier today, that I was really concerned. I am glad you seem so much better."

"Who would not feel better after sharing a bottle of champagne and a sumptuous meal with a wonderful companion? I think I may be tipsy. You would not take advantage of me, would you doctor?" she smiled.

"It may be very difficult, but I was raised to be a gentleman, and I have always had great respect for the ladies, especially beautiful, intelligent, wonderful ones like you. Perhaps we should take a walk along the pier and enjoy the delightful evening. You may hold on to my arm if you are feeling the least bit unstable."

They walked out of the restaurant and down to the base of the lighthouse. "Would you be up to climbing to the top of the lighthouse? The view is phenomenal," Jeff suggested.

"That would be grand."

They climbed, arm in arm, up the winding stairs of the lighthouse and out on to the balcony. At that point, Jeff dropped to one knee and said, "Rose, you are the light of my life. Would you do me the great honor of marrying me?" He took out a blue Tiffany box, opened it and offered her a solitaire diamond ring.

"I thought you said you would not take advantage of me, Jeff?" Mary Rose said as tears flowed down her cheeks.

"Please do not cry, my precious. The last thing I wanted to do was make you cry. On my trip I realized I do not want to live without you. I missed you so much."

"But, Jeff, how can we work out our differences?"

"I spoke with my rabbi and asked his advice. He said that if we are truly in love, and willing to work hard, we can make a very happy union. I promise I will do all I can to make you happy, Rose. I will never interfere with the practice of your religion. The children may be raised Catholic."

"This morning, I spoke with a priest. You caught me when I was returning from church. He advised me there were no priests that would bless such a union. How can we get married?"

"Rabbi Levy suggested that we get married by a judge, and then a priest will be willing to bless the marriage at a later date. Please say yes and make my world complete. I love you, Mary Rose Wenban, more than I have ever loved anyone. I did not know what true love was until I met you."

"I need time to think about this when my head is not spinning so wildly. I am not saying 'no,' just give me some time. I have been praying a lot about this possibility and asking the Blessed Mother to show me the way, and she keeps making me bump into you. I am beginning to think she is telling me that you are the way for me. Keep that beautiful ring in a safe place."

Jeff gently put his arms around her and pulled her to him. He kissed the tears from her eyes, and said: "I will give you as much time as you need to say yes." He then kissed her again and again. She swooned in his arms.

"I think I had better get you home before I cannot keep my promise about not taking advantage of you. I love you so much."

"Jeff, I love you too. I also have never known love, and the more I am with you the more deeply I fall in love with you. When I watched you today with the young boy, my heart was beating so fast, I thought everyone could hear it. Rodney figured it out. He asked me if I loved you as much as you loved me. He is a very smart lad."

"Perhaps he will dance at our wedding," Jeff smiled as he helped Mary Rose down the winding staircase. They called for the buggy, and rode home with Jeff's arm snuggly around Mary Rose.

CHAPTER FIFTY

The Wedding

It took several months before Mary Rose finally accepted Jeff's proposal. Mary Ellen had been doing everything she could to persuade her that Jeff was the man of her dreams, and that she would never find someone better than he. When the announcement was made of the engagement, Sister Agnes sought out Mary Rose and took her aside.

"My dear child, you are the answer to my prayers. You know I cannot publicly approve of this marriage, because it is not recognized by the Church, but I know you will see to it that it is blessed as soon as you can. I know you are the tool God sent to finally get Dr. Bloom to convert. He will tell you how long I have worked on him, but to no avail. You have my blessing, be assured. May you have a long and happy life together." She hugged Mary Rose and wiped the tears from her eyes.

Sister Marianna's response was not quite as warm. "I cannot believe that one of my nurses is disgracing the Hotel Dieu, after all we have done for you. We opened our arms to you, and have made you family for so many years now. And what do you do? You trick one of our finest doctors into marrying you. And he is a Jew! I can only imagine how distraught your own Sister John must be upon hearing your news. You know, of course, that you will no longer be associated with the hospital after your civil ceremony. How could you do such a thing?"

"Sister Marianna, I am so sorry to disappoint you. Be assured, I fought my feelings for Dr. Bloom for many years. I too am very unhappy that we cannot be married in the Church, but I hope one day soon to have our marriage blessed by a priest. I assure you that I did not pursue or trick Dr. Bloom. We are very much in love and would appreciate your blessing on our union. If you cannot give it, I understand. I will be resigning my position one week before our wedding, and will be moving out of the Nurses' Residence at that time. I have loved my time at Hotel Dieu. You have been my family and I love all of you dearly. I came to teach, but I learned much more. I hope my nine years here have benefited the hospital and the city, but I must follow my heart."

The wedding was held on a Wednesday evening, May 30, 1906, at the home of George Mugnier on Toledano Street. Palms, ferns and flowers could be seen tucked into every nook and cranny, and the chandeliers, doorways and windows were draped with asparagus ferns. Mary Rose chose a gown of white silk mull over white silk elaborately embroidered with lace. Her long flowing tulle veil was held in place by orange blossoms. Her only attendant was Mary Ellen. She entered the main room on the arm of Dr. Danna. When she saw Jeff standing next to Judge Wynne Rodgers, her heart skipped a beat and tears came to her eyes. 'How could anyone be so very happy,' she thought. The room was filled with friends. Following the ceremony, a light buffet was served, and the newly married couple spent their first night together at the Saint Charles Hotel.

As they lay in their nuptial bed, Mary Rose asked: "And, Dr. Bloom, exactly what mysterious honeymoon are we going on? You sent over that huge steamer trunk and told me to pack all of my clothing, but refuse to give me any idea of where we are going."

"Well, my dear Mrs. Bloom, tomorrow at noon we will board the S.S. Nicaraguan, one of the most elaborate ships of the Leyland Line, and head for the Continent. Our first stop will be in Liverpool where we will visit with Professor Boyce, the Dean of the School of Tropical Medicine. I met him last summer in New Orleans and had an opportunity to learn some wonderful ideas, and now I hope to learn how we should incorporate them into our practices. You know the English hospitals are model institutions, and I have plans to visit several. After traveling through England, we will go north to Scotland where I have arranged to meet with Dr. Joseph Lister and his wife in Glasgow."

Mary Rose gasped.

"I thought that would please you," he continued. "Then over to Ireland, where I hear the southern part is filled with jovial, happy folk, always in good humor. The men in Northern Ireland are reserved and circumspect, very much like the English. The new land law is in successful operation and the tenants are buying the land they farm, and there is much less emigration. From there we will go to Paris and Switzerland. I hear the mountains of Switzerland are breathtaking, and Paris is much like New Orleans. Our itinerary will then take us to Germany, especially to Alsace, where my father's people live. I hope to meet some of them. I have made arrangements to meet with physicians in hospitals in each major city to learn their newest techniques. I have taken an extended leave from the hospital, and I did not think you would mind being a part of my study, my dear."

Mary Rose kissed him firmly, and snuggled into his side to dream of the wonderful adventures ahead.

Dr. Jefferson Davis Bloom   *Mary Rose Wenban*

CREDITS

Writing the story of Mary Rose has been quite an adventure. There are so many people I need to give credit for their help and assistance.

- First of all, my husband, Arthur, who has supported and encouraged me throughout my endeavors.
- My daughter, Katie Martin, who was my first and most honest critic.
- My son, Mike, who helped design the cover and developed my web page.
- My sister, Barbara Edmond, who helped me dig up information.
- Janie Dawson and Debi Griffin, two English teachers, who corrected my grammar and punctuation, and often suggested better words.
- Cathy Hoffmann and Cindy Ohberg who were excellent proofreaders.
- Catherine Kahn, archivist of Touro Infirmary, who just happens to be a cousin.
- Jeanne Baronowsky, a much closer cousin, who helped with ancestry research.
- Sister Josie Cusimano, DC, who explained what it was like to be a Daughter of Charity for over 70 years.
- Eira Tansey, Tulane University Matas Library, who helped me weed through volumes of material.
- Elizabeth Schexnyder of the National Hansen's Disease Center in Carville, who introduced me to one of the patients who had been at the center for most of his life.
- Jim Morris of the Louisiana State Archives who found treasures for me.
- Lenora Costa, archivist at Longue Vue House and Gardens, who introduced me to my great Aunt Hannah.

And finally and most importantly,

- My dear grandmother, Mary Rose, whom I often implored to channel me and help me tell the true story.

Appendix One

Real people (in order of appearance)

Mary Rose Wenban Bloom
Elizabeth Wenban (Sister John)
Edward Wenban
Clara Wenban
Veronica Wenban
Jeff Bloom
Isaac Bloom
Hannah Bloom Stern
Maurice Stern
Louis Bloom
Arthur Bloom
Phillip Sartorius
Governor Francis T. Nicholls
Dr. Albert B. Miles
Dr. Rudolph Matas
Paul Tulane
Governor Samuel Douglas McEnery
Edgar Bloom Stern
Dr. F. Loeber
Dr. Joseph Lister
Judah Touro
Louis Pasteur
Sister Agnes, DC
Dr. Robert Koch

Dr. Julius Petri
Florence Nightingale
Dan Holiday
Sir Thomas Albutt
Bernard Marigny de Mandeville
Dr. Isadore Dyer
Tommy Lofton
Henry Howard
Robert Coleman Camp
Henry J. Budington
Fr. Boblioi
Capt. F.S. Dugmore
Dr. Edward Jenner
Governor Murphy Foster
Colonel Samuel L. James
Andrew Carney
Mary Ellen Faircloth
Richard and Deborah Milliken
Phillip Werlein
Sister Mariana, DC
William Morris
Dr. Sidney Theard
Dr. Joseph Lovell
Dr. H. A. Veazie

Dr. Alfred Danna
Marie Laveau
King Louis XIV
Andrew Jackson
Zachary Taylor
Baroness Pontalba
Dietrich Einsiedel
Lawrence Fabacher and his family
P.T. Barnum
A.C. Hutchinson
Governor William W. Heard
Chief Justice E.T. Merrick
Honorable T.J. Kernan
Dr. E.S. Lewis
May E. Waters

May Campbell
Lily Mae Scooler
Morris Hayman
Dr. Adolph Lorenz
Dr. George Brown
Dr. Alonzo Garcelona
Captain Jacob E. Bloom
Dr. J. M. Batchelor
Dr. J.A. Danna
Dr. S.W. Stafford
Dr. Adolph Lorenz
St. Anne-de-Beaupre
George Mugnier
Judge Wynne Rodgers
Professor Rubert Boyce

Appendix Two

Glossary of perhaps unfamiliar terms

Alee—the leeward side, away from the wind
Alsace—a region between France and Germany that frequently changed nationality
Aseptic practices—sanitation and disinfection
Barge—an open vessel used to transport goods that has no power of its own, but is pushed by a tug boat
Bayou—a flowing body of water that runs through the swamps
Beignet—a fried pastry covered with powdered sugar
Blanc—white
Cadavers—dead human bodies used for experimental studies
Café Au Lait—coffee with milk
Calliope—an organ usually associated with steamboats or merry-go-rounds
Call-outs—the first dances at a Mardi Gras ball where the ladies are "called" to come meet their partner for that dance
Carpetbaggers—northerners who came south after the Civil War
Cesspool—an underground container for sewage where it decomposes
Chapeau—hat
Chiffarobe—an armoire or bureau, usually with an area for hanging clothes
Cistern—a huge tank that collects rain water for use in the house
Congenital—something you are born with
Cornette—an elaborate headpiece worn by the Daughters of Charity
Croissants—rolls
Darkies—slang for Negroes
Dead house—morgue

Debutantes—young ladies who are being introduced into society

Dueling in the courtyard—refers to two doctors who actually fired rounds at each other over who was to care for a patient.

Eggs Benedict—an English muffin, covered with ham or bacon, topped with a poached egg and smothered in Hollandaise sauce

Garden district—an area of very exclusive mansions in uptown New Orleans

Germaphobe—someone with an unusual fear of germs

Gris gris—Voodoo spells

Grits—ground corn cooked into a porridge

Grits and grillades—grits covered with slices of pork roast and gravy

Hard sauce—a mixture of confectioner's sugar and either brandy, rum, or bourbon

Hooligan—a person of disreputable character

House surgeon—the doctor who is the head of a hospital

Hovel—poor people

Hush puppies—fried cornbread nuggets

Indigent—poor

Inmate—a patient in the hospital

Jim Crow laws—required separation of the races

Joie de vivre—joy of life; happiness

Lessez le bon temps rouler—let the good times roll

Liveried—uniformed

Milk toast—very bland and boring

Naysayer—someone who always disagrees

North shore—St. Tammany Parish which is across Lake Ponchartrain from New Orleans

Novena—nine days of prayer to receive special graces

Octo libra—a threat my mother always used

Okra—a pod shaped vegetable commonly used in gumbo

Opium narcosis—overdose of opium causing a person to stop breathing

Palman qui meruit ferat—let he who earns the palm bear it—a reference from Sparta where a palm branch was the symbol of achievement

Paregoric—a commonly used medicine to treat diarrhea that contains opium

Pest house—a building used to care for patients with highly contagious diseases

Petit four—a small cube of cake covered with fondant icing

Pirogue—a flat bottomed boat with a squared off bow and stern used in shallow waters

Poboy—a large sandwich made with French bread

Roseville—a region in New Orleans known for its houses of prostitution

Saffron scourge—yellow fever

Schnitzel—a typical German dish usually made of veal cutlets, flattened and fried

Sea sponge—the simplest animal with a body full of pores and channels

Shrimp creole—a stew made with shrimp as the main ingredient, usually served over rice

Shiva—a Jewish custom of mourning for one week

Skiagraph—X-ray

Soiree—evening party

Spanish moss—a plant related to the pineapple that is made up of fine, curly, gray strands that grows on the limbs and branches of trees

Tableau—a dramatic presentation

Torah—the first five books of the *Bible* which cite the principles and laws of the Jewish religion

Trolley—streetcar

Voodoo—a religion brought to New Orleans by slaves from Jamaica

Yellow jack—yellow fever

BIBLIOGRAPHY

A History of the Southern Jewish Community http://www.isjl.org/history/

A History of Tulane Medical Center. http://www.depaultulane.com/

A Short History of the Sisters of Charity.
http://www.emmitsburg.net/archive_list/articles/history/stories/sister

About.com/inventors. http://inventors.about.com/library/inventors/
blthermometer.htm

American Association of Thoracic Surgeons,
http://www.aats.org/annualmeeting/Program-Books/50th-Anniversary-
Book/Biography-Rudolph-Matas.html

Angola Museum, Louisiana State Penitentiary Museum Foundation, http://
angolamuseum.org/?q=History#history

"Antebellum Louisiana Life," *The Cabildo*
http://lsm.crt.state.la.us/cabildo/cab9.htm

Atlanta on line, http://www.atlantaga.gov/government/urbandesign_mrich.aspx

Barth, Rabbi Lewis M. "The Power of Deathbed Promises," *The Board
of Rabbis of Southern California,* http://www.boardofrabbis.org/
The-Power-of-Deathbed-Promises

Bath, Dr. Thomas W. "Opium Narcosis," *California and Western Medicine,*
Vol XXXIX, No 5. http://www.ncbi.nlm.nih.gov/pmc/articles/ 1658864/
pdf/calwestmed00429-0047.pdf

Boston City Hospital Training School for Nurses. Boston: Boston City Hospital,
ca 1900.

Carney Hospital, Boston. http://www.caritascarney.org

Carnival Collection. Tulane University, Special Research Collection,
http://www.louisianadigitallibrary.org/cdm4/results.php?CISOOP1=
all&CISOFI

*Charity Hospital Annual Report to the General Assembly of the State of
Louisiana, 1902.* http://www.tulane.edu/~matas/CHR/CHR1902.pdf

City of Vicksburg http://web.vicksburg.org/Vicksburg/Default.aspx?tabid=73 http://www3.telus.net/st_simons/cr9801.htm

Clifford, Sir Thomas, *Britannica Encyclopedia* http://www.britannica.com/EBchecked/topic/16002/Sir-Thomas-Clifford-Allbutt

"Cuban American Treaty" *Wikipedia* http://en.wikipedia.org/wiki/CubaUSrelations

"Diptheria," *Health Scout.* http://www.healthscout.com/ency/68/466/main.html#cont,

Foote, Edward Milton, MD. *A Text-Book of Minor Surgery.* http://rlbatesmd.blogspot.com/2009/09/historic-treatment-of-burns.html

Garrett, Tracy. Petticoats and Pistols. http://petticoatsandpistols.com/2010/05/14 /steaming-on-the-mighty-mississippi/

Hebrew Rest Cemeteries No. 1,2 and 3. http://www.nolacemeteries.com/hebrew.html

Henderson, Luana. Louisiana Leper Home Records. Special Collections, Hill Memorial Library, Louisiana State University Library, Baton Rouge, Louisiana, 2006.

Hird, The Reverand Ed. "Dr. Joseph Lister." *St. Simon's Anglican Church* 1917.

"History of Electric Vehicles". *About.com. Inventors* http://inventors.about.com/od/estartinventions/a/History-Of-Electric-Vehicles.htm

History of the Jews of Louisiana, http://www.archive.org/stream/historyofjewsofl00jewi#page/138/mode/2up

History of Gambling in the United States, http://www.library.ca.gov/crb/97/03/Chapt2.html

History of St. Louis Cathedral, http://stlouiscathedral.org/early_history.html

Husband, Joseph. *The Story of the Pullman Car.* A. C. Mc Clug & Company, Chicago, 2009.

"Independence in Cuba" *Wikipedia* http://en.wikipedia.org/wiki/Cuba_

Jackson, Robert. W., and Fabian E. Pollo. "The Legacy of Professor Adolf Lorenz, the 'bloodless surgeon of Vienna", *Baylor University Medical Center Proceedings,* January 2004

Jackson Square, great public places. http://www.pps.org/great_public_spaces/one?public_place_id=72

Jax Brewery, The Shops http://jacksonbrewery.com/about.html

Joseph Lister, http://campus.udayton.edu/~hume/Lister/lister.htm

Henderson, Luana. *Louisiana Leper Home Records.* Special Collections, Hill Memorial

Klug, Lisa. "Jewish Funeral Custom: Saying Goodbye to a Loved One." *Jewish Life.* http://www.jewishfederations.org/page.aspx?id=937

Knapp, Bliss. *The Ninety-first Psalm.* http://www.christianscience.org/BKPs91.htm

Lost: Louisiana Tiffany Windows, http://southeasternarchitecture.blogspot. com/2009_04_01_archive.html

Louisiana Secretary of State Website, http://www.sos.louisiana.gov/tabid/358/ Default.aspx

"Louisiana Winning Her Fight with Leprosy." *New York Times*, undated.

LSU Health Systems, http://www.mclno.org/MCLNO//Menu/Hospital/ History/CharitysBeginnings.aspx

National Governors Association, http://www.nga.org/portal/site/nga/menuitem.

National Hansen's Disease Center, http://www.hrsa.gov/hansens/history.htm

"New Orleans," *The Catholic encyclopedia; an international work of reference on the constitution, doctrine, and history of the Catholic church*; (1913)

New Orleans Hospitals: Info and Vintage Images, http://old-new-orleans.com/ NO_hospitals.html

Rhodes, James Ford. *The History of the Civil War*. The Macmillan Company, New York, 1917

Richardon, Joe M. "Edgar B. Stern: A White New Orleans Philanthropist Helps Build a Black University," *The Journal of Negro History*, Vol. 82, No. 3 (Summer, 1997), p.328-342.

Rudolph Matas Library. *Louisiana Research Collection, La.History and Archives*, Tulane University, New Orleans,. http://medlib.tulane.edu/historical

Salvaggio, John, M.D. *New Orleans' Charity Hospital: A Story of Physicians, Politics, and Poverty*. Louisiana State University Press, Baton Rouge, LA, 1992

Saint Anne de Beaupre Sanctuary and Shrine, http://www.shrinesaintanne.org

Saint Louis Cemetary #1, http://www.nolacemeteries.com/louis1.html

Sugar, Streetcar, and the Sisters-the Story of a Forgotten Hospital http://www.medschool.lsuhsc.edu/pediatrics/docs/Sugar,%20Streetcars, %20and%20the%20Sisters-3.pdf

The Court of Two Sisters, http://www.courtoftwosisters.com/?nav=history

The Daughters of Charity, Northeast Province. http://www.dc-northeast.org/ archives.aspx

Tulane University Health Sciences, Rudolph Matas Library, http://www.tulane. edu/~matas/historical/medschool/founders.htm

The Living City/New York http://www.livingcityarchive.org/htm/framesets/themes/sanitation/ fs_1895.htm

McNabb, Donnald & Louis E. "Lee" Madere, Jr. *A History of New Orleans*. http://www.madere.com/history.html

Philip Werlein, http://medianola.tulane.edu/index.php/Werlein_Music_Store

The Telltale Heart, diagnosing cardiovascular illness.

http://www.hhmi.org/biointeractive/museum/exhibit98/content/b6_
17info.html
Vicksburg, http://web.vicksburg.org/Vicksburg/Default.aspx?tabid=73
Vintage New Orleans Hospitals, http://old-new-orleans.com/NO_hospitals.html
Wilds, John. *Crises, Clashes and Cures: A Century of Medicine in New Orleans.*
Orleans Parish Medical Society, 1978.

The many newspapers of New Orleans whose clippings I used. Unfortunately they were unidentified, but proved invaluable in telling the story. They probably include:

- *The Daily Picayune*
- *The Daily States*
- *The New Orleans Item*

But may also include:

- *The American*
- *The Country Visitor*
- *The Daily City Items*
- *Evening Chronicle*
- *The Harlequin*
- *The Issue*
- *The Times Democrat*

All of these papers, and more, were in publication during this time period.

ABOUT THE AUTHOR

Carol Bloom Paine was born and raised in New Orleans. She graduated from Louisiana State University in Baton Rouge, eighty miles upriver, where she met her husband and has remained ever since. She taught middle and high school for over thirty years, and received many awards for her teaching. She was named a "Fellow" by both the Woodrow Wilson National Foundation and the Academic Distinction Fund. Carol has served as an instructor of classes for teachers at LSU and Southern University, as well as mentored many new teachers. She has two wonderful children and five fantastic grandchildren.